Pitt Press Series.

AN
APOLOGIE FOR POETRIE

BY

SIR PHILIP SIDNEY,

EDITED FOR THE SYNDICS OF THE UNIVERSITY PRESS

(FROM THE TEXT OF 1595)

WITH NOTES, ILLUSTRATIONS, AND GLOSSARY,

BY

EVELYN S. SHUCKBURGH, M.A.
LIBRARIAN AND LATE FELLOW OF EMMANUEL COLLEGE, CAMBRIDGE.

CAMBRIDGE:
AT THE UNIVERSITY PRESS.
1891

CAMBRIDGE UNIVERSITY PRESS
Cambridge, New York, Melbourne, Madrid, Cape Town, Singapore,
São Paulo, Delhi, Dubai, Tokyo, Mexico City

Cambridge University Press
The Edinburgh Building, Cambridge CB2 8RU, UK

Published in the United States of America by Cambridge University Press, New York

www.cambridge.org
Information on this title: www.cambridge.org/9780521166218

First published 1891
First paperback edition 2010

A catalogue record for this publication is available from the British Library

ISBN 978-0-521-16621-8 Paperback

AN

APOLOGIE FOR POETRIE

PREFACE.

AMONG the many services rendered by Mr Arber to the study of early English literature not the least is the fact that his reprints have been usually from the oldest obtainable editions of the works with which he was dealing. These first editions are not, of course, without faults of their own; but they at any rate are free from a numerous class of mistakes accumulated by successive errors of the press, and by arbitrary alterations and conjectures of successive editors. In the case of Sidney's *Apologie for Poetry* the reproduction of the first edition of 1595 has been particularly valuable: for, on examination, it will be found to have been printed much more carefully, and perhaps from a better MS. than the second, which is contained in the folio edition of Sidney's works (1598), although the latter is said to have been issued under the direction of the Countess of Pembroke. From this all subsequent editions have been derived. They all contain the two passages omitted in the 1595 edition[1]; they all exhibit certain blunders in common, some of which I shall mention presently; and in certain cases, where the edition of 1598 merely sinned by omitting one or more words, the subsequent editions shew that their editors filled up the blank, not by referring to the first edition of 1595, but by their own conjectures.

I have collated altogether seven editions. These are

---

[1] See pp. 37, 58.

(1) the first edition of 1595, printed by Henry Olney and reprinted by Mr Arber in 1868.   (2) The folio printed by William Ponsonbie in 1598, which contains the 3rd edition of the *Arcadia*, and the 2nd of the *Apologie* [or 'the *Defense*,' as it is henceforward entitled].   (3) The folio of 1623 'printed by H. L. for Mathew Lownes,' which contains the 6th edition of the *Arcadia* and the 5th of the *Apologie*.   (4) A copy contained in the collected works of Sidney, 3 vols. 4to., Lond. 1724.   The *Defense* occupies vol. 3, 'Poetical Works,' pp. 1—52.   (5) *The defence of Poetry*, Glasgow, 1752, 4to. printed by G. R. Urie.   (6) An edition of 1787 by Wharton combined with extracts from the *Discoveries* of Ben Jonson.   (7) The *Defence of Poetry*, printed by W. Bulmer and Co., Lond. 1810, and edited for private circulation, according to a MS. note in the British Museum copy, by Lord Thurlow.   I did not know of Flugel's edition (1889) in time to use it.

None of these have been edited with any particular care. They reproduce one after the other, as I said, the blunders of the edition of 1598, and seldom introduce any real correction of value.   Of about 120 divergences from the first edition, nearly all, with a few exceptions to be mentioned hereafter, and with a few more which are simply alterations in orthography, are for the worse.   It was evidently therefore first of all necessary to be certain of the readings of the edition of 1595.   I therefore began by collating Mr Arber's reprint with the copy in the British Museum, which is one of a very few known to exist, and I have marked some few instances in which Mr Arber's printer has played him false.   These it will be useful to give here, as the readers of Mr Arber's edition may like to make the alterations in their copies, and Mr Arber may himself have an opportunity of introducing the corrections in a future edition.

		Arber.	Copy in British Museum.
p. 4, l. 17.		Appolos	Apollos
p. 10, l. 16.		hymes	hymnes
p. 17, l. 8.		fruitfull	fruitlesse (*a mistake*)
p. 20, l. 30.		of Xenophon	in Xenophon
p. 25, l. 7.		humane	humaine
p. 27, l. 10.		farre set	farre fet
p. 29, l. 30.		ludit.	ludit,
p. 30, l. 18.		Danus	Davus
p. 31, l. 1.		Vicers	Ulcers
p. 49, l. 23.		sinxit	finxit
,, l. 28.		paper-blurers	paper-blurrers
p. 53, l. 33.		Hecuba	by Hecuba
p. 57, l. 18.		assectation	affectation
,, ,,		farre sette	farre fette
p. 58, l. 7.		senatum	in senatum
,, l. 23.		Fow	Now

Having thus satisfied myself to the best of my ability that I had got the text of 1595, I proceeded to compare it with the later editions mentioned above. It became clear to me, as I said, that they were all derived not from this first edition, but from that of 1598. It must be remembered that none of Sidney's works were printed in his lifetime; but that they were circulated in MS. privately. We cannot tell where Henry Olney got his copy. It differed from that from which the edition of 1598 was printed first in its title *An Apologie* instead of *A Defence*, and secondly in not containing the two passages found on pp. 37 and 58 of this edition. Probably also some of the blunders oi the subsequent editions may be attributed to this second MS.; but most of them are, I think, rather to be assigned to more careless printing or editing. I will give here some of the more striking instances. In p. 5, l. 7, the first edition has the word *Areytos* from the Spanish *Aréito*. But the printer of 1598 not knowing the word gave *Arento*, and so it has appeared in every edition since, no one having taken the trouble to use a Spanish dictionary. The first edition rightly attributed the advice (p. 10, l. 24) 'to sing psalmes,' to *St James:* the printer of 1598 either found in his MS. or evolved from his own ignorance, *St Paul;* and all the editors since have adopted the mistake. In p. 23, l. 25, the first edition rightly gives the word *occidendos.* The 1598 printer, not knowing the meaning, produced *occidentes:* and *occidentes,* making actual nonsense, has stood in the text ever since. In p. 24, l. 18, the first edition gives a perfectly intelligible sentence, " And howe *Praxis* cannot be, without being mooved to practise, it is no hard matter to consider." By changing *cannot* to *can* the 1598 printer contrived to make nonsense of the sentence: but every edition since has followed him. So in p. 42, l. 6 he has done the same by inserting a *not.* In 1595 we have 'sith no memory is so auncient, that hath the precedence of Poetry.' A great deal of Sidney's argument has turned on this point, that Poetry was the oldest of sciences, older than all history. Our 1598 printer however contrives to make nonsense by printing 'that hath *not* the precedence of poetry.' In this case subsequent editors saw the difficulty; but instead of referring to the first edition they conjectured ' that gives not the precedence to poetry,' which without being absolute nonsense, is much less clear and simple than the original. Another instance will shew how an intelligent use of the first edition might have saved considerable difficulty. In 1595 we have (p. 14, l. 8) 'Wherein if wee can shew the poets noblenes, by setting him before his other competitors.' Sense is easily restored by striking out 'if.' But in 1598 the 'if' is retained, and confusion worse confounded by omitting 'nobleness' also, and the sentence thus re-constructed: 'wherein if we can shew, the poet is worthy to have it

before any other competitor.' The next editor (1623) will
not have this, but writes, 'Wherein easily we can shew the
poet is worthy' etc. But the subsequent editors reinstated
'if'; and the prevailing form of the sentence in them all is,
'Wherein if we can shew it rightly, the poet is worthy to
have it before any other competitors.' But if we look at
the passage attentively we shall see that the 'if' clause is
quite inappropriate. Sidney is comparing the various
sciences in the light of their powers of contributing to
the 'ending end' of all sciences—virtuous action. 'In
this point of view'—he argues—'we can shew the poet's
superiority by comparing him with his competitors.' There
is no condition required, and indeed nothing for 'it' to
refer to in the imaginary clause 'if we can shew it rightly.'
Sometimes the mistakes of 1598 running through all subse-
quent editions are less serious, amounting to nothing but a
slight change of expression, as in p. 21, l. 3, 'foule and ill-
favoured' is changed to 'full ill-favoured': I have no doubt
the first is right, but the change is not important. More
important on the other hand is the change of *seates* to *states*
in p. 18, l. 30. Sidney is not thinking of the representation
of the passions *as* they actually are so much as of *where*
they actually are. Poetry, he says, gives examples of
them, not by abstract description, but by representing them
actually influencing individuals; you see them as it were
in their natural 'seates,' the breasts of men and women.

Many more instances might be given; but enough has
been said to shew that the foundation of a text of the
Apologie must be the edition of 1595. In a few cases
a change in subsequent editions is obviously right, as in
p. 59, l. 25, *knacks* for the *tracks* of 1595; p. 37, l. 23 *eare*
or *ear* for *erre*; and p. 63, l. 1, *cataract* for the *cataphract*
of 1595: but on the whole the present edition, with some

sparing changes of spelling and punctuation, reproduces
that of 1595.

The illustrations in the notes have been taken generally
from writers contemporary with Sidney or immediately pre-
ceding or succeeding him. They might have been largely
increased; and perhaps some will think that they might
advantageously have been curtailed. To real students of
the Elizabethan literature doubtless most of them are
familiar; but there are many who may enjoy this essay
of Sidney's who have neither time nor opportunity for such
reading; or who, if they have time, may find it convenient
to have their attention directed to other writers of the
16th century. To such these notes and illustrations are
addressed. The language of Sidney is sufficiently modern
to cause no real difficulty to a reader of our time. Still
his usages are at times far enough removed from those at
present prevailing to make it worth while to trace the origin
of words, and the history of their use, and it is with this
end that the Glossarial Index has been drawn up. Like most
men of education of his day Sidney was steeped in classical
literature; it is therefore necessary in illustrating him con-
tinually to refer to Greek and Latin writers. It has been
my object not to make this portion of my notes more
prominent than was absolutely necessary. Finally, it is
right to say that the various quotations in the notes have
for the most part been marked by myself in the course of
reading the authors referred to: when they are taken
second-hand it is generally notified. Yet I have of course
been greatly assisted by such works as Schmidt's *Shakespeare
Lexicon;* W. A. Wright's *Bible Word-Book;* Skeat's *Dic-
tionary;* and the excellent indexes now happily attached to
most of our Early Poets. I am obliged to Mr W. A. Wright
also for other help.

SIR PHILIP SIDNEY.

PHILIP SIDNEY was born November 30[1], 1554, and died October 17, 1586. He had not therefore completed his thirty-second year. Of this short life seventeen years must be assigned to childhood, and the education of boyhood at Shrewsbury and Oxford, which last he quitted in 1571, three more to the foreign travel looked upon as also a part of education, and the remaining twelve years are all that are left for the achievements of manhood. These years do not contain any incidents of a great or startling nature. Putting aside the last few months of his life, and its heroic close, there is nothing specially memorable to relate. Still it remains true that hardly any one, of whose career we have record, made so decisive an impression on his contemporaries, or one that time has shewn to be so lasting and vivid. Thousands know the story of the draught of water given to the dying soldier who have very faint ideas as to why there was fighting at Zutphen. To many men and

---

[1] The MS. Psalter in Trinity College Library, referred to below, gives this date, not the 29th as usually stated. The entry is 'The nativitie of Phillippe Sydney sonne and heire of S* Henrie Sydney Knighte and the Lady Marie his wyfe, eldest daughter of Iohn. duke of Northumb. was one fryday the last of November being Saincte Andrewes day, a quarter before fyve in the morning, Annis R Regis Philippi et Marie R Regine primo et secundo et anno D'ni, milesimo quingentessimo, quinquagesimo quarto. His godfathers were the greate king, Phillippe, king of Spaine, and the noble John Russell erle of Bedford. And his godmother the most vertuous Ladie Jane Duchesse of Northumb. his grandmother.'

women his 'radiant figure' shines through the mists of ages, in a halo of purity and chivalry, to whom the great names and brilliant achievements of the heroes of the Elizabethan age have become vague and uncertain echoes of a half-forgotten tale. 'To be the most beloved of English writers,' says Thackeray of Goldsmith, 'what a title is that for a man!' To be the best beloved of all the men in Court and camp with whom English history makes us acquainted,—that has rightly or wrongly been Sidney's portion. It is worth while to spend a short time in considering why this should be so. In the first place, then, he impressed his contemporaries with the greatest admiration and affection. There seems no variation in this respect. It was so at school, at Oxford, abroad, in the Court, and finally in his government of Flushing. The friends he made at school or College were his friends for life, and two of them, Fulke Grevil and E. Dyer, walked by the side of his coffin. Abroad he inspired an almost romantic affection in the heart of the old politician, philosopher and reformer Languet; secured the respect and admiration of two such opposite characters as Don John of Austria, and William the Silent; while the artists and men of letters in Italy seem to have been one and all captivated by him. When his Court life began, the same story was repeated. His uncle, the Earl of Leicester, was devoted to him; the Queen called him 'her Philip,'—though she was a trying patroness, as Sidney found,— and early in his Court career entrusted him with a mission of some importance at the Court of the new Emperor Rudolph. By most of the other courtiers he was thought of with a special kind of regard, deeper and more earnest than was usual in that scene of frivolity or selfish emulation. Nor was this feeling secured by any lack of spirit. He shewed enough of that in the quarrel with the Earl of Oxford; as well as in his demeanour to the Earl of Ormond, when he found him in hostility to his father. Nor was it from any superhuman faultlessness of temper. He was, indeed, prone to outbursts of somewhat violent anger, in which he did not hesitate to speak with unwise vehemence, as in the case of his letter to

Molineux, whom he wrongly suspected of having divulged the contents of his correspondence with his father. Even to the Queen he ventured to speak with firmness and candour, both in the interview in which she reproved him for his behaviour to Lord Oxford; and in the celebrated letter, in which he boldly put before her the objections to her proposed marriage with Anjou. It was no want of spirit, no impeccable sweetness of temper, I repeat, that made him so beloved. It was something more; a character unstained by the coarse vices of those among whom he lived,—and how coarse they were only students of the more remote materials of Elizabethan history know,—a temper which, if not perfect, was in the highest degree reasonable, placable, and transparently sincere; honour untarnished; loyalty to his country, his friends, and his family unquestioned; depth of thought, and a poet's temperament: all these qualities went to form a character, the nobility of which made so deep an impression on his contemporaries, that its fame has survived after more than three hundred years with unique distinctness. We may add to these sources of attraction that splendid beauty, which still lives in the pictures at Penshurst and Warwick, and which seems still to fascinate our eyes, and inspire us with the conviction that we are looking at a man of keenest intelligence, most tremulous sensibility, and loftiest purity. Again, Sidney's sympathies were catholic, and embraced all that was brightest and best in the movements of his time. Loving letters and learning, he made his mark as a student at Oxford. When he travelled, he not only read widely in French and Italian literature, but took the keenest pleasure in Art, and in the society of artists and men of letters. In politics he felt with profound sincerity for the Protestant cause, then struggling for life in the face of a Catholic revival; and which was being supported by so many princes and statesmen by such dubious means and with such mixed motives. He told his friend Fulke Grevil.

'That our true-heartednesse to the Reformed Religion, in the beginning, brought Peace, Safetie, and Freedome to us; concluding that the wisest and best way was that of the famous William Prince of

Orange, who never divided the consideration of estate from the cause of religion, nor gave that sound party occasion to be jealous or distracted upon any appearance of safety whatsoever; prudently resolving that to temporize with the Enemies of our Faith, was but (as among Sea-gulls) a strife, not to keep upright, but aloft upon the top of the billow: which false-heartednesse to God and man would in the end find itself forsaken of both.'

Another movement of the day which keenly interested Sidney was the exploration of the New World. He watched eagerly the reports of Frobisher and Drake, and at one time actually was on the eve of embarking on an expedition with the latter. Thus great movements touched him : but he was equally alive to the less prominent, though perhaps not less important, developments of the fancy or ingenuity of mankind, which was being manifested in a revival of literature, and improvements in mechanical contrivances. Fulke Grevil must again illustrate this side of his hero, for whom his love was so sincere, and on the whole so wise, that it serves to keep alive and make readable what is otherwise a dull and ill-constructed little book :

'Indeed he was a true modell of Worth; a man fit for Conquest, Plantation, Reformation, or what Action soever is greatest, and hardest amongst men : Withall, such a lover of Mankind and Goodnesse, that whatsoever had any reall parts, in him found comfort, participation, and protection to the uttermost of his power; like *Zephyrus* he giving life where he blew. The Universities abroad, and at home, accompted him a generall Mecaenas of Learning; dedicated their books to him; and communicated every Invention or Improvement of Knowledge with him. Souldiers honoured him, and were so honoured by him, as no man thought he marched under the true Banner of *Mars*, that had not obtained *Sir Philip Sidney's* approbation. Men of Affairs in most parts of Christendome entertained correspondency with him. But what speak I of these, with whom his own waies and ends did concur? since (to descend) his heart and capacity were so large, that there was not a cunning Painter, a skilfull Engenier, an excellent Musician, or any other Artificer of extraordinary fame, that made not himself known to this famous spirit, and found him his true friend without hire; and the common *Rendez-vous* of Worth in his time.'

If Sidney gave to such men his money or his support, or, better still, his sympathy and appreciation, he has been well repaid by the affection of many generations:

> 'And sure full dear of all he loved was.'

So says Spenser in the noble verses which enshrine the memory of 'the most noble and valorous knight Sir Philip Sidney.'

> ' For from the time that first the Nymph his mother
> Him forth did bring, and taught his lambs to feed;
> A sclender swaine, excelling far each other,
> In comely shape, like her that did him breed,
> He grew up fast in goodnesse and in grace,
> And doubly faire wax both in mynd and face.
> Which daily more and more he did augment,
> With gentle usage and demeanure myld ;
> That all mens hearts with secret ravishment
> He stole away, and weetingly beguyled.
> Ne spight itselfe, that all good things doth spill,
> Found ought in him, that she could say was ill.'

The not very numerous incidents of Sidney's life have been often told ; and must be very briefly recapitulated here. Mr Fox Bourne's *Memoir*, and Mr J. A. Symonds' *Sidney*, in the 'English Men of Letters' series, will give the reader generally all the information attainable. His *correspondence with Languet*, and the documents in the first volume of the *Sidney papers* are the principal original sources of information, and will be studied by those who wish to form an independent judgment[1].

[1] The *Sidney Papers*, 2 vols. fo. edited by Arthur Collins, 1746. Sidney's *Correspondence with Languet*, translated, with the Latin text of Sidney's letters and two letters to his brother Robert, and a prefatory *Memoir*, by Stewart A. Pears, London, Pickering (1845). Besides these there are *Lives* by W. Gray, Oxford (1829); R. A. Grosart, *Early English Poets* series (1877), T. Zouch, York (1808); J. Lloyd (1862). All these may be consulted with advantage. There are besides innumerable shorter notices and essays in Historians, Biographical

INTRODUCTION.

Philip Sidney was the eldest son of Sir Henry Sidney, Kt., by his wife Lady Mary, daughter of John Dudley, Duke of Northumberland, who perished on the scaffold for his part in the plot to put his daughter-in-law, Lady Jane, upon the throne, at the death of Edward VI. Sir Henry [b. 21 July, 1529] had taken no part in this plot. He had been closely attached to the young king, who indeed died in his arms ; and upon his death had retired to Penshurst, the house which he had inherited from his father Sir William. Edward VI. died 6 July, 1553 ; Philip Sidney was born on the 30th of November of the following year. In the course of these sixteen months his mother had had to mourn the death of her father Northumberland (22 Aug., 1553), her brother Guildford and his wife Lady Jane (12 Feb., 1554) on the scaffold; and of her brother John Dudley, who came from the Tower to Penshurst so enfeebled, that he died on the 21st of October, 1554. But though Penshurst was thus a house of mourning at the time of Sidney's birth, his father, Sir Henry, had no cause to be dissatisfied with his own position. He seems to have enjoyed the Queen's favour from the first ; he named his son after her husband Philip of Spain, whom she married in July preceding the boy's birth ; and within two years he was sent to Ireland as Vice-Treasurer. He remained there in that office under the Lord Deputy (his brother-in-law Lord Fitz-Walter, afterwards the Earl of Sussex), and as Lord Justice, until the years 1559—60 ; and must have been constantly absent from Penshurst. In 1560 he was constituted Lord President of the Marches of Wales, still retaining his office in Ireland for some years to come, with a brief interval. As President of Wales his official residence

Dictionaries and the like. See especially Holinshed's *Chronicles*, Camden's *Britannia*, Hazlitt's *Age of Elizabeth*, Masson's *English Novelists*, Motley's *United Netherlands*. The first in point of time, and, in a sense, first in point of interest, as the work of a friend and contemporary, is *The Life of the renowned Sir Philip Sidney*, by Sir Fulke Grevil, Lord Brooke, first published separately after his death, 1652. Letters on Sidney's death will be found in the *Leycester Correspondence*, Ed. J. Bruce for the Camden Society, 1844; and an account of his funeral in Ellis, *Letters*, series 1. vol. 3, p. 16.

was at Ludlow Castle ; but he seems to have been much at Penshurst also, for some of his children appear to have been born there[1]. Still the residence at Ludlow caused Philip to be sent to Shrewsbury, at which school he was entered on the 19th of November, 1564, along with his lifelong friend and biographer Fulke Grevil. Of his school life we know nothing except the report of Grevil :

'Though I lived with him and knew him from a child, yet I never knew him other than a man : with such staiednesse of mind, lovely, and familiar gravety, as carried grace and reverence above greater years. His talk ever of knowledge, and his very play tending to enrich his mind ; so as even his teachers found something in him to observe and learn, above that which they had usually read or taught.'

This, and the fact gathered from the letter addressed to him by his father (1566), that at 12 years old he could write

[1] Sir Henry was married to Lady Mary Dudley at Asser, 29 March, 1551, the ceremony being repeated publicly at Ely Place, Holborn, in the Whitsuntide following. They had issue, (1) A daughter who died in infancy, (2) Philip, b. 30 Nov., 1554, (3) Ambrozia, d. at Ludlow Castle, 22 Feb., 1574, said to be 'nearly twenty years old,' (4) Margaret, d. 10 April, 1558, 1¾ years old (according to the tablet in Penshurst Church), she was therefore born July, 1556, (5) Mary, b. at Ticknell near Beudlie, in the Marches of Wales, 27 October, 1561, m. Henry Earl of Pembroke, 21 April, 1577, d. in London, 25 Sept. 1621, (6) Robert (afterwards Earl of Leicester), b. 19 Nov., 1563, at Penshurst, d. 13 July, 1626, (7) Thomas, b. at Hogsdon by London, 25 March, 1569. He was 'assistant to the chief mourner' at his brother's funeral; and is said to have led a military life, serving among other things in the Netherlands. 'Young Sidney' is mentioned as being one in a pair of combatants in jousts (1591) celebrated in Peele's *Polyhymnia*

> 'Sidney, at which name I sigh,
> Because I lack the Sidney that I lov'd,
> And yet I love the Sidneys that survive.'

[Some of these dates,—as of Mary and Thomas—do not appear in the usual books of reference, but are taken from a MS. *Psalter once belonging to Sir Henry, and now in The Library of Trinity College, Cambridge, kindly pointed out to me by Mr W. A. Wright.]*

in Latin and French, is all we know of his school life.   The
'staiednesse' of the boy remained with the man.   In 1574 he
admitted to Languet that he was 'often graver than suited his
age or employments,' but claimed that the best cure of this
melancholy he had always found to be some difficult mental
exercise[1].   'I have given over the delights in the world,' he
says to his brother in 1580; and he found it necessary to defend
himself from the charge of pride, which his grave manner brought
upon him, in a sonnet which is so personal that it is worth
quoting here for this reason alone, to say nothing of its grace:

> 'Because I oft in darke abstracted guise
>   Seame most alone in greatest company,
>   With dearth of words or answers quite awry,
>   To them that would make speech of speech arise,
>   They deeme, and of their doom the rumour flies
>   That poison foul of babbling pride doth lie
>   So in my swelling breast, that only I
>   Fawn on myself, and others do despise.
>   Yet pride I think doth not my soul possesse
>   (With looks too oft in his unflattering glasse):
>   But one worse fault, ambition, I confesse
>   That makes me oft my best friends overpasse,
>   Unseene, unheard, while thought to highest place
>   Bends all his powers, even unto Stella's grace.'

From Shrewsbury he went in 1568 when 14 years old to
Christchurch, Oxford, where he stayed till 1571; leaving, with-
out a degree, to travel.   That he took full advantage of all
the learning that was to be got at Oxford seems certain.   We
know that he considered himself to have made considerable
progress in Logic there; and his Latin letters to Languet shew
that he possessed readiness and skill in the use of the language,
even if the *Ciceronianism,* of which he speaks with disapproval,
is not to be found in them.   On one occasion we hear of his
disputing in the schools in the presence of his uncle the Earl

---

[1] Letter to Languet, 4 Feb., 1574, *Facile me confiteor tristiorem saepe
esse quam aut aetas aut occupationes postulant,* etc.

of Leicester, who was Chancellor of the University. No doubt his relationship to this powerful nobleman helped to spread his fame in the University; but the charm of his own person and character, and the love which he shewed for letters and learned men must have been felt there, as afterwards in the wider world to which he presently passed. His friend Fulke Grevil was at Oxford with him,—and how well we could have spared some of his praiseworthy remarks on the politics of the time for a Boswellian report of one conversation between the friends! There too he made acquaintance with Ed. Dyer[1], who remained a close friend till his death. The Oxford residence, after a time spent at Ludlow with his family, was followed by over three years of foreign travel (May, 1572, to May 31, 1575). The most striking incident of these travels was Sidney's presence in Paris while the Bartholomew Massacre was raging (August 24, 1572). He took refuge in the house of the English ambassador, Francis Walsingham, who was afterwards to be his father-in-law. But though the sight of Paris during that terrible week no doubt influenced and confirmed his political and religious views; yet it was but an incident in his three years' experiences. His friendship with the veteran Huguenot Languet; his insight into the Courts of Paris, Vienna and Prague; his intercourse with the German Princes, and with William the Silent; his visits among the nobles of Venice, as well as the artists' studios there and at Padua; his wide reading in French and Italian; the steadiness with which he followed other studies,—reading Cicero, Aristotle, Plutarch and other classical authors, and even on Languet's advice attempting, though not it seems with great success, to master German: all this it was that combined to send him home not the ordinary travelled Englishman, a by-word in those times for foppery and corruption, but a thoroughly accomplished man and finished gentleman, of wide knowledge and cultivated taste in literature, as well as with

---

[1] Author of the well-known verses beginning 'My mind to me a kingdom is.'

clear and decided views on statecraft and the politics of Europe.

Sidney returned to London, on the last day of May, 1575, to find his family lessened by the death of one sister, while his only surviving sister Mary, was in the service of the Queen; and his uncle, Lord Leicester, was at the height of his favour and influence. Philip therefore entered upon public life with brilliant prospects. In these days he would have gone at once into Parliament, and have looked for office as the natural result of high position and acknowledged talents. In the reign of Elizabeth a young man of his connexions and genius had no other chance of rising but from the favour of the Queen, gained either directly, or at the instigation of her trusted servants. He must hang about the Court, appearing at all proper times, and with such splendour and shew of personal devotion as were calculated to gain the notice and approbation of the sovereign, now a maiden of the mature age of 42, who still believed that her courtiers were not only loyal to her dynasty, but wildly in love with her person. It is true that, in spite of this personal vanity, Elizabeth had a keen eye for a really able and useful minister; and it was natural for Sidney to hope that his qualifications would meet with recognition at no distant date. Accordingly an employment was soon found for him. In 1576 he was sent on an embassy to the Emperor Rudolph II. to congratulate him on his accession, with further instructions 'to visit and treat with other Princes in Germany,'—with a view, that is, to the possibility of a union among the Protestant Princes for the defence of the Protestant interest in Europe generally. The biographies of Sidney enlarge much on the splendour, not to say ostentation, with which he performed this mission. He returned in June 1577, and a letter from Walsingham (now Sir Francis, and a Privy Councillor) to his father will shew that he was considered to have done well (11 June, 1577):

'I am to impart to you the returne of the yonge gentleman, Mr Sidney, your sonne, whose message verie sufficientlie performed, and the relating therof, is no lesse gratefullye received and well liked of her

Majestie, then the honorable opinion he hathe left behind him with all the Princes, with whom he had to negociate, hathe left a most sweet savor and gratfull remembraunce of his name in those Parts. The Gentleman hathe given no small argument of great Hope, the fruits wherof I doubt not but your Lordship shall reape, as the benefits of the good Parts which ar in him, and wherof he hathe given some tast in this Voyage, is to redounde to more then your Lordship and himself.'

The 'no small argument of great hope' however was long in bringing the desired fruit. The Queen liked and admired him; but was also prone to criticise and find fault with him; and had not yet, it seems, made up her mind that he was the man for a really important post. In his absence his sister Mary had left her position in Court to be the wife of the Earl of Pembroke (21 April, 1577); and perhaps the Queen, who never liked her ladies to marry, even though she gave her consent, was less inclined to advance him. At any rate things were not so cheerful for Philip as before. His father was in somewhat troubled water. His government in Ireland, though successful, had been expensive; and the Queen hated spending money. The Earl of Ormond conceived himself wronged by him, and was at Court busy in bringing his case before the Queen. Sidney entered hotly into his father's cause; behaved with marked haughtiness to the Earl of Ormond; and was in constant communication with Sir Henry and his agents as to the means of composing his defence, on which he eventually drew up a written statement in his own hand, part of which is still extant, and which was much admired[1]. Still all this was against his own personal promotion; and he was for the next few years to experience all those heartaches and that fever of hope deferred, which, according to Spenser, was the lot of the courtier:

[1] E. Waterhouse to Sir H. Sidney, 30 Sept., 1577 (from Windsor) 'Mr Philip hath gathered a collection of all the articles which have been enviously objected to your government, whereunto he hath fraimid an answer in way of discours, the most excellently (if I have any judgement) that ever I red in my Lief: the substance whereof is now approvid in your letters and notes by Mr Whitten. But let no man compare with Mr Philips pen.' Sidney Papers, Vol. I. p. 228.

    'To loose good dayes that might be better spent;
    To wast long nights in pensive discontent;
    To speed to day, to be put back tomorrow;
    To feed on hope, to pine with feare and sorrow;
    To have thy Princes grace, yet want her Peeres;
    To have thy asking, yet wait manie yeeres;
    To fret thy soule with crosses and with cares;
    To eat thy heart through comfortless despaires;
    To fawne, to crouche, to waite, to ride, to ronne,
    To spend, to give, to want, to be undone.
    Unhappy wight, borne to disastrous end,
    That doth his life in so long tendence spend[1].'

Sidney felt much of this; and, longing to be doing a man's work somewhere, more than once planned to make a voyage to the West Indies, the accounts of which enflamed his imagination. One great source of comfort he had in the society of his sister at Wilton. He was there with his mother and brothers, in the summer of 1577; and again, after two more years' idle shew in attendance upon the Court, and the progresses of the Queen, he found a pleasant refuge there for some months in 1580, after his quarrel with the Earl of Oxford. The next three years of his life, 1580—1584, were full ones in regard to literary work, as well as emotion. Four years before (1576) we find that a match had been talked of between him and Penelope Devereux, the daughter of the Earl of Essex. What hindered the completion of this marriage we do not know. If we are to believe the poems in *Astrophel and Stella*, Sidney would not when he could, and found when too late that his heart was wholly hers. How much of this is actual fact, and how much of the poems are imaginary and dramatic, we cannot tell. For myself, I believe that the passion is mainly a poet's passion, not wholly fictitious, and yet not to be construed literally, nor all its various hot and cold fits interpreted to the letter. It was the fashion of expiring chivalry for each knight to have a lady, to whom he was attached by a passion not wholly spiritual, nor wholly of the earth. Dante and

---

[1] Spenser, *Mother Hubberd's Tale.*

Beatrice, Petrarch and Laura, were perhaps the models on which such dramatic emotions were framed ; and Lord Surrey's famous devotion to Geraldine was a more recent example. Editors of Sidney's works have chosen to interpret *Astrophel and Stella* literally; and have disputed on the order of the poems as marking the phases of the passion.   I cordially agree with Mr Symonds in thinking that the order, as it stands, is right : but I cannot think the poems themselves biographical in the ordinary sense, or that they present material for a real history of events.   They are something more: they are the history of a great soul touched with passion ; they are greater than mere facts, just as tragedy is greater, because more universal, than history[1].   Can we believe that if this devotion had been other than poetical, Spenser could have written in his *Astrophel*, dedicated to Sidney's widow, such lines as these?

> 'Stella the faire, the fairest star in skie,
>   As fair as Venus or the fairest faire,
>   (A fairer star saw never living eie,)
>   Shot her sharp pointed beams through purest air.
>   Her he did love, her he alone did honour,
>   His thoughts, his rimes, his songs were all upon her.
>   To her he vowed the service of his daies,
>   On her he spent the riches of his wit:
>   For her he made hymnes of immortal praise,
>   Of onely her he sung, he thought, he writ.
>   Her, and but her, of love he worthie deemed;
>   For all the rest but little he esteemed.'

Her first marriage with a man, who seems to have been of bad character, was apparently not the end, but the beginning

---

[1] Penelope Devereux married Lord Rich in 1580 or 1581; was divorced from him in 1605 and married Henry Blount, Earl of Devonshire, by whom she had already had children.   The curious thing is that, though her connexion with Lord Devonshire had been avowed and condoned at Court, her marriage after divorce, in the lifetime of the first husband, was regarded with great horror and anger by James I. Some letters of Penelope's are printed in Grosart's *Memoir* of Sidney.

of the drama of emotion in Sidney, and we may date the poems therefore probably as being composed in 1581 to 1582. Sidney had already it seems composed part or all of the *Arcadia*. Both are the offspring of retirement, a retirement sought in discontent at the writer's chances of promotion in the public service. Coming back to Court in the summer of 1580, he opposed himself to the party in favour of the Queen's marriage with the Duke of Anjou; and wrote the celebrated letter of remonstrance, which in spite of its boldness seems not to have offended her. Nor indeed did it prevent Sidney playing a principal part, in the course of the following year, in the displays of chivalry got up to do honour to Anjou, when he came to London to press his suit. In 1581 he also sat in Parliament for Kent, besides being much occupied with attendance at Court. The *Apologie for Poetrie* was probably written at the beginning of this or at the end of the previous year, in which he also lost his friend and correspondent Languet. In the next year (1582) we can make out very little of what he was doing. He was with his father on the Marches of Wales in the summer, and anxious to be named in the Council of Wales[1]. He had proved so useful to his father, that upon some suggestion of sending Sir Henry again to Ireland in this year, he let his son know that he would only go on condition of being accompanied by him, and with an understanding from the Queen that he was to be succeeded by him. This suggestion however seems to have come to nothing; nor do we hear anything more of Philip's appointment to the Council of Wales. He was without place or definite employment, eager as he was to obtain a chance of distinguishing himself. In the first month of 1583 he was knighted, on the occasion of serving as deputy for Prince Casimir of the Palatinate in his installation as a Knight of the Garter; and 21st September the same year married Frances Walsingham. We know nothing of their married life, or of the relations between them. A daughter was born early in 1584, and we find Frances determined on joining her husband, rather against his wishes, at

---

[1] Sidney Papers, Vol. I. p. 296.

Flushing, where he said there were things to do 'not suited for the feminine gender.' That she was possessed of attractions is shewn by the fact of her winning the affections of two husbands in succession, the famous Earl of Essex in 1590, by whom she had five children, and the Earl of Clanricarde in 1602. She hastened also to Sidney's side when he was wounded, and her exertions or her sorrow, or both, caused the child, with which she was pregnant, to be still-born. A letter of hers to Cecil praying for his intercession in behalf of her husband Essex, when sentenced to death in 1601, gives a favourable idea both of her abilities and her heart[1]. In this same year he again sat in Parliament, till March 1585; and in the same period seems to have been engaged in composing the defence of his uncle, Lord Leicester, against the libel known as *Leicester's Commonwealth:* and was at length nominated to a distinct office, that of *Master of Ordnance*, which he was to share with his uncle. But he was still restless and dissatisfied, and had his eyes fixed on America. While in Parliament he had

---

[1] The picture of Sidney's widow and daughter now at Penshurst is stated by its inscription to have been painted in 1590, 'Aet. 40.' If this were the case Frances would have been four years her husband's senior, and have been born in 1550; but her father, Sir Francis, is generally stated to have been born in 1536, which would make the date on the Penshurst picture impossible. On the other hand the date of Sir Francis Walsingham's birth depends likewise on an inscription upon a picture: writers before that picture had been known or observed stating that he was born in 1500 and died in his 90th year. It seems impossible to settle the question: I am inclined to believe the Penshurst date, and to suppose that Sir Francis was born about 1526, instead of 1536, which would make him about contemporary with his brother-in-law Sir W. Mildmay. I think Frances being older than her husband would account for the apparent want of any enthusiastic feeling for her, which one cannot help suspecting. It is true that this involves the birth of five children by Lord Essex between her 40th and 50th year, which is only not impossible, and the birth of one child by Lord Clanricarde when she was fifty. But it is to be observed that this last child seems to have cost her her life.

been engaged in considering and helping to pass a bill for the settlement of Virginia by Sir Walter Raleigh. This doubtless had filled his mind still more with thoughts of the West. He had already had a license from the Queen in 1583 'to discover, search, find out, and view certain parts of America;' and 'to enjoy, to him, his heirs and assignees for ever' what would be about 3,000,000 acres of this undiscovered country. This license had not been acted upon. But now Philip was fully set upon taking part in the expedition, upon which Sir Francis Drake was for the last time about to start. The fleet was to meet at Plymouth; and Sidney went thither under cover of a mission to receive Don Antonio of Portugal who was about to arrive there. His real design was kept carefully concealed, for he felt sure that the Queen would forbid it. He arrived at Plymouth in company with his friend Fulke Grevil, but found that Sir Francis Drake, though he had been glad of Sidney's countenance and support in preparing his expedition, was far from anxious to have his own authority divided by the presence of a man, whose rank and influence would make it impossible to refuse him a part in the command. While Sidney was being tantalised by what seemed the endless delay in starting the fleet, a peremptory order arrived from the Queen that he should return to Court; but at the same time offering him an employment which would at last give him the desired opportunity for active service. In 1585 Elizabeth had at length made up her mind, after endless hesitations, debates and delays, to give active assistance to the Netherlanders in their revolt against the Spanish government. In return for the men and money to be sent under the direction of Lord Leicester, she was to hold as security three 'Cautionary Towns,' Flushing, Enkhuysen and Brill. Sidney was to proceed at once to take up the office of 'Governor of Flushing and Rammekins,' with the military rank of General of Horse. He arrived at Flushing in November, and was ready, in company with Prince Maurice of Nassau, to receive his uncle in state on the 19th of December. Sidney had for some time held the opi-

---

[1] Ellis's *Letters*, 1, 3, p. 56.

nion that the more hopeful plan for weakening Spain was that of attacking her West India possessions, rather than by joining in the Dutch revolt. Nor did he find affairs in the Netherlands in a very encouraging state. The Spanish governor, the Prince of Parma, was a splendid soldier; the States were divided by jealousies and fears; the English soldiers already in the country were in a miserable state of poverty and disorganisation; and unless Leicester's coming should introduce some order and discipline in the troops, and some unity of action among the States, the prospect of final success was remote. By general consent Sidney's carriage in this difficult position was worthy of all praise. Of actual achievements in the field there are only two to record. First the storming of Axel (16 July, 1586) under his direction[1]; and secondly, the battle near Zutphen, in which he received his death wound. On the 2nd October, 1586, a small force, accompanied by the leading English nobles and gentlemen, who were serving, some as volunteers, on Leicester's staff,—Essex, Audley, Stanley, Pelham, Russel, Philip and Robert Sidney,—was posted near the Church of Warnsfeld to intercept a convoy of provisions which the Spaniards were trying to throw into Zutphen. It was a misty morning, and the creaking of the wagons could be heard before the troops convoying them could be seen. When the mist suddenly lifted, the small English force found themselves, a body of 50 in all, in the presence of an enemy numbering fully three thousand. The scene which followed has been too often narrated to be repeated here. Three times this little band of heroes charged: and three times broke the enemy's lines. In the third charge Sidney, who had already had a horse killed under him, and who from a rather overstrained feeling of chivalry had thrown off his cuisses, because he met Sir William Pelham in light armour,—received a bullet in the leg, three inches above the knee, shattering the bone. He had ridden through the enemy close up to their intrenchments, and now in terrible pain rode back again, unwilling even then to

---

[1] See *Leycester Correspondence*, Ed. Bruce, p. 237. Motley's *United Netherlands*, Vol. 2, p. 32.

leave the field. But his horse was restive; he could not manage it, maimed and bleeding as he was, and had to be lifted off and carried to the English camp. It was while being thus conveyed that the incident occurred, which more than almost any tale of heroism has touched the heart and fancy of the world. It must be given in Fulk Grevil's own words :

'In which sad progress, passing along by the rest of the army, where his uncle the General was, and being thirstie with excess of bleeding, he called for drink, which was presently brought him; but as he was putting the bottle to his mouth, he saw a poor Souldier carryed along, who had eaten his last at the same Feast, gastly casting up his eyes at the bottle. Which Sir Philip perceiving, took it from his head, before he drank, and delivered it to the poor man, with these words, *Thy necessity is yet greater than mine.*'

That cup of cold water, given, in the highest sense, in Christ's name to a brother mortal in his agony, has had its reward in the admiring love of countless kind hearts of men, women, and children. Sidney was carried by water to Arnheim and survived until October 17, watched over by brother, wife, and friends most tenderly; bearing his sufferings with heroic courage and sweetness of temper. His body was embalmed and taken to Flushing, and thence to London, where it was buried with the honours of a magnificent public funeral at the expense of the Crown 16 Feb., 1587[1]. The Court and the country generally wore mourning for him; and a universal feeling of admiring pity was excited, which may be said to have lasted to this day. His father and mother had both died in the earlier part of the same year (May and August), and at his death Sidney was possessed of the family property. Still, he died deeply in debt. Nor is this wonderful. He had always been inclined to somewhat splendid and lavish expenditure; and his father had begged him and his brother in this respect 'often to remember whose sons they were, and seldom whose nephews.' Moreover he had been compelled to equip himself for his

---

[1] See a description of his funeral in Ellis's *Letters*, Vol. III., p. 16.

governorship at his own charges, and any pay likely to come from the Queen was sure to be cut down to the lowest possible amount, and dealt out in small driblets and with many delays. Then too the misery of many of the soldiers, whom he found serving in the Low Countries, had been too much for his generous heart; and he had liberally relieved them from his own somewhat straitened resources. And though he was now the owner of Penshurst and other properties, he had come into possession so recently, that he could have derived as yet little or no pecuniary benefit from his estates, while further debts to the Crown for 'reliefs' would have been incurred. Philip had provided, as he thought, for the payment of his creditors by ordering the sale of enough land to satisfy them. But difficulties arose as to the power of sale under the will; and we do not know how the business was finally settled.

Such, in brief outline, were the events of Sidney's life. It remains to glance briefly also at his position in literature, and the circumstances in which the *Apologie for Poetrie* was written. It may be taken as certain that the period of Sidney's literary activity lies between 1578 and 1584. Up to the former date was his season of preparation, after the latter his mind was set on other things. Chaucer had been dead nearly 180 years, and no English poet of first-rate importance had lived since. Sidney himself enumerates the names of those who, as he thought, had done good work since Chaucer[1]; and although the list might perhaps be increased by a few names, such as Lydgate, Howes, Wyat, and even Skelton, yet it remained true that there seemed some paralysing influence at work which stopped the free exercise of English genius in the art of poetry. Prose composition was hardly in better case. Malory's *Morte d'Arthur*, Elyot's *Governour*, More's *History of Richard III.*, and R. Robynson's translation of his *Utopia*, Tyndale's *Translation of the Bible*, and the English *Prayer-book* itself, had indeed appeared, and shewn what an English prose style might be; still there was

---

[1] p. 51.

very far from being a good standard of such composition, or signs of the mine being worked with fruitful result. There was a pause before the splendid outburst of the last sixteen years of Elizabeth. Naturally enough the younger men, who, like Sidney, had been trained up in the literature of Greece and Rome, when dreaming of a reform and revival of English poetry, sought for principles on which they were to proceed in the rules of classical verse. Accordingly, Sidney began by forming what he called an Areopagus, or Senate of Poets, who were to draw up rules for this versifying. The nucleus of this self-constituted literary tribunal consisted of the three school and college friends, Sidney, Fulke Grevil and E. Dyer. These were afterwards joined by Spenser and Gabriel Harvey, and some few others. The idea with which they started, of improving the structure of English verse by introducing the principles of classical quantitative metre, was soon found to be a mistaken one. Sidney, indeed, produced some specimens, which had better not have been preserved; and Spenser wasted some time and ingenuity in attempts hardly more successful. The latter happily soon abandoned an enterprise, of which it is doubtful whether he ever seriously approved. And Sidney himself, when his muse had bidden him 'look in his heart and write' followed the dictates of common sense, and the genius of the English language; nor is there much trace in the *Apologie* of a hankering after the old error. His position as a poet must be determined by *Astrophel and Stella:* and though its plan is not original in the strictest sense,—for a series of detached poems, combined into one by unity of motive, could claim several Italian ancestors, going back indeed to the *Amores* of Ovid,— yet it was an original attempt in English literature, and may in a sense be regarded as the progenitor of Shakespeare's *Sonnets;* and in modern times of Tennyson's *In Memoriam;* for different as the motive of this last-named poem may be, yet they have this in common: in both deep personal emotions lead the writer's thoughts to deeper questions still,—to the mysteries of nature and human life and thought. The care and correctness also with which the intricate structure of the sonnet is managed form a distinct advance on his predecessors. As for their poetical and dramatic merits, different judgments will be passed by different minds. So good a critic as Charles Lamb found a great charm in them, and accounted them 'among the best of their kind:' and it may safely be said of the best of them that they are still alive and capable of stirring emotion. They are interspersed with lyrical songs, which, with some of the poems in the *Arcadia*, have at least the merit of good rhythm, and at times of real lyrical passion. The use of the sonnet in such poems as those of Sidney and Shakespeare was not destined to hold its ground in English literature; but it is interesting, both as an attempt to introduce Italian correctness and artistic perfection into England; and as a specimen of a poem of passion founded on personal experience, and yet dramatised by imagination.

As a prose writer Sidney has also a distinct place of his own. The form and machinery of the *Arcadia* is again Italian; the classical scenery and imagery is the natural outcome of the renaissance; but the harmonious beauty of the style is Sidney's own. In appreciation of the charms of nature it is ahead of its age: and though its lack of plot and its prolix descriptions make it wearisome to the modern reader, it was by far the most 'popular novel' of its time. The *Apologie* does not labour under the reproach of prolixity or tediousness. Though some of its arguments and theories would be rejected to-day, it is full of insight and clear statement, and delivers sober judgments which are as applicable now as when Sidney penned them. The charm of the style has often been remarked, and it has been declared by competent critics to be the first piece of really harmonious prose in our language. Without committing ourselves to so general an assertion, we may yet recognise the beauty of such passages as these: 'With a tale forsooth he commeth to you, with a tale which holdeth children from play, and old men from the chimney corner; and, pretending no more, doth intend the winning of the mind from wickedness to virtue' (p. 25): 'So is it in men,—most of which are childish in the best things, till they be cradled in their grave' (p. 25): or the description of the historian 'better acquainted with a thousand years ago, than with the present age, and yet better knowing how this world goeth, than how his own wit runneth; curious for antiquities, and inquisitive of novelties; a wonder to young folks, and a tyrant in table-talk' (p. 15): or the definition of learning as 'this purifying of wit, this enritching of memory, enabling of judgment, and enlarging of conceit' (p. 13): or of reading as 'the gathering of many knowledges' (p. 42). Another noticeable feature of the essay is its originality. True, the ancients are ransacked for examples, and the dicta of Greek or Roman writers regarded as settling questions, as though by the voice of nature: still the writer is also continually speaking of what he has seen and known. Thus the essay begins with a reference to a personal experience; the illustrations from Italy, Hungary, Ireland and Wales are from his own knowledge; his references to West Indian customs are the fruit of his own intense interest in the great discoveries of the age; his own discontent prompts his reference to the 'over-faint quietness of the time;' his own taste is expressed in his criticism on the cold artificiality of the love poetry of the day, even to the pedantic tricks of 'coursing of a letter[1].' Though he uses Aristotle's and Scaliger's *Poetics* freely in his classification of poets, and in many of his definitions, yet he uses them with the independence which comes of study at first hand; and his classical quotations are as a rule not too hackneyed or obvious, and seem generally to be made from memory and with such alterations as suited him. With no author was he apparently more entirely familiar than with Plutarch; a familiarity shewn not indeed by direct quotation, but by numerous expressions which came evidently from an almost unconscious reproduction of thoroughly assimilated thoughts.

Like all that Sidney wrote, the *Apologie* was not printed until some time after his death. The first edition is that of 1595, when he had been nine years dead. There is no certain proof therefore of the time of its composition; yet we have the means of making a fairly certain conjecture. In the first place

---

[1] Compare Sonnets XV. LIV.

we have a letter written to his brother Robert abroad, dated from Leicester House, 18 October, 1580, in which many of the thoughts suggest those of the *Apologie.* Thus we have the various functions of the historian, orator, natural and moral philosopher and poet sketched in much the same spirit. There is also a remark as to the Ciceronianism of the day, which directly recalls the reference to the 'Nizolian paper-books' (p. 57), 'So you can speak and write Latin not barbarously; I never require great study in Ciceronianism, the chief abuse of Oxford, "*qui dum verba sectantur, res ipsas negligunt.*"' In many minute points the letter suggests that the writer had in his thoughts the matter which is dealt with in the *Apologie.* The next piece of evidence is in the well-known letter of Spenser to G. Harvey, dated also from Leicester House, October 1579. After mentioning his intimacy with Sidney and Dyer, he says: 'Newe books I heare of none, but only one, that writing a certain booke called *The Schoole of Abuse,* and dedicating it to Maister Sidney, was for his labour scorned: if at leaste it be in the goodnesse of that nature to scorne.' The author of this work, Stephen Gosson, was a native of Kent, born the year before Sidney, and educated at Christ Church, which he entered the year after Sidney left Oxford. He had in early life written poems and plays; but about 1578—9 was caught by the Puritan feeling that was growing up against plays, and ceased writing for the stage. The *Schoole of Abuse* was produced in August 1579, followed soon after by the second part, or *An Apologie of the Schoole of Abuse.* Now, though Sidney shews throughout his defence of poetry that he is answering various criticisms and common prejudices, yet a few extracts from the *Schoole of Abuse* will shew that he must also have had this work in his mind, both as the latest in date, and as being dedicated to himself, and thereby, as it were, challenging his sympathy and assent. The *Schoole of Abuse,* however, though containing general reflections on poets, is mainly concerned with the dramatic poets and the corruptions of the theatres. It is therefore when Sidney comes to speak of plays that he mostly has Gosson in mind. Of the more general reflections on poets, to which Sidney's answer refers, these specimens will suffice:

'These are the cuppes of *Circes*, that turne reasonable creatures into brute beastes, the balles of Hippomenes, that hinder the course of Atalanta; and the blocks of the Divel that are caste in our wayes, to cut off the race of toward wittes.   No marveyle though Plato shut them out of his Schoole, and banished them quite out of his common wealth, as effeminate writers, unprofitable members, and utter enemies to vertue,' p. 20, Ed. Arber.

'Dion sayth that english men could suffer watching and labour, hunger and thirst, and bear all stormes with hed and shoulders. ...The men in valure not yeelding to Scithia, the women in courage passing the Amazons.   The exercise of both was shootyng and darting, running and wrestling, and trying such maisteries, as eyther consisted in swiftnesse of feete, agilitie of body, strength of armes, or Martiall discipline. But the exercise that is nowe among us is banqueting, playing, pipyng and dauncing, and all suche delightes as may win us to pleasure or rocke us to sleepe.'   p. 34.

'Therefore let me hold the same proposition still, which I set down before, and drewe out of Tully, that ancient Poetes are fathers of lies, Pipes of vanitie, and schooles of Abuse.'   p. 66.

These generally are the charges against poetry which called forth the reply of the *Apologie*. After a short introduction (pp. 1—2), Sidney's essay falls into three parts: I. (pp. 2—28) a general defence of poetry, as the earliest form of literature, as holding up a mirror to nature, as contributing better than philosophy or history to the end of all teaching—virtuous action. II. (pp. 28—47) answers to objections to the several kinds of poetry, which are enumerated and classified.   III. (pp. 47—63) an enquiry into the state of English poetry and the reasons for its disrepute, with certain suggestions.   Each part ends with a recapitulation of the arguments employed.   It is in the second of these divisions that it falls in with Sidney's plan to defend the work of the dramatist : and the charges generally brought against it may be seen in the following extract from Gosson :

'Nowe are the abuses of the worlde revealed, Every man in a play may see his owne faultes, and learne by this glasse, to amende his manners. *Curculio* may chatte til his heart ake, ere any be offended with his gyrdes.   Deformities are checked in jeast and mated in earnest. The sweetnesse of musicke, and pleasure of sportes, temper the bitternesse of rebukes, and mitigate the tartenesse of every taunt according to this

> Omne vafer vitium ridenti Flaccus amico
> Narrat, et admissus circum praecordia ludit.
> *Flaccus* among his friends with fawning Muse
> Doth nip him neere, that fostreth foule abuse.

Therefore they are either so blinde, that they cannot, or so blunt that they will not see why this exercise should not be suffered as a profitable recreation,' p. 31.

'I accuse them (the poets) for bringing their cunning into theaters: that I say they have wilfully left, or with ignorance loste those warlike tunes which were used in auncient times to stirre up in us a manly motion, and found out new descant with the dauncers of Sybaris to rocke us a sleepe in all ungodlieness.' p. 69.

It will be seen that Sidney takes up the sarcastic challenge of the first of these extracts almost in the words of the writer. But in truth, Gosson's invective is directed chiefly against the immorality of the play-*houses*, or other places where plays were acted, rather than against the plays themselves; these were chiefly guilty as contributing to gather the assemblies where such breaches of morality took place. On this head Sidney says nothing. He confines his defence to the moral effects of the scenes represented.

To appreciate the third part of the *Apologie* (pp. 47—63), in which Sidney examines the causes of the admitted defects in English poetry, and especially in English plays, it is necessary to remember how little of what we now regard as first-rate work had been done in poetry since Chaucer[1]; and that nothing of what was really great had been produced in the English drama, although Sidney could truly say that such composition was the most common of all in England. If he wrote in 1580/1, it was seven years before Marlowe's *Tamburlaine*, eight years before Shakespeare's *Love's Labour Lost*, fifteen years before Ben Jonson's *Every Man in his Humour*. Green had apparently not left Cambridge, and it is very unlikely that any of his plays had yet been seen in London. Peele's *Arraignment of Paris* may have

---

[1] See *ante*, p. xxix.

been acted; but it is hardly possible that any of Nash's plays could have been. Sidney was therefore criticising those tragedies and comedies which had not salt enough in them to keep them sweet, even if some of them were afterwards restored to a greater and more lasting life by the magic touch of Shakespeare. It is some credit to him in these circumstances that he was not discouraged as to the future of English letters, and would not listen to those who held that our language was rude, and unfitted to be an instrument of the higher literature; it is, he emphatically declares, 'indeed capable of any excellent exercising of it.'

AN APOLOGIE FOR POETRIE.

WHEN the right vertuous *Edward Wotton* and I were at the Emperors Court together, wee gave our selves to learne horse-manship of *Iohn Pietro Pugliano;* one that with great commendation had the place of an Esquire in his stable.   And hee, according to the fertilnes of the Italian wit, did not onely afoord us the demonstration of his practise, but sought to enrich our mindes with the contemplations therein, which hee thought most precious.   But with none 10 I remember mine eares were at any time more loden, then when (either angred with slowe paiment, or mooved with our learner-like admiration) he exercised his speech in the prayse of his facultie.   Hee sayd, Souldiours were the noblest estate of mankinde, and horsemen the noblest of 15 Souldiours.   Hee sayde, they were the Maisters of warre, and ornaments of peace : speedy goers, and strong abiders : triumphers both in Camps and Courts.   Nay, to so unbe-leeved a poynt hee proceeded, as that no earthly thing bred such wonder to a Prince, as to be a good horseman.   Skill 20 of government was but a *Pedanteria* in comparison.   Then would hee adde certain prayses, by telling what a peerlesse

Introduc-
tion.
Each artist
maintains the
importance of
his own art. 5

beast a horse was : the onely serviceable Courtier without flattery, the beast of most beutie, faithfulnes, courage ; and such more, that, if I had not beene a peece of a Logician before I came to him, I think he would have perswaded 5 mee to have wished my selfe a horse. But thus much at least with his no fewe words hee drave into me, that selfe-love is better then any guilding to make that seeme gorgious wherein our selves are parties. Wherein, if *Pugliano* his strong affection and weake arguments will not satisfie you, 10 I wil give you a neerer example of my selfe, who (I knowe not by what mischance) in these my not old yeres and idelest times, having slipt into the title of a Poet, am provoked to say somthing unto you in the defence of that my unelected vocation; which if I handle with more good 15 will then good reasons, beare with me, sith the scholler is to be pardoned that foloweth the steppes of his Maister. And yet I must say, that as I have iust cause to make a pittiful defence of poore Poetry, which, from almost the highest estimation of learning, is fallen to be the laughing- 20 stocke of children; so have I need to bring some more availeable proofes : sith the former is by no man barred of his deserved credite, the[1] silly latter hath had even the names of Philosophers used to the defacing of it, with great danger of civill war among the Muses.

25   And first, truly to al them that professing learning inveigh against Poetry may iustly be obiected, *Poetry is the* EARLIEST *form of compo-sition in all literatures.* that they goe very neer to ungratfulnes, to seek to deface that, which in the noblest nations and languages that are knowne, hath been the 30 first lightgiver to ignorance, and first Nurse, whose milk by little and little enabled them to feed afterwards of tougher

---

[1] 'whereas the', in some later Edd.

knowledges: and will they now play the Hedghog, that being received into the den, drave out his host? or rather the Vipers, that with theyr birth kill their Parents? Let learned Greece, in any of her manifold Sciences, be able to shew me one booke before *Musaeus, Homer*, and *Hesiodus:* 5 all three nothing els but Poets. Nay, let any historie be brought, that can say any Writers were there before them, if they were not men of the same skil, as *Orpheus, Linus*, and some others are named: who, having beene the first of that Country that made pens deliverers of their knowledge 10 to their posterity, may iustly challenge to bee called their Fathers in learning: for not only in time they had this priority (although in it self antiquity be venerable), but went before them as causes, to drawe with their charming sweetnes the wild untamed wits to an admiration of know- 15 ledge. So as *Amphion* was sayde to move stones with his Poetrie to build Thebes; and *Orpheus* to be listened to by beastes, indeed stony and beastly people: so among the Romans were *Liuius Andronicus*, and *Ennius;* so in the Italian language, the first that made it aspire to be a 20 Treasure-house of Science were the Poets *Dante, Boccace*, and *Petrarch;* so in our English were *Gower* and *Chawcer*.

After whom, encouraged and delighted with theyr excellent fore-going, others have followed, to beautifie our mother tongue, as wel in the same kinde as *Even philoso-* 25 in other Arts. This did so notably shewe it *phy was first taught in verse.* selfe, that the Philosophers of Greece durst not a long time appeare to the worlde but under the masks of Poets. So *Thales, Empedocles, Parmenides* sange their naturall Philosophie in verses: so did *Pythagoras* and 30 *Phocilides* their morral counsells: so did *Tirteus* in war matters, and *Solon* in matters of policie: or rather, they beeing Poets dyd exercise their delightful vaine in those

points of highest knowledge, which before them lay hid to
the world. For that wise *Solon* was directly a Poet it is
manifest, having written in verse the notable fable of the
Atlantick Iland, which was continued by *Plato.*

5   And truely, even *Plato,* whosoever well considereth,
shall find, that in the body of his work, though
Plato's dia- the inside and strength were Philosophy, the
logues are
themselves skinne as it were and beautie depended most
poetical.
of Poetrie : for all standeth upon Dialogues,
10 wherein he faineth many honest Burgesses of Athens to
speake of such matters, that, if they had been sette on the
racke, they would never have confessed them. Besides,
his poetical describing the circumstances of their meetings,
as the well ordering of a banquet, the delicacie of a walke,
15 with enterlacing meere tales, as *Giges* Ring, and others,
which who knoweth not to be flowers of Poetrie did never
walke into Apollo's Garden.

And even Historiographers, although theyr lippes
sounde of things doone, and veritie be written
Historians
20 *imitate poetic* in theyr fore-heads, have been glad to borrow
methods.
both fashion, and perchance weight of Poets.
So *Herodotus* entituled his Historie by the name of the nine
Muses : and both he, and all the rest that followed him,
either stole or usurped of Poetrie their passionate describ-
25 ing of passions; the many particularities of battailes which
no man could affirme; or, if that be denied me, long Orations
put in the mouthes of great Kings and Captaines, which it
is certaine they never pronounced. So that truely, neyther
Philosopher nor Historiographer coulde at the first have
30 entred into the gates of populer iudgements, if they had
not taken a great pasport of Poetry, which in all Nations at
this day, wher learning florisheth not, is plaine to be seene:
in all which they have some feeling of Poetry. In Turky,

besides their lawe-giving Divines, they have no other Writers
but Poets.   In our neighbour Countrey Ireland,
where truelie learning goeth very bare, yet are *It is respected in the most*
theyr Poets held in a devoute reverence. *barbarous countries.*
Even among the most barbarous and simple 5
Indians where no writing is, yet have they their Poets, who
make and sing songs which they call *Areytos*, both of theyr
Auncestors deedes, and praises of theyr Gods : a sufficient
probabilitie, that, if ever learning come among them, it
must be by having theyr hard dull wits softened and sharp- 10
ened with the sweete delights of Poetrie.   For untill they
find a pleasure in the exercises of the minde, great promises
of much knowledge will little perswade them that knowe
not the fruites of knowledge.   In Wales, the true remnant
of the auncient Brittons, as there are good authorities to 15
shewe the long time they had Poets which they called
Bardes ; so thorough all the conquests of Romaines, Saxons,
Danes, and Normans, some of whom did seeke to ruine all
memory of learning from among them, yet doo their Poets
even to this day last : so as it is not more notable in soone 20
beginning then in long continuing.   But since the Authors
of most of our Sciences were the Romans, and before them
the Greekes, let us a little stand upon their authorities, but
even so farre as to see what names they have given unto
this now scorned skill. 25

Among the Romans a Poet was called *Vates*, which is
as much as a Diviner, Fore-seer, or Prophet, as
by his conioyned wordes *Vaticinium* and *Vati-* THE ESTIMA-TION OF POE-
cinari is manifest : so heavenly a title did that TRY (1) *among the Romans.*
excellent people bestow upon this hart-ravish- 30
ing knowledge.   And so farre were they carried into the
admiration thereof, that they thought in the chaunceable

hitting upon any such verses great fore-tokens of their
following fortunes were placed.   Whereupon grew the
worde of *Sortes Virgilianae*, when by suddaine opening
Virgils booke, they lighted upon any verse of hys making :
5 whereof the histories of the Emperors lives are full: As of
Albinus the Governour of our Iland, who in his childehoode
mette with this verse

Arma amens capio nec sat rationis in armis :

and in his age performed it.   Which although it were a very
10 vaine and godles superstition, as also it was to think that
spirits were commaunded by such verses,—whereupon this
word charmes, derived of *Carmina* commeth,—so yet
serveth it to shew the great reverence those wits were
helde in.   And altogether not without ground, since both
15 the Oracles of *Delphos* and *Sibillas* prophecies where wholy
delivered in verses.   For that same exquisite observing of
number and measure in words, and that high flying liberty
of conceit proper to the Poet, did seeme to have some
dyvine force in it.

20   And may not I presume a little further, to shew the
reasonablenes of this worde *Vates?*   And say
(2) Among the Hebrews. that the holy *Davids* Psalmes are a divine
Poem?   If I doo, I shall not do it without the
testimonie of great learned men, both auncient and
25 moderne.   But even the name Psalmes will speake for mee,
which, being interpreted, is nothing but songes : then that it
is fully written in meeter, as all learned Hebricians agree,
although the rules be not yet fully found : lastly and
principally, his handeling his prophecy, which is meerely
30 poetical.   For what els is the awaking his musicall instru-
ments ; the often and free changing of persons ; his notable
Prosopopeias, when he maketh you as it were, see God

comming in his Maiestie; his telling of the Beastes ioyful-
nes, and hills leaping, but a heavenlie poesie, wherein
almost hee sheweth himselfe a passionate lover of that
unspeakable and everlasting beautie to be seene by the eyes
of the minde, only cleered by fayth? But truely nowe 5
having named him, I feare mee I seeme to prophane that
holy name, applying it to Poetrie, which is among us throwne
downe to so ridiculous an estimation: but they that with
quiet iudgements will looke a little deeper into it, shall finde
the end and working of it such, as, beeing rightly applyed, 10
deserveth not to bee scourged out of the Church of God.

But now, let us see how the Greekes named it, and
howe they deemed of it. The Greekes called
him a Poet[1], which name hath, as the most *(3) Among the Greeks.*
excellent, gone thorough other Languages. It 15
commeth of this word *Poiein*, which is to make: wherein I
know not, whether by lucke or wisedome, wee Englishmen
have mette with the Greekes in calling him a maker: which
name, how high and incomparable a title it is, I had rather
were knowne by marking the scope of other Sciences, then 20
by my partiall allegation.

There is no Arte delivered to mankinde, that hath not
the workes of Nature for his principall obiect,
without which they could not consist, and on *The poet is a creator in a*
which they so depend, as they become Actors *fuller sense than others.* 25
and Players, as it were, of what Nature will
have set foorth. So doth the Astronomer looke upon the
starres, and by that he seeth setteth downe what order
Nature hath taken therein. So doe the Geometrician, and
Arithmetician, in their diverse sorts of quantities. So doth 30

---

[1] Later Editions have the Greek word ποιητὴν, and so in the case of
other Greek words throughout.

the Musitian in times tel you which by nature agree, which
not.   The naturall Philosopher thereon hath his name, and
the Morrall Philosopher standeth upon the naturall vertues,
vices, and passions of man : ‘and followe Nature’ (saith
5 hee) ‘therein, and thou shalt not erre.’   The Lawyer sayth
what men have determined.   The Historian what men have
done.   The Grammarian speaketh onely of the rules of
speech : and the Rethorician, and Logitian, considering
what in Nature will soonest prove and perswade, thereon
10 give artificial rules, which still are compassed within the
circle of a question, according to the proposed matter.
The Phisition waigheth the nature of a mans bodie, and
the nature of things helpeful or hurtefull unto it.   And the
Metaphisick, though it· be in the seconde and abstract
15 notions, and therefore be counted supernaturall, yet doth
hee indeede builde upon the depth of Nature.   Onely the
Poet, disdayning to be tied to any such subiection, lifted up
with the vigor of his owne invention, dooth growe in effect
another nature, in making things either better than Nature
20 bringeth forth, or, quite anewe, formes such as never were
in Nature, as the *Heroes*, *Demigods*, *Cyclops*, *Chimeras*,
Furies, and such like : so as hee goeth hand in hand with
Nature, not inclosed within the narrow warrant of her guifts,
but freely ranging onely within the Zodiack of his owne
25 wit.

Nature never set forth the earth in so rich tapistry, as
divers Poets have done, neither with so plesant

The poet even transcends nature. rivers, fruitful trees, sweet smelling flowers, nor
whatsoever els may make the too much loved
30 earth more lovely.   Her world is brasen, the Poets only
deliver a golden.   But let those things alone and goe to
man, for whom as the other things are, so it seemeth in him
her uttermost cunning is imployed, and knowe whether

shee have brought foorth so true a lover as *Theagines*, so
constant a friende as *Pilades*, so valiant a man as *Orlando*,
so right a Prince as *Xenophons Cyrus*, so excellent a man
every way as *Virgils Aeneas:* neither let this be iestingly
conceived, because the works of the one be essensiall, the 5
other, in imitation or fiction: for any understanding knoweth
the skil of the Artificer standeth in that *Idea* or fore-conceite
of the work, and not in the work it selfe.   And that the
Poet hath that *Idea*, is manifest, by delivering them forth in
such excellencie as hee hath imagined them.   Which deliver- 10
ing forth also, is not wholie imaginative, as we are wont to
say by them that build Castles in the ayre: but so farre
substantially it worketh, not onely to make a *Cyrus*, which
had been but a particuler excellencie as Nature might have
done, but to bestow a *Cyrus* upon the worlde, to make 15
many *Cyrus's*, if they wil learne aright why and how that
Maker made him.

Neyther let it be deemed too sawcie a comparison to
ballance the highest poynt of mans wit with the
efficacie of Nature: but rather give right honor   *This creative* 20
to the heavenly Maker of that maker; who   *faculty is the*
highest human
faculty.
having made man to his owne likenes, set him
beyond and over all the workes of that second nature:
which in nothing hee sheweth so much as in Poetrie; when,
with the force of a divine breath, he bringeth things forth far 25
surpassing her dooings, with no small argument to the
incredulous of that first accursed fall of *Adam:* sith our
erected wit maketh us know what perfection is, and yet our
infected will keepeth us from reaching unto it.   But these
arguments wil by fewe be understood, and by fewer granted. 30
Thus much (I hope) will be given me, that the Greekes,
with some probabilitie of reason, gave him the name above
all names of learning.   Now let us goe to a more ordinary

opening of him, that the trueth may be more palpable : and
so I hope, though we get not so unmatched a praise as the
Etimologie of his names wil grant, yet his very description,
which no man will denie, shall not iustly be barred from a
5 principall commendation.

Poesie therefore is an arte of imitation, for so *Aristotle*
termeth it in his word *Mimesis*, that is to say, a
representing, counterfetting, or figuring foorth :
to speake metaphorically, a speaking picture :
with this end, to teach and delight ; of this have
beene three severall kindes.

Poetry is the ART OF IMITA-TION *or* GRA-PHIC REPRE-SENTATION.
10

The chiefe both in antiquitie and excellencie, were they
that did imitate the inconceivable excellencies
of GOD.   Such were, *David* in his Psalmes,
Salomon in his song of Songs, in his Ecclesiastes,
and Proverbs : *Moses* and *Debora* in theyr Hymnes, and the
writer of *Iob;* which beside other, the learned *Emanuell
Tremilius* and *Franciscus Iunius*, doe entitle the poeticall
part of the Scripture.   Against these none will speak that
20 hath the holie Ghost in due holy reverence.   In this kinde,
though in a full wrong divinitie, were *Orpheus, Amphion,
Homer* in his hymnes, and many other, both Greekes and
Romaines : and this Poesie must be used, by whosoever will
follow *S. Iames* his counsell, in singing Psalmes when they
25 are merry : and I knowe is used with the fruite of comfort by
some, when, in sorrowfull pangs of their death-bringing
sinnes, they find the consolation of the never-leaving good-
nesse.

SUBJECTS (1) *the Divine excellencies.*
15

The second kinde is of them that deale with matters
Philosophicall ; eyther morrall, as *Tirteus, Pho-
cilides* and *Cato* : or naturall, as *Lucretius* and
Virgils Georgicks: or Astronomicall, as *Manilius,*

30 *(2) Morals, physics and history.*

and *Fontanus:* or historical, as *Lucan:* which who mislike, the faulte is in their iugdements quite out of taste, and not in the sweet foode of sweetly uttered knowledge.

But because thys second sorte is wrapped within the folde of the proposed subiect, and takes not the course of his owne invention, whether they properly be Poets or no, let Gramarians dispute: and goe to the thyrd, indeed right Poets, of whom chiefly this question ariseth ; betwixt whom, and these second is such a kinde of difference, as betwixt the meaner sort of Painters (who counterfet onely such faces as are sette before them) and the more excellent, who having no law but wit, bestow that in cullours upon you which is fittest for the eye to see : as the constant though lamenting looke of *Lucrecia*, when she punished in her selfe an others fault. Wherein he painted not *Lucrecia*, whom he never sawe, but painteth the outwarde beauty of such a vertue. For these third be they which most properly do imitate to teach and delight, and to imitate, borrow nothing of what is, hath been, or shall be : but range, onely rayned with learned discretion, into the divine consideration of what may be and should be. These bee they, that, as the first and most noble sorte may iustly bee termed *Vates*, so these are waited on in the excellentest languages and best under-standings with the fore described name of Poets. For these indeede doo meerely make to imitate ; and imitate both to delight and teach ; and delight to move men to take that goodnes in hande, which without delight they would flye as from a stranger ; and teach, to make them know that goodnes whereunto they are mooved : which being the noblest scope to which ever any learning was directed, yet want there not idle tongues to barke at them.

(3) Abstract qualities exhibited in imaginary persons.

These be subdivided into sundry more speciall denomi-

Classification of right poets. They do not necessarily write in metre.

nations. The most notable bee the *Heroick, Lirick, Tragick, Comick, Satirick, Iambick, Ele-giack, Pastorall,* and certaine others. Some
5 of these being termed according to the matter they deale with, some by the sorts of verses they liked best to write in, for indeede the greatest part of Poets have apparelled their poeticall inventions in that numbrous kinde of writing which is called verse: indeed but appa-
10 relled, verse being but an ornament and no cause to Poetry; sith there have beene many most excellent Poets that never versified, and now swarme many versifiers that neede never aunswere to the name of Poets. For *Xenophon,* who did imitate so excellently as to give us *effigiem iusti imperij,* the
15 portraiture of a iust Empire, under the name of *Cyrus* (as *Cicero* sayth of him), made therein an absolute heroicall Poem. So did *Heliodorus* in his sugred invention of that picture of love in *Theagines* and *Cariclea.* And yet both these writ in Prose: which I speak to shew, that it is not
20 riming and versing that maketh a Poet, no more then a long gowne maketh an Advocate; who though he pleaded in armor should be an Advocate and no Souldier. But it is that fayning notable images of vertues, vices, or what els, with that delightfull teaching, which must be the right
25 describing note to know a Poet by. Although indeed the Senate of Poets have chosen verse as their fittest rayment, meaning, as in matter they passed all in all, so in maner to goe beyond them: not speaking (table talke fashion, or like men in a dreame,) words as they chanceably fall from
30 the mouth, but peyzing each sillable of each worde by iust proportion according to the dignitie of the subiect.

Nowe therefore it shall not bee amisse first to waigh this

latter sort of Poetrie by his works, and then by his partes ;
and if in neyther of these Anatomies hee be con-
demnable, I hope wee shall obtaine a more
favourable sentence. This purifing of wit, this
enritching of memory, enabling of iudgment,
and enlarging of conceyt, which commonly we
call learning, under what name soever it com forth, or to
what immediat end soever it be directed, the final end is,
to lead and draw us to as high a perfection, as our degene-
rate soules, made worse by theyr clayey lodgings, can be 10
capable of. This, according to the inclination of the man,
bred many formed impressions : for some that thought this
felicity principally to be gotten by knowledge, and no know-
ledge to be so high and heavenly as acquaintance with the
starres, gave themselves to Astronomie ; others, perswading 15
themselves to be *Demigods* if they knewe the causes of
things, became naturall and supernaturall Philosophers ;
some an admirable delight drew to Musicke ; and some the
certainty of demonstration to the Mathematickes. But all,
one and other, having this scope—to knowe, and by know- 20
ledge to lift up the mind from the dungeon of the body to
the enioying his owne divine essence. But when, by the
ballance of experience, it was found that the Astronomer
looking to the starres might fall into a ditch, that the
enquiring Philosopher might be blinde in himselfe, and the 25
Mathematician might draw foorth a straight line with a
crooked hart : then loe, did proofe, the over ruler of
opinions, make manifest that all these are but serving
Sciences, which as they have each a private end in them-
selves, so yet are they all directed to the highest end of the 30
mistres Knowledge, by the Greekes called *Arkitecktonike,*
which stands (as I thinke) in the knowledge of a mans selfe,
in the Ethicke and politick consideration, with the end of

well dooing and not of well knowing onely: even as the
Sadlers next end is to make a good saddle, but his farther
end to serve a nobler facultie, which is horsemanship: so the
horsemans to souldiery, and the Souldier not onely to have
5 the skill, but to performe the practice of a Souldier: so that,
the ending end of all earthly learning being vertuous action,
those skilles that most serve to bring forth that have a most
iust title to bee Princes over all the rest: wherein wee can[1]
shewe the Poets noblenes, by setting him before his other
10 Competitors.

Among whom as principall challengers step forth the

Compared (1) *with moral philosophy:*

morrall Philosophers: whom, me thinketh, I see
comming towards me with a sullen gravity, as
though they could not abide vice by day light;
15 rudely clothed for to witnes outwardly their contempt of
outward things; with bookes in their hands agaynst glory,
whereto they sette theyr names; sophistically speaking
against subtility; and angry with any man in whom they
see the foule fault of anger. These men casting larges as
20 they goe of Definitions, Divisions, and Distinctions, with
a scornefull interogative doe soberly aske, whether it bee
possible to finde any path so ready to leade a man to
vertue, as that which teacheth what vertue is? and teacheth
it not onely by delivering forth his very being, his causes,
25 and effects; but also, by making known his enemie vice,
which must be destroyed, and his combersome servant
Passion, which must be maistered; by shewing the generali-
ties that contayneth it, and the specialities that are derived
from it. Lastly, by playne setting downe how it extendeth it
30 selfe, out of the limits of a mans own little world, to the go-
vernment of families, and maintayning of publique societies.

The Historian, scarcely giveth leysure to the Moralist

---

[1] The first Edition has 'if we can', which makes nonsense. In later
Editions various alterations have been adopted. See Preface.

to say so much, but that he,—loden with old Mouse-eaten
records, authorising himselfe (for the most part)   (2) *with*
upon other histories, whose greatest authori-   *History.*
ties are built upon the notable foundation of Heare-say,
having much a-doe to accord differing Writers, and to pick 5
trueth out of partiality; better acquainted with a thousande
yeeres a goe, then with the present age, and yet better
knowing how this world goeth, then how his owne wit
runneth; curious for antiquities, and inquisitive of novelties;
a wonder to young folkes, and a tyrant in table talke,—de- 10
nieth in a great chafe, that any man for teaching of vertue,
and vertuous actions, is comparable to him. I am *Lux
vitæ, Temporum Magistra, Vita memoriæ, Nuncia vetus-
tatis. &c.* 'The philosopher' (sayth hee) 'teacheth a
'disputative vertue, but I doe an active : his vertue is ex- 15
'cellent in the dangerlesse Academie of *Plato*, but mine
'sheweth foorth her honorable face, in the battailes of
'*Marathon, Pharsalia, Poitiers*, and *Agincourt.* Hee teach-
'eth vertue by certaine abstract considerations, but I onely
'bid you follow the footing of them that have gone before 20
'you. Olde-aged experience goeth beyond the fine-witted
'Philosopher, but I give the experience of many ages.
'Lastly, if he make the Song-booke, I put the learners
'hande to the Lute: and if hee be the guide, I am the
'light.' Then woulde hee alledge you innumerable ex- 25
amples, conferring storie by storie, how much the wisest
Senatours and Princes have beene directed by the credite
of history, as *Brutus, Alphonsus* of *Aragon*, and who not,
if need bee? At length, the long lyne of theyr disputation
maketh a poynt in thys, that the one giveth the precept, 30
and the other the example.

Nowe, whom shall wee finde (sith the question stand-
eth for the highest forme in the Schoole of learning) to bee

Moderator? Trulie, as me seemeth, the Poet; and if not a
Moderator, even the man that ought to carrie the
title from them both, and much more from all
other serving Sciences. Therefore compare we
the Poet with the Historian, and with the Morrall
Philosopher, and, if hee goe beyond them
both, no other humaine skill can match him. For as for
the Divine, with all reverence it is ever to be excepted, not
only for having his scope as far beyonde any of these, as
10 eternitie exceedeth a moment, but even for passing each
of these in themselves. And for the Lawyer, though *Ius*
bee the Daughter of Iustice, and Iustice the chiefe of
Vertues; yet because hee seeketh to make men good
rather *Formidine pœnœ*, then *Virtutis amore*, or, to say
15 righter, dooth not indevour to make men good, but that
their evill hurt not others,—having no care, so hee be a
good Cittizen, how bad a man he be : therefore, as our
wickednesse maketh him necessarie, and necessitie maketh
him honorable, so is hee not in the deepest trueth to stande
20 in rancke with these ; who all indevour to take naughtines
away, and plant goodnesse even in the secretest cabinet of
our soules. And these foure are all that any way deale
in that consideration of mens manners, which beeing the
supreme knowledge, they that best breed it deserve the
25 best commendation.

The Philosopher therfore and the Historian are they
which would win the gole : the one by precept,
the other by example. But both not having
both, doe both halte. For the Philosopher,
30   setting downe with thorny argument the bare
rule, is so hard of utterance, and so mistie to bee conceived,
that one that hath no other guide but him shall wade in
him till hee be olde, before he shall finde sufficient cause

*Between these
Poetry (setting
aside divinity)
is a better
moderator
than Law.*

*The short-
comings of
Philosophy
and History.*

to bee honest: for his knowledge standeth so upon the abstract and generall, that happie is that man who may understande him, and more happie that can applye what hee dooth understand. On the other side, the Historian, wanting the precept, is so tyed, not to what shoulde bee, 5 but to what is; to the particuler truth of things, and not to the general reason of things; that hys example draweth no necessary consequence, and therefore a lesse fruitfull doctrine.

Nowe dooth the peerelesse Poet performe both: for 10 whatsoever the Philosopher sayth shoulde be doone, hee giveth a perfect picture of it in some one, by whom hee presupposeth it was done. So as hee coupleth the generall notion with the particuler example. A perfect picture I say, 15 for hee yeeldeth to the powers of the minde an image of that whereof the Philosopher bestoweth but a woordish description: which dooth neyther strike, pierce, nor possesse the sight of the soule so much as that other dooth. For as in outward things, to a man that had never 20 seene an Elephant or a Rinoceros, who should tell him most exquisitely all theyr shapes, cullour, bignesse, and perticular markes; or of a gorgeous Pallace the Architecture[1], with declaring the full beauties might well make the hearer able to repeate as it were by rote all hee had 25 heard, yet should never satisfie his inward conceit[2] with being witnes to it selfe of a true lively knowledge. But the same man, as soone as hee might see those beasts well painted, or the house wel in moddel, should straightwaies grow, without need of any description, to a iudicial comprehend- 30

Their short-comings are supplied by Poetry, which gives concrete examples as well as precepts.

[1] Later Edd. 'an architect,' a note of interrogation being put after 'markes.' But 'who' = 'he who.' See note.

[2] Ed. 1595 'conceits.'

ing of them. So no doubt the Philosopher with his learned definition, bee it of vertue, vices, matters of publick policie, or privat government, replenisheth the memory with many infallible grounds of wisdom; which, notwithstanding, lye
5 darke before the imaginative and iudging powre, if they bee not illuminated or figured foorth by the speaking picture of Poesie.

    Tullie taketh much paynes, and many times not without poeticall helpes, to make us knowe the force
10 love of our Countrey hath in us. Let us but heare old *Anchises* speaking in the middest of Troyes flames, or see *Ulisses*, in the fulnes of all *Calipso's* delights, bewayle his absence from barraine and beggerly *Ithaca*. Anger the *Stoicks* say, was a short
15 maddnes: let but *Sophocles* bring you *Aiax* on a stage, killing and whipping Sheepe and Oxen, thinking them the Army of Greeks with theyr Chiefetaines *Agamemnon* and *Menelaus*: and tell mee if you have not a more familiar insight into anger, then finding in the Schoolemen his *Genus* and *differ-*
20 *ence?* See whether wisdome and temperance in *Ulisses* and *Diomedes*, valure in *Achilles*, friendship in *Nisus* and *Euri-alus*, even to an ignoraunt man, carry not an apparent shyning; and contrarily, the remorse of conscience in *Oe-dipus*, the soone repenting pride of *Agamemnon*, the selfe-
25 devouring crueltie in his Father *Atreus*, the violence of ambition in the two *Theban* brothers, the sowre-sweetnes of revenge in *Medæa;* and, to fall lower, the *Terentian Gnato*, and our *Chaucers* Pandar, so exprest, that we nowe use their names to signifie their trades. And finally, all
30 vertues, vices, and passions, so in their own naturall seates layd to the viewe, that wee seeme not to heare of them, but cleerely to see through them. But even in the most excellent determination of goodnes, what Philosophers

Examples of concrete treat-ment of moral questions by the poets.

counsell can so redily direct a Prince, as the fayned *Cyrus* in *Xerophon?* or a vertuous man in all fortunes, as *Aeneas* in *Virgill?* or a whole Common-wealth, as the way of Sir *Thomas Moore's Eutopia?* I say the way, because where Sir *Thomas Moore* erred, it was the fault of the man and not of the Poet, for that way of patterning a Common-wealth was most absolute, though hee perchaunce hath not so absolutely perfourmed it. For the question is, whether the fayned image of Poesie, or the regular instruction of Philosophy, hath the more force in teaching: wherein, if the Philosophers have more rightly shewed themselves Philosophers then the Poets have obtained to the high top of their profession, as in truth,

Mediocribus esse poetis,

Non Di, non homines, non concessere Columnæ:
it is I say againe, not the fault of the Art, but that by fewe men that Arte can bee accomplished. Certainly, even our Saviour Christ could as well have given the morrall common places of uncharitablenes and humblenes, as the divine narration of *Dives* and *Lazarus:* or of disobedience and mercy, as that heavenly discourse of the lost Child and the gratious Father; but that hys through-searching wisdom knewe the estate of *Dives* burning in hell, and of *Lazarus* being in *Abrahams* bosome, would more constantly (as it were) inhabit both the memory and iudgment. Truly, for my selfe, mee seemes I see before my eyes the lost Childes disdainefull prodigality, turned to envie a Swines dinner: which by the learned Divines are thought not historicall acts, but instructing Parables. For conclusion, I say the Philosopher teacheth, but he teacheth obscurely, so as the learned onely can understande him; that is to say, he teacheth them that are already taught: but the Poet is the foode for the tenderest stomacks, the Poet is indeed the

right Popular Philosopher, whereof *Esops* tales give good
proofe; whose pretty Allegories, stealing under the formall
tales of Beastes, make many, more beastly then Beasts, begin
to heare the sound of vertue from these dumbe speakers.

5   But now may it be alledged, that if this imagining **of**
matters be so fitte for the imagination, then
must the Historian needs surpasse, who bring-
eth you images of true matters, such as indeede
were doone, and not such as fantastically

Aristotle on the rival qualities of poetry and history.

10 or falsely may be suggested to have been doone. Truely
Aristotle himselfe in his discourse of Poesie, plainely deter-
mineth this question, saying, that Poetry is *Philosophoteron*
and *Spoudaioteron*, that is to say, it is more Philosophicall,
and more studiously serious, then history. His reason is,
15 because Poesie dealeth with *Katholou*, that is to say, with
the universall consideration; and the history with *Kathe-
kaston*, the perticuler; 'nowe' sayth he, 'the universall
'wayes what is fit to bee sayd or done, eyther in likelihood
'or necessity, (which the Poesie considereth in his imposed
20 'names); and the perticuler onely marks, whether *Alcibiades*
'did or suffered this or that.' Thus farre *Aristotle:* which
reason of his (as all his) is most full of reason. For indeed,
if the question were whether it were better to have a perti-
cular acte truly or falsly set down, there is no doubt which
25 is to be chosen; no more then whether you had rather have
Vespasians picture right as hee was, or at the Painters
pleasure nothing resembling. But if the question be for
your owne use and learning, whether it be better to have it
set downe as it should be, or as it was: then certainely is
30 more doctrinable the fained Cyrus of *Xenophon* then the
true *Cyrus* in *Iustine:* and the fayned *Aeneas* in *Virgil*, then
the right *Aeneas* in *Dares Phrygius*. As to a Lady that
desired to fashion her countenance to the best grace, a

Painter should more benefite her to portraite a most sweet face, wryting *Canidia* upon it, then to paynt *Canidia* as she was, who *Horace* sweareth was foule and ill favoured.

If the Poet doe his part a-right, he will shew you in *Tantalus*, *Atreus*, and such like, nothing that is not to be shunned: in *Cyrus*, *Aeneas*, *Ulisses*, each thing to be followed; where the Historian, bound to tell things as things were, cannot be liberall (without hee will be poeticall) of a perfect patterne; but, as in *Alexander* or *Scipio* himselfe, shew dooings, some to be liked, some to be misliked. And then how will you discerne what to followe but by your owne discretion, which you had without reading *Quintus Curtius?* And whereas a man may say, though in universall consideration of doctrine the Poet prevaileth; yet that the historie, in his saying such a thing was doone, doth warrant a man more in that hee shall follow. The aunswere is manifest, that if hee stande upon that was; as if hee should argue, because it rayned yesterday, therefore it shoulde rayne to day, then indeede it hath some advantage to a grose conceite. But if he know an example onlie, informes a coniectured likelihood, and so goe by reason, the Poet dooth so farre exceede him, as hee is to frame his example to that which is most reasonable, be it in warlike, politick, or private matters; where the Historian in his bare *Was*, hath many times that which wee call fortune to over-rule the best wisedome. Manie times, he must tell events, whereof he can yeelde no cause: or, if hee doe, it must be poeticall.

For that a fayned example hath asmuch force to teach, as a true example (for as for to moove, it is cleere, sith the fayned may bee tuned to the highest key of passion) let us take one example, wherein a Poet and a Historian doe concur.

Poetry can give examples of what is entirely to be shunned or followed. History can only shew mixed characters.

Examples of the power of fiction to rouse emotion.

Herodotus and *Iustine* do both testifie that *Zopirus*, King
Darius faithful servaunt, seeing his Maister long resisted by
the rebellious *Babilonians*, fayned himselfe in extreame
disgrace of his King : for verifying of which, he caused his
5 own nose and eares to be cut off, and so flying to the
Babylonians, was received : and for his knowne valour so
far credited, that hee did finde meanes to deliver them over
to *Darius*.　Much like matter doth *Livie* record of *Tar-*
quinius and his sonne.　*Xenophon* excellently faineth such
10 another stratageme, performed by *Abradates* in *Cyrus* behalfe.
Now would I fayne know, if occasion bee presented unto
you, to serve your Prince by such an honest dissimulation,
why you doe not as well learne it of *Xenophons* fiction as of
the others verity : and truely so much the better, as you
15 shall save your nose by the bargaine ; for *Abradates* did not
counterfet so far.　So then the best of the Historian is
subiect to the Poet ; for whatsoever action, or faction, what-
soever counsell, pollicy, or warre stratagem the Historian is
bound to recite, that may the Poet (if he list) with his
20 imitation make his own ; beautifying it both for further
teaching, and more delighting, as it pleaseth him : having
all, from *Dante*, his heaven to hys hell, under the authoritie
of his penne.　Which if I be asked what Poets have done
so, as I might well name some, yet say I, and say againe, I
25 speak of the Arte, and not of the Artificer.

　　Nowe, to that which commonly is attributed to the
prayse of histories, in respect of the notable
learning is gotten by marking the successe, as
though therein a man should see vertue exalted,
and vice punished.　Truly that commendation
is peculiar to Poetrie, and farre of from History.

Poetical
justice pro-
vokes to virtue
more certainly
30 *than historical*
truth.

For indeede Poetrie ever setteth vertue so out in her best
cullours, making Fortune her wel-wayting hand-mayd, that

one must needs be enamored of her. Well may you see *Ulisses* in a storme, and in other hard plights ; but they are but exercises of patience and magnanimitie, to make them shine the more in the neere-following prosperitie. And of the contrarie part, if evill men come to the stage, they ever goe out (as the Tragedie Writer answered to one that mis-liked the shew of such persons) so manacled, as they little animate folkes to followe them. But the Historian, beeing captived to the trueth of a foolish world, is many times a terror from well dooing, and an incouragement to unbrideled wickednes. For, see wee not valiant *Milciades* rot in his fetters? The iust *Phocion*, and the accomplished *Socrates*, put to death like Traytors? The cruell *Severus* live pros-perously? The excellent *Severus* miserably murthered? *Sylla* and *Marius* dying in theyr beddes? *Pompey* and *Cicero* slaine then, when they would have thought exile a happinesse? See wee not vertuous *Cato* driven to kyll himselfe? and rebell *Cæsar* so advaunced, that his name yet, after 1600 yeares, lasteth in the highest honor? And marke but even *Cæsars* own words of the fore-named *Sylla*, (who in that onely did honestly, to put downe his dishonest tyrannie,) *Literas nescivit :* as if want of learning caused him to dce well. Hee meant it not by Poetrie, which not con-tent with earthly plagues, deviseth new punishments in hel for Tyrants : nor yet by Philosophie, which teacheth *Occi-dendos esse :* but no doubt by skill in Historie ; for that indeede can affoord your *Cipselus, Periander, Phalaris, Dionisius,* and I know not how many more of the same kennell, that speede well enough in theyr abhominable uniustice or usurpation.

I conclude therefore, that hee excelleth Historie, not onely in furnishing the minde with knowledge, but in setting it forward, to that which deserveth to be called and

accounted good : which setting forward, and mooving to
well dooing, indeed setteth the Lawrell crowne
upon the Poet as victorious, not onely of the
Historian, but over the Philosopher: howsoever
in teaching it may bee questionable. For suppose
it be granted (that which I suppose with great reason may be
denied) that the Philosopher, in respect of his methodical
proceeding, doth teach more perfectly then the Poet: yet do
I thinke that no man is so much *Philophilosophos*, as to
compare the Philosopher in mooving with the Poet.   And
that mooving is of a higher degree then teaching, it may by
this appeare, that it is wel nigh the cause and the effect of
teaching.   For who will be taught, if hee bee not mooved
with desire to be taught? and what so much good doth that
teaching bring forth (I speak still of morrall doctrine), as
that it mooveth one to doe that which it dooth teach? for
as *Aristotle* sayth, it is not *Gnosis*, but *Praxis* must be the
fruit.   And howe *Praxis* cannot be, without being mooved
to practise, it is no hard matter to consider.

The Philosopher sheweth you the way, hee informeth
you of the particularities, as well of the tediousnes of the
way, as of the pleasant lodging you shall have when your
iourney is ended, as of the many by-turnings that may
divert you from your way.   But this is to no man but to
him that will read him, and read him with attentive studious
painfulnes.   Which constant desire, whosoever hath in him,
hath already past halfe the hardnes of the way, and there-
fore is beholding to the Philosopher but for the other halfe.
Nay truely, learned men have learnedly thought, that, where
once reason hath so much over-mastred passion as that the
minde hath a free desire to doe well, the inward light each
minde hath in it selfe, is as good as a Philosophers booke;
seeing in nature we know it is wel to doe well, and what is

*Poetry is also
a better moral
teacher than
philosophy.*

well and what is evill, although not in the words of Arte
which Philosophers bestowe upon us; for out of naturall
conceit, the Philosophers drew it: but to be moved to doe
that which we know, or to be mooved with desire to knowe,
Hoc opus: Hic labor est. 5

Nowe therein of all Sciences (I speak still of humane, and
according to the humane conceits) is our Poet
the Monarch.   For he dooth not only shew the *For the Poet not only teaches, but also attracts.*
way, but giveth so sweete a prospect into the
way, as will intice any man to enter into it. 10
Nay, he dooth, as if your iourney should lye through a fayre
Vineyard, at the first give you a cluster of Grapes; that, full
of that taste, you may long to passe further.   He beginneth
not with obscure definitions, which must blur the margent
with interpretations, and load the memory with doubtful- 15
nesse: but hee commeth to you with words set in de-
lightfull proportion, either accompanied with, or prepared
for the well inchaunting skill of Musicke; and with a tale
forsooth he commeth unto you, with a tale which holdeth
children from play, and old men from the chimney corner; 20
and, pretending no more, doth intende the winning of the
mind from wickednesse to vertue: even as the childe is
often brought to take most wholsom things, by hiding them
in such other as have a pleasant tast: which, if one should
beginne to tell them the nature of *Aloes* or *Rubarb*[1] they 25
shoulde receive, woulde sooner take their Phisicke at their
eares then at their mouth.   So is it in men (most of which
are childish in the best things, till they bee cradled in their
graves,) glad they will be to heare the tales of *Hercules,*
Achilles, Cyrus, and *Aeneas:* and hearing them, must needs 30
heare the right description of wisdom, valure, and iustice;

---

[1] Later Edd. '*rhubarbarum.*'

which, if they had been barely, that is to say, Philosophically set out, they would sweare they bee brought to schoole againe.

That imitation, wherof Poetry is, hath the most conveniency to Nature of all other: in somuch that, as *Aristotle* sayth, those things which in themselves are horrible, as cruell battailes, unnaturall Monsters, are made in poeticall imitation delightfull. Truely I have knowen men, that even with reading *Amadis de Gaule*, (which God knoweth wanteth much of a perfect Poesie) have found their harts mooved to the exercise of courtesie, liberalitie, and especially courage. Who readeth *Aeneas* carrying olde *Anchises* on his back, that wisheth not it were his fortune to perfourme so excellent an acte? Whom doe not the words of *Turnus* moove? (the tale of *Turnus* having planted his image in the imagination,)

Examples of the attractive- ness of poetry.

Fugientem hæc terra videbit?
Usque adeone mori miserum est?

Where the Philosophers, as they scorne to delight, so must they bee content little to moove: saving wrangling whether Vertue bee the chiefe or the onely good: whether the contemplative or the active life doe excell. Which *Plato* and *Boethius* well knew; and therefore made Mistres Philosophy very often borrow the masking rayment of Poesie. For even those harde harted evill men, who thinke vertue a schoole name, and knowe no other good but *indulgere genio*, and therefore despise the austere admonitions of the Philosopher, and feele not the inward reason they stand upon, yet will be content to be delighted; which is al the good felow Poet seemeth to promise: and so steale to see the forme of goodnes (which seene they cannot but love) ere themselves be aware, as if they tooke a medicine of Cherries.

Infinite proofes of the strange effects of this poeticall invention might be alledged, onely two shall serve, which are so often remembred, as I thinke all men knowe them. The one of *Mene-nius Agrippa*, who, when the whole people of Rome had resolutely devided themselves from the Senate, with apparant shew of utter ruine, though hee were (for that time) an excellent Oratour, came not among them upon trust of figurative speeches, or cunning insinuations: and much lesse, with farre fet *Maximes* of Philosophie, which (especially if they were *Platonick*) they must have learned Geometrie before they could well have conceived: but forsooth he behaves himselfe, like a homely, and familiar Poet. Hee telleth them a tale, that there was a time, when all the parts of the body made a mutinous conspiracie against the belly, which they thought devoured the fruits of each others labour: they concluded they would let so unprofitable a spender starve. In the end, to be short, (for the tale is notorious, and as notorious that it was a tale,) with punishing the belly they plagued themselves. This applied by him wrought such effect in the people, as I never read that ever words brought forth but then so suddaine and so good an alteration; for, upon reasonable conditions, a perfect reconcilement ensued. The other is of *Nathan* the Prophet, who when the holie *David* had so far forsaken God, as to confirme adulterie with murther: when hee was to doe the tenderest office of a friende, in laying his owne shame before his eyes, sent by God to call againe so chosen a servant: how doth he it? but by telling of a man, whose beloved Lambe was ungratefullie taken from his bosome: the applycation most divinely true, but the discourse it selfe, fayned: which made *David*, (I speake of the second and instrumentall cause) as in a glasse, to see

his own filthines, as that heavenly Psalme of mercie wel
testifieth.

By these therefore examples and reasons, I think it may
be manifest, that the Poet with that same hand
of delight doth draw the mind more effectually
then any other Arte dooth: and so a conclusion
not unfitlie ensueth, that as vertue is the most
excellent resting place for all worldlie learning to make his
end of: so Poetrie, beeing the most familiar to teach it, and
most princelie to move towards it, in the most excellent
work is the most excellent workman.

But I am content, not onely to decipher him by his
workes, (although works, in commendation or
disprayse, must ever holde an high authority)
but more narrowly will examine his parts: so
that (as in a man) though all together may carry
a presence ful of maiestie and beautie, perchance in some
one defectious peece, we may find a blemish: now in his
parts, kindes, or *Species* (as you list to terme them) it is to
be noted, that some Poesies have coupled together two or
three kindes, as Tragicall and Comicall, wher-upon is risen
the Tragi-comicall. Some in the like manner have mingled
Prose and Verse, as *Sanazzar* and *Boetius.* Some have
mingled matters Heroicall and Pastorall. But that commeth
all to one in this question, for, if severed they be good, the
coniunction cannot be hurtfull. Therefore perchaunce for-
getting some, and leaving some as needlesse to be remem-
bred, it shall not be amisse in a worde to cite the speciall
kindes, to see what faults may be found in the right use of
them.

Is it then the Pastorall Poem which is misliked? (for
perchance, where the hedge is lowest they will soonest

leape over.)   Is the poore pype disdained, which some-
time out of *Melibeus* mouth can shewe the miserie
of people under hard Lords or ravening Soul-   (1) *Pastoral.*
diours?   And again, by *Titirus*, what blessednes is derived
to them that lye lowest from the goodnesse of them that sit 5
highest?   Sometimes, under the prettie tales of Wolves and
Sheepe, can include the whole considerations of wrong
dooing and patience; sometimes shew, that contention for
trifles can get but a trifling victorie.   Where perchaunce a
man may see, that even *Alexander* and *Darius*, when they 10
strave who should be Cocke of thys worlds dunghill, the
benefit they got was, that the after-livers may say,

> *Hæc memini et victum frustra contendere Thirsin:*
> *Ex illo Coridon Coridon est tempore nobis.*

Or is it the lamenting Elegiack, which in a kinde hart 15
would moove rather pitty then blame, who
bewailes, with the great Philosopher *Heraclitus*,   (2) *Elegiac.*
the weakenes of man-kind and the wretchednes of the world:
who surely is to be praysed, either for compassionate
accompanying iust causes of lamentation, or for rightly 20
paynting out how weake be the passions of wofulnesse.   Is
it the bitter but wholsome Iambick, which rubs
the galled minde, in making shame the trumpet   (3) *Iambic.*
(4) *Satiric.*
of villanie, with bolde and open crying out
against naughtines; or the Satirick, who   25

> *omne vafer vitium ridenti tangit amico?*

Who sportingly never leaveth, until hee make a man laugh
at folly, and at length ashamed to laugh at himselfe; which
he cannot avoyd, without avoyding the follie.   Who while

> *circum praecordia ludit*   30

giveth us to feele, how many head-aches a passionate life bringeth us to : how, when all is done,

Est Ulubris, animus si nos non deficit æquus.

No perchance it is the Comick, whom naughtie Play-makers
5 (5) *Comic.* and Stage-keepers have iustly made odious. To the argument of abuse I will answer after. Onely thus much now is to be said, that the Comedy is an imitation of the common errors of our life, which he repre-senteth in the most ridiculous and scornefull sort that may
10 be ; so as it is impossible that any beholder can be content to be such a one. Now, as in Geometry, the oblique must bee knowne as wel as the right; and in Arithmetick, the odde aswell as the even: so, in the actions of our life, who seeth not the filthines of evil wanteth a great foile to per-
15 ceive the beauty of vertue. This doth the Comedy handle so in our private and domestical matters, as with hearing it we get, as it were, an experience what is to be looked for of a nigardly *Demea:* of a crafty *Davus:* of a flattering *Gnato:* of a vaine glorious *Thraso:* and not onely to know
20 what effects are to be expected, but to know who be such, by the signifying badge given them by the Comedian. And little reason hath any man to say, that men learne evill by seeing it so set out : sith, as I sayd before, there is no man living but, by the force trueth hath in nature, no sooner
25 seeth these men play their parts, but wisheth them in *Pistrinum :* although perchance the sack of his owne faults lye so behinde hys back, that he seeth not himselfe daunce the same measure : whereto yet nothing can more open his eyes, then to finde his own actions contemptibly set forth.
30 So that the right use of Comedy will (I thinke) by no body be blamed, and much lesse of the high
(6) *Tragedy.* and excellent Tragedy, that openeth the greatest

wounds, and sheweth forth the Ulcers that are covered
with Tissue; that maketh Kinges feare to be Tyrants,
and Tyrants manifest their tirannicall humors; that with
stirring the affects[1] of admiration and commiseration, teach-
eth the uncertainety of this world, and upon how weake 5
foundations guilden roofes are builded. That maketh us
knowe,

> *Qui sceptra saevus duro imperio regit,*
> *Timet timentes, metus in aucthorem redit.*

But how much it can moove, *Plutarch* yeeldeth a 10
notable testimonie of the abhominable Tyrant *Alexander
Pheraeus;* from whose eyes a Tragedy, wel made and repre-
sented, drewe aboundance of teares : who without all pitty,
had murthered infinite numbers, and some of his owne
blood. So as he, that was not ashamed to make matters 15
for Tragedies, yet coulde not resist the sweet violence of a
Tragedie.   And if it wrought no further good in him, it was
that he, in despight of himselfe, withdrewe himselfe from
harkening to that, which might mollifie his hardened heart.
But it is not the Tragedy they doe mislike : For it were too 20
absurd to cast out so excellent a representation of whatso-
ever is most worthy to be learned.

Is it the Lyricke that most displeaseth, who with his
tuned Lyre, and wel accorded voyce, giveth
praise, the reward of vertue, to vertuous acts; (7) *Lyric.*   25
who gives morrall precepts, and naturall Problemes ; who
sometimes rayseth up his voice to the height of the heavens,
in singing the laudes of the immortall God? Certainly
I must confesse my own barbarousnes, I never heard the
olde song of *Percy* and *Duglas,* that I found not my heart 30
mooved more then with a Trumpet: and yet is it sung but

___
[1] Some later Edd. 'affections.'

by some blinde Crouder, with no rougher voyce then rude
stile: which being so evill apparrelled in the dust and cob-
webbes of that uncivill age, what would it worke trymmed
in the gorgeous eloquence of *Pindar?* In *Hungary* I
5 have seene it the manner at all Feasts, and other such
meetings, to have songes of their Auncestours valour; which
that right Souldier-like Nation thinks the chiefest kindlers
of brave courage. The incomparable *Lacedemonians* did
not only carry that kinde of Musicke ever with them to the
10 field; but even at home, as such songs were made, so were
they all content to bee the singers of them, when the lusty
men were to tell what they dyd, the olde men what they had
done, and the young men what they wold doe. And where
a man may say, that *Pindar* many times prayseth highly
15 victories of small moment, matters rather of sport then
vertue: as it may be aunswered, it was the fault of the Poet,
and not of the Poetry; so indeede the chiefe fault was in
the tyme and custome of the Greekes, who set those toyes at
so high a price, that *Phillip* of *Macedon* reckoned a horse-
20 race wonne at *Olympus* among hys three fearefull felicities.
But as the unimitable *Pindar* often did, so is that kinde
most capable and most fit to awake the thoughts from the
sleep of idlenes, to imbrace honorable enterprises.

There rests the Heroicall, whose very name (I thinke)
25   should daunt all back-biters; for by what con-
(8) The Heroic, ceit can a tongue be directed to speake evill of
which is the
highest kind that, which draweth with it, no lesse Champions
of poetry.
            then *Achilles, Cyrus, Aeneas, Turnus, Tydeus,*
and *Rinaldo?* who doth not onely teach and move to a
30 truth, but teacheth and mooveth to the most high and
excellent truth. Who maketh magnanimity and iustice
shine, throughout all misty fearefulnes and foggy desires.
Who, if the saying of *Plato* and *Tullie* bee true, that who

could see Vertue would be wonderfully ravished with the
love of her beauty: this man sets her out to make her more
lovely in her holyday apparell to the eye of any that will daine
not to disdaine, untill they understand. But if any thing be
already sayd in the defence of sweete Poetry, all concurreth 5
to the maintaining the Heroicall, which is not onely a
kinde, but the best and most accomplished kinde of Poetry.
For as the image of each action stirreth and instructeth
the mind, so the loftie image of such Worthies most in-
flameth the mind with desire to be worthy, and informes 10
with counsel how to be worthy.   Only let *Aeneas* be worne
in the tablet of your memory; how he governeth himselfe in
the ruine of his Country; in the preserving his old Father,
and carrying away his religious ceremonies; in obeying the
Gods commandement to leave *Dido*, though not onely all 15
passionate kindenes, but even the humane consideration of
vertuous gratefulnes, would have craved other of him; how
in storms; howe in sports; howe in warre; howe in peace;
how a fugitive; how victorious; how besiedged; how be-
siedging; howe to strangers; howe to allyes; how to enemies; 20
howe to his owne: lastly, how in his inward selfe, and how
in his outward government.   And I thinke, in a minde not
preiudiced with a preiudicating humor, hee will be found in
excellencie fruitefull: yea, even as *Horace* sayth

melius Chrisippo et Crantore.   25

But truely I imagine, it falleth out with these Poet-
whyppers, as with some good women, who often are sicke,
but in fayth they cannot tel where.   So the name of
Poetrie is odious to them, but neither his cause nor effects,
neither the sum that containes him, nor the particularities 30
descending from him, give any fast handle to their carping
disprayse.

Sith then Poetrie is of all humane learning the most auncient, and of most fatherly antiquitie, as from whence other learnings have taken theyr beginnings: sith it is so universall, that no learned Nation dooth despise it, nor no barbarous Nation is without it: sith both Roman and Greek gave divine names unto it, the one of prophecying, the other of making: and that indeede, that name of making is fit for him; considering, that, whereas other Arts retaine themselves within their subiect, and receive as it were their beeing from it, the Poet onely bringeth his owne stuffe, and dooth not learne a conceite out of a matter, but maketh matter for a conceite: Sith neither his description nor his ende contayneth any evill, the thing described cannot be evill: Sith his effects be so good as to teach goodnes and to delight the learners: Sith therein (namely in morrall doctrine, the chiefe of all knowledges) hee dooth not onely farre passe the Historian, but, for instructing, is well nigh comparable to the Philosopher; and, for moving, leaves him behind him: Sith the holy scripture (wherein there is no uncleannes) hath whole parts in it poeticall, and that even our Saviour Christ vouchsafed to use the flowers of it: Sith all his kindes are not onlie in their united formes, but in their severed dissections fully commendable; I think (and think I thinke rightly) the Lawrell crowne, appointed for triumphing Captaines, doth worthilie (of al other learnings) honor the Poets triumph.

But because wee have eares aswell as tongues, and that the lightest reasons that may be will seeme to weigh greatly, if nothing be put in the counterballance: let us heare, and, aswell as wee can, ponder, what obiections may bee made against this Arte, which may be worthy eyther of yeelding, or answering.

The claims of poetry to a first place among the arts recapitulated.

Objections *to poetry generally.*

First truely I note, not onely in these *Misomousoi* Poet-haters, but in all that kinde of people, who seek a prayse by dispraysing others, that they doe prodigally spend a great many wandering wordes in quips and scoffes; carping and taunting at each thing, which by stirring the Spleene, may 5 stay the braine from a through beholding the worthines of the subiect. Those kinde of obiections, as they are full of very idle easines, sith there is nothing of so sacred a maiestie, but that an itching tongue may rubbe it selfe upon it : so deserve they no other answer, but, in steed of laugh- 10 ing at the iest, to laugh at the iester. Wee know a playing wit can prayse the discretion of an Asse ; the comfortable-nes of being in debt ; and the iolly commoditie of beeing sick of the plague. So of the contrary side, if we will turne *Ovids* verse,   15

> *Ut lateat virtus proximitate mali,*

that good lye hid in neerenesse of the evill: *Agrippa* will be as merry in shewing the vanitie of Science, as *Erasmus* was in commending of follie. Neyther shall any man or matter escape some touch of these smyling raylers. But for *Eras-* 20 *mus* and *Agrippa*, they had another foundation then the superficiall part would promise. Mary, these other pleasant Fault-finders, who wil correct the Verbe, before they under stande the Noune, and confute others knowledge before they confirme theyr owne : I would have them onely remember, 25 that scoffing commeth not of wisedom. So as the best title in English they gette with their merriments, is *The folly of rhyming and versifying.* to be called good fooles : for so have our grave Fore-fathers ever termed that humorous kinde of iesters : but that which gyveth greatest scope to their 30 scorning humors, is ryming and versing. It is already sayde (and, as I think, trulie sayde) it is not ryming and

versing that maketh Poesie.   One may bee a Poet without
versing, and a versifier without Poetry.   But yet,
Answer (1) rhyme and metre not necessary to poetry, presuppose it were inseparable (as indeede it
seemeth *Scaliger* iudgeth) truelie it were an
5   inseparable commendation.   For if *Oratio*, next
to *Ratio*, Speech next to Reason, bee the greatest gyft
bestowed upon mortalitie: that can not be praiselesse, which
dooth most pollish that blessing of speech, which
(2) yet they present lan- guage in its considers each word, not only (as a man may
10 *highest per- fection,* say) by his forcible qualitie, but by his best
measured quantitie, carrying even in themselves,
a Harmonie (without perchaunce Number, Measure, Order,
Proportion, be in our time growne odious.)   But lay a side
the iust prayse it hath, by beeing the onely fit speech for
15 Musick (Musick, I say, the most divine striker of the
sences), thus much is undoubtedly true, that if reading bee
foolish without remembring, memorie being the onely
treasurer of knowledge, those words which are fittest for
memory, are likewise most convenient for knowledge.
20   Now, that Verse farre exceedeth Prose in the knitting
up of the memory, the reason is manifest.   The
(3) and are of the greatest assistance to memory. words, besides theyr delight (which hath a great
affinitie to memory), beeing so set, as one word
cannot be lost, but the whole worke failes:
25 which accuseth it selfe, calleth the remembrance backe to
it selfe, and so most strongly confirmeth it; besides, one
word so as it were begetting another, as, be it in ryme or
measured verse, by the former a man shall have a neere
gesse to the follower: lastly, even they that have taught the
30 Art of memory, have shewed nothing so apt for it, as a
certaine roome devided into many places well and throughly
knowne.   Now, that hath the verse in effect perfectly:
every word having his naturall seate, which seate, must

needes make the words remembred. But what needeth more in a thing so knowne to all men? who is it that ever was a scholler, that doth not carry away some verses of *Virgill*, *Horace*, or *Cato*, which in his youth he learned, and even to his old age serve him for howrely lessons[1]? But the fitnes 5 it hath for memory, is notably proved by all delivery of Arts: wherein for the most part, from Grammer, to Logick, Mathematick, Phisick, and the rest, the rules chiefely necessary to bee borne away, are compiled in verses. So that, verse being in it selfe sweete and orderly, and beeing 10 best for memory, the onely handle of knowledge, it must be in iest that any man can speake against it.

Nowe then goe wee to the most important imputations laid to the poore Poets. For ought I can yet learne, they are these: first, that there beeing *Particular* OBJECTIONS 15 *to poetry, (1) its uselessness,* many other more fruitefull knowledges, a man might better spend his tyme in them, then in this. Secondly, that it is the mother of lyes. Thirdly, that it is the Nurse of abuse, infecting us with many (2) *its false-hood,* (3) *im-* 20 *morality.* pestilent desires: with a Syrens sweetnes, drawing the mind to the Serpents tayle of sinfull fancy:—and heerein especially, Comedies give the largest field to ere, as *Chaucer* sayth:—howe both in other Nations and in ours, before Poets did soften us, we were full of courage, given to martiall exercises; the pillers of manlyke 25 liberty, and not lulled a sleepe in shady idlenes with Poets pastimes. And lastly, and chiefely, they cry (4) *Plato's verdict against it.* out with an open mouth, as if they out shot

---

[1] In the 1598 and subsequent editions there follows here

  "as, *Percontatorem fugito, nam garrulus idem est.* 30
    Dum sibi quisque placet credula turba sumus."

The first from Horace (Epp. 1, 18, 69); the second from Ovid (Remed. Amor. 686).

Robin Hood, that *Plato* banished them out of hys Commonwealth.   Truely, this is much, if there be much truth in it.

First to the FIRST : that a man might better spend his tyme, is a reason indeede : but it doth (as they say) but *Petere principium :* for if it be as I affirme, that no learning is so good, as that which teacheth and mooveth to vertue ; and that none can both teach and move thereto so much as Poetry : then is the conclusion manifest, that Incke and Paper cannot be to a more profitable purpose employed. And certainly, though a man should graunt their first assumption, it should followe (me thinkes) very unwillingly, that good is not good, because better is better.   But I still and utterly denye, that there is sprong out of earth a more fruitefull knowledge.   To the SECOND therefore, that they should be the principall lyars ; I aunswere paradoxically, but, truely, I thinke truely ; that of all Writers under the sunne, the Poet is the least lier : and though he would, as a Poet can scarcely be a lyer, the Astronomer, with his cosen the Geometrician, can hardly escape, when they take upon them to measure the height of the starres.   How often, thinke you, doe the Phisitians lye, when they aver things good for sicknesses, which afterwards send *Charon* a great nomber of soules drowned in a potion before they come to his Ferry.   And no lesse of the rest, which take upon them to affirme.   Now, for the Poet, he nothing affirmes, and therefore never lyeth.   For, as I take it, to lye is to affirme that to be true which is false.   So as the other Artists, and especially the Historian, affirming many things, can in the cloudy knowledge of mankinde hardly escape from many lyes.   But the Poet (as I sayd before) never affirmeth.   The Poet never maketh any circles

---

Marginal notes:

ANSWERS.
(1) *To call it useless is to beg the question.*

(2) *Instead of being the falsest of arts, poetry is the truest ; for it does not pretend to historical truth.*

Line numbers: 5, 10, 15, 20, 25, 30

about your imagination, to coniure you to beleeve for true
what he writes.   Hee citeth not authorities of other Histo-
ries, but even for hys entry calleth the sweete Muses to
inspire into him a good invention: in troth, not labouring
to tell you what is, or is not, but what should or should not 5
be: and therefore, though he recount things not true, yet,
because hee telleth them not for true, he lyeth not, without
we will say that *Nathan* lyed in his speech before alledged
to *David.*   Which as a wicked man durst scarce say, so
think I none so simple would say that *Esope* lyed in the 10
tales of his beasts: for who thinks that *Esope* writ it for
actually true were well worthy to have his name chronicled
among the beastes hee writeth of.   What childe is there, that
comming to a Play, and seeing *Thebes* written in great
Letters upon an olde doore, doth beleeve that it is *Thebes?* 15
If, then, a man can arive at that childs age to know that the
Poets persons and dooings are but pictures of[1] what should
be, and not stories of[1] what have beene, they will never give
the lye to things not affirmatively, but allegorically and figura-
tivelie written.   And therefore, as in Historie, looking for 20
trueth, they goe away full fraught with falshood: so in
Poesie, looking for fiction, they shal use the narration but
as an imaginative groundplot of a profitable invention.

But heereto is replyed, that the Poets gyve names to
men they write of, which argueth a conceite of 25
an actuall truth, and so, not being true, prooves *Nor is the use*
a falshood.   And doth the Lawyer lye then, *of definite*
names a bar
when under the names of *Iohn a stile* and *Iohn* *to this plea.*
a noakes, hee puts his case?   But that is easily answered.
Theyr naming of men, is but to make theyr picture the 30
more lively, and not to builde any historie.   Paynting men,
they cannot leave men namelesse.   We see we cannot play

---

[1] *of* inserted by Ed.

at Chesse, but that wee must give names to our Chesse-
men ; and yet, mee thinks, hee were a very partiall Cham-
pion of truth, that would say we lyed for giving a peece of
wood the reverend title of a Bishop.   The Poet nameth
5 *Cyrus* or *Aeneas* no other way, then to shewe what men of
theyr fames, fortunes, and estates, should doe.

    Their THIRD is, how much it abuseth mens wit, trayning
it to wanton sinfulnes, and lustfull love : for
indeed that is the principall, if not the onely
10 abuse I can heare alledged.   They say, the
Comedies rather teach, then reprehend, amo-
rous conceits.   They say, the Lirick is larded with pas-
sionate Sonnets.   The Elegiack weepes the want of his
mistresse.   And that even to the Heroical *Cupid* hath
15 ambitiously climed.   Alas Love, I would thou couldest as
well defende thy selfe, as thou canst offende others !   I
would those, on whom thou doost attend, could eyther put
thee away, or yeelde good reason why they keepe thee !   But
grant love of beautie to be a beastlie fault, (although it be
20 very hard, sith onely man, and no beast, hath that gyft to
discerne beauty.)   Grant, that lovely name of Love to
deserve all hatefull reproches : (although even some of my
Maisters the Philosophers, spent a good deale of theyr
Lamp-oyle, in setting foorth the excellencie of it.)   Grant, I
25 say, what soever they wil have granted; that not onely love,
but lust, but vanitie, but (if they list) scurrilitie, possesseth
many leaves of the Poets bookes : yet thinke I, when
this is granted, they will finde theyr sentence may, with
good manners, put the last words foremost : and not say,
30 that Poetrie abuseth mans wit, but that mans wit abuseth
Poetrie.   For I will not denie, but that mans wit may make
Poesie, which should be *Eikastike* (which some learned
have defined, figuring foorth good things,) to be *Phanta-*

(3) As to the
immorality of
poetry, this is
its abuse, not
its use.

stike: which doth, contrariwise, infect the fancie with un-
worthy obiects. As the Painter, that shoulde give to the
eye eyther some excellent perspective, or some fine pic-
ture, fit for building or fortification: or contayning in it
some notable example, as *Abraham*, sacrificing his Sonne 5
Isaack, Iudith killing *Holofernes, David* fighting with
Goliah, may leave those, and please an ill-pleased eye with
wanton shewes of better hidden matters.

But what ! shall the abuse of a thing make the right use
odious? Nay truely, though I yeeld, that Poesie may not 10
onely be abused, but that beeing abused, by the reason of
his sweete charming force, it can doe more hurt then any
other Armie of words: yet shall it be so far from con-
cluding, that the abuse should give reproch to the abused,
that contrariwise it is a good reason, that whatsoever 15
being abused dooth most harme, beeing rightly used
(and upon the right use each thing conceiveth his title)
doth most good.

Doe wee not see the skill of Phisick (the best rampire
to our often-assaulted bodies), beeing abused, teach poyson 20
the most violent destroyer? Dooth not knowledge of Law,
whose end is to even and right all things, being abused,
grow the crooked fosterer of horrible iniuries? Doth not
(to goe to the highest) Gods word abused breed heresie?
and his Name abused become blasphemie? Truely, a 25
needle cannot doe much hurt, and as truely (with leave of
Ladies be it spoken) it cannot doe much good. With a
sword, thou maist kill thy Father, and with a sword thou
maist defende thy Prince and Country. So that, as in their
callirg Poets the Fathers of lyes, they say nothing : so in 30
this theyr argument of abuse, they proove the commenda-
tion.

They alledge heere-with, that before Poets beganne to

be in price, our Nation hath set their harts delight
upon action, and not upon imagination: rather
doing things worthy to bee written, then writing
things fitte to be done.   What that before
5 tyme was I thinke scarcely *Sphinx* can tell:
sith no memory is so auncient, that hath the
precedence of Poetrie.   And certaine it is, that
in our plainest homelines, yet never was the
Albion Nation without Poetrie.   Mary, thys argument,
10 though it bee leaveld against Poetrie, yet is it indeed a
chaine-shot against all learning or bookishnes, as they
commonly tearme it. Of such minde were certaine *Gothes*, of
whom it is written, that having in the spoile of a famous Citie
taken a fayre librarie, one hangman (bee like fitte to execute
15 the fruites of their wits who had murthered a great number of
bodies) would have set fire on it: 'no' sayde another very
gravely, 'take heede what you doe, for whyle they are busie
'about these toyes, wee shall with more leysure conquer
'their Countries.'   This indeede is the ordinary doctrine of
20 ignorance, and many wordes sometymes I have heard spent
in it: but because this reason is generally against all learn-
ing, aswell as Poetrie; or rather, all learning but Poetry:
because it were too large a digression to handle, or at least
too superfluous, (sith it is manifest, that all government of
25 action is to be gotten by knowledg, and knowledge best by
gathering many knowledges, which is reading,) I onely with,
Horace, to him that is of that opinion,

Iubeo stultum esse libenter:

for as for Poetrie it selfe, it is the freest from thys obiection;
30 for Poetrie is the companion of the Campes.

I dare undertake, *Orlando Furioso*, or honest King
Arthur, will never displease a Souldier: but the quiddity of

Ens and *Prima materia,* will hardely agree with a Corslet : and therefore, as I said in the beginning, even Turks and Tartares are delighted with Poets. *Homer*, a Greek, florished before Greece florished : and if to a slight coniecture a coniecture may be opposed, truly it may seeme, that as by him their learned men tooke almost their first light of knowledge, so their active men received their first motions of courage. Onlie *Alexanders* example may serve, who by *Plutarch* is accounted of such vertue, that Fortune was not his guide but his foote-stoole : whose acts speake for him, though *Plutarch* did not, to be[1] indeede the Phœnix of warlike Princes. This *Alexander* left his Schoolemaister, living *Aristotle,* behinde him, but tooke deade *Homer* with him : he put the Philosopher *Calisthenes* to death for his seeming philosophicall, indeed mutinous stubburnnes ; but the chiefe thing he ever was heard to wish for, was, that *Homer* had been alive. He well found he received more braverie of minde bye the patterne of *Achilles,* then by hearing the definition of Fortitude : and therefore, if *Cato* misliked *Fulvius,* for carying *Ennius* with him to the fielde ; it may be aunswered, that if *Cato* misliked it, the noble *Fulvius* liked it, or els he had not doone it : for it was not the excellent *Cato Uticensis,* (whose authority I would much more have reverenced), but it was the former ; in truth a bitter punisher of faults, but else a man that had never wel sacrificed to the Graces. Hee misliked and cryed out upon all Greeke learning, and yet being 80 yeeres olde began to learne it ; be-like fearing that *Pluto* understood not Latine. Indeede, the Romaine lawes allowed no person to be carried to the warres, but hee that was in the Souldiers role : and therefore, though *Cato* misliked his unmustered person, hee misliked not his

And in fact poetry has always been the companion of soldiers.

---

[1] *to be,* omitted in Ed. of 1595.

worke. And if hee had, *Scipio Nasica*, iudged by common consent the best Romaine, loved him. Both the other *Scipio* Brothers, who had by their vertues no lesse surnames, then of *Asia* and *Affrick*, so loved him, that they caused 5 his body to be buried in their Sepulcher. So as *Cato*, his authoritie being but against his person, and that aunswered with so farre greater then himselfe, is heerein of no validitie.

(4) As to Plato's expul- 10 *sion of Poets from his com-monwealth. In the first place, though he of all others used it most, philosophers are apt to be* 15 *jealous of poets: for*

But now indeede my burthen is great; now *Plato* his name is layde upon mee, whom I must confesse, of all Philosophers, I have ever esteemed most worthy of reverence; and with great reason, sith of all Philosophers he is the most poeticall. Yet if he will defile the Foun-taine, out of which his flowing streames have proceeded, let us boldly examine with what reasons hee did it.

First truly, a man might maliciously obiect, that *Plato*, being a Philosopher, was a naturall enemie of

poetry is more influential than philo- 20 *sophy.*

Poets: for indeede, after the Philosophers had picked out of the sweete misteries of Poetrie the right discerning true points of knowledge, they forthwith, putting it in method, and making a Schoole-arte of that which the Poets did onely teach by a divine delightful-nes, beginning to spurne at their guides, like ungratefull 25 Prentises, were not content to set up shops for themselves, but sought by all meanes to discredit their Maisters; which by the force of delight beeing barred them, the lesse they could overthrow them, the more they hated them. For indeede, they found for *Homer* seaven Cities strove who 30 should have him for their Citizen: where many Citties banished Philosophers, as not fitte members to live among them. For onely repeating certaine of *Euripides* verses, many *Athenians* had their lyves saved of the *Syracusians:*

when the *Athenians* themselves thought many Philosophers unwoorthie to live. Certaine Poets, as *Simonides*, and *Pindarus* had so prevailed with *Hiero* the first, that of a Tirant they made him a iust King, where *Plato* could do so little with *Dionisius*, that he himselfe, of a Philosopher, was 5 made a slave. But who should doe thus, I confesse, should requite the obiections made against Poets, with like cavillation against Philosophers, as likewise one should doe, that should bid one read *Phædrus*, or *Symposium* in *Plato*, or the discourse of love in *Plutarch*, and see whether any Poet 10 doe authorize abhominable filthines, as they doe. Againe, a man might aske out of what Common-wealth *Plato* did banish them? insooth, thence where he himselfe alloweth communitie of women. So as belike, this banishment grewe not for effeminate wantonnes, sith little should poeti- 15 call Sonnets be hurtfull, when a man might have what woman he listed. But I honor philosophicall instructions, and blesse the wits which bred them, so as they be not abused : which is likewise stretched to Poetrie.

S. *Paule* himselfe (who yet for the credite of Poets 20 alledgeth twise two Poets, and one of them by the name of a Prophet) setteth a watch-word upon Philosophy, indeede upon the abuse. So dooth *Plato* upon the abuse, not upon Poetrie. *Plato* found fault, that the Poets of his time filled the worlde with wrong opinions of the Gods, making light 25 tale of that unspotted essence ; and therefore would not have the youth depraved with such opinions. Heerin may much be said. Let this suffice : the Poets did not induce such opinions, but dyd imitate those opinions already induced. For all the Greek stories can well testifie, that 30 the very religion of that time stoode upon many and many-fashioned Gods, not taught so by the Poets, but followed according to their nature of imitation. Who list, may reade

in *Plutarch* the discourses of *Isis* and *Osiris*, of the cause
why Oracles ceased, of the divine providence : and see
whether the Theologie of that nation stood not upon such
dreames, which the Poets indeed supersticiously observed,
5 and truly (sith they had not the light of Christ) did much
better in it then the Philosophers, who, shaking off supersti-
tion, brought in Atheisme.

 Plato therefore, (whose authoritie I had much rather
Plato's true   iustly conster then uniustly resist) meant not
10 *meaning.*   in general of Poets, in those words of which
Iulius Scaliger saith : *Qua authoritate barbari quidam
atque hispidi abuti velint ad Poetas e republica exigendos:*
but only meant, to drive out those wrong opinions of
the Deitie (whereof now, without further law, Christianity
15 hath taken away all the hurtful beliefe) perchance, as he
thought, norished by the then esteemed Poets. And a man
need goe no further then to *Plato* himselfe to know his mean-
ing; who in his Dialogue called *Ion* giveth high and rightly
divine commendation to Poetrie. So as *Plato*, banishing
20 the abuse not the thing, not banishing it but giving due
honor unto it, shall be our Patron and not our adversarie.
For indeed I had much rather (sith truly I may doe it)
shew theyr mistaking of *Plato*, under whose Lyons skin they
would make an Asse-like braying against Poesie, then goe
25 about to overthrow his authority, whom the wiser a man is,
the more iust cause he shall find to have in admiration :
especially, sith he attributeth unto Poesie more then my
selfe doe ; namely, to be a very inspiring of a divine force,
farre above mans wit, as in the afore-named Dialogue is
30 apparant.

 Of the other side, who wold shew the honors have been
by the best sort of iudgements granted them, a whole Sea
of examples woulde present themselves. *Alexanders,*

Cæsars, *Scipios* al favorers of Poets. *Lelius*, called the Romane *Socrates*, himselfe a Poet; so as part of *Heautontimorumenon* in *Terence*, was supposed to be made by him. And even the Greek *Socrates*, whom *Apollo* confirmed to be the onely wise man, is sayde to have spent part of his old tyme in putting *Esops* fables into verses. And therefore, full evill should it become his scholler *Plato* to put such words in his Maisters mouth against Poets. But what need more? *Aristotle* writes the Arte of Poesie: and why if it should not be written? *Plutarch* teacheth the use to be gathered of them, and how if they should not be read? And who reades *Plutarchs* eyther historie or philosophy shall finde hee trymmeth both theyr garments with gards of Poesie.

Ancient testimonies in favour of poetry.

But I list not to defend Poesie with the helpe of her underling, Historiography. Let it suffise, that it is a fit soyle for prayse to dwell upon: and what dispraise may set upon it is eyther easily over-come, or transformed into iust commendation. So that, sith the excellencies of it may be so easily and so iustly confirmed, and the low-creeping obiections so soone troden downe; it not being an Art of lyes, but of true doctrine: not of effeminatenes, but of notable stirring of courage: not of abusing mans witte, but of strengthning mans wit: not banished, but honored by *Plato:* let us rather plant more Laurels, for to engarland our Poets heads, (which honor of beeing laureat, as besides them onely triumphant Captaines weare, is a sufficient authority to shewe the price they ought to be had in,) then suffer the ill-favouring breath of such wrong-speakers once to blowe upon the cleere springs of Posie.

Recapitulation of the claims of poetry.

But sith I have runne so long a careere in this matter,

me thinks, before I give my penne a fulle stop, it shalbe
but a little more lost time, to inquire, why England (the
Mother of excellent mindes) should bee growne
so hard a step-mother to Poets, who certainly
in wit ought to passe all other: sith all onely
proceedeth from their wit, being indeede makers
of themselves, not takers of others.   How can
I but exclaime,

An enquiry
into the causes
5 of the low
repute of
poetry in
England.

Musa mihi causas memora, quo numine læso.

10 Sweete Poesie, that hath aunciently had Kings, Emperors,
Senators, great Captaines, such, as besides a thousand others,
David, *Adrian*, *Sophocles*, *Germanicus*, not onely to favour
Poets, but to be Poets.   And of our neerer times, can
present for her Patrons, a *Robert*, king of Sicil, the great
15 king *Francis* of France, King *Iames* of Scotland.   Such
Cardinals as *Bembus* and *Bibiena*.   Such famous Preachers
and Teachers, as *Beza* and *Melancthon*.   So learned Philo-
sophers, as *Fracastorius* and *Scaliger*.   So great Orators,
as *Pontanus* and *Muretus*.   So piercing wits, as *George*
20 *Buchanan*.   So grave Counsellors, as besides many, but
before all, that *Hospitall* of Fraunce: then whom (I thinke)
that Realme never brought forth a more accomplished iudge-
ment, more firmely builded upon vertue.   I say these, with
numbers of others, not onely to read others Poesies, but to
25 poetise for others reading.   That Poesie, thus embraced in
all other places, should onely finde in our time a hard wel-
come in England, I thinke the very earth lamenteth it, and
therfore decketh our Soyle with fewer Laurels then it was
accustomed.   For heertofore Poets have in England also
30 florished; and, which is to be noted, even in those times
when the trumpet of *Mars* did sounde loudest.   And now,
that an over-faint quietnes should seeme to strew the house

for Poets, they are almost in as good reputation, as the *Mountibancks* at *Venice.*

Truly even that, as of the one side it giveth great praise to Poesie, which like *Venus* (but to better purpose) hath rather be troubled in the net with *Mars,* then enioy the homelie quiet of *Vulcan :* so serves it for a peece of a reason, why they are lesse gratefull to idle England, which nowe can scarce endure the payne of a pen.

FIRST CAUSE. *Want of spirit in the age.*

Upon this necessarily followeth, that base men with servile wits undertake it; who think it inough if they can be rewarded of the Printer. And so, as *Epaminondas* is sayd with the honor of his vertue to have made an office, by his exercising it, which before was contemptible to become highly respected : so these, no more but setting their names to it, by their owne disgracefulnes disgrace the most gracefull Poesie. For now, as if all the Muses were gotte with childe to bring foorth bastard Poets, without any commission they doe poste over the banckes of *Helicon,* tyll they make the readers more weary then Post-horses : while in the mean tyme, they

SECOND CAUSE. *The inferiority of the men engaging in it, and their mercenary spirit.*

Queis meliore luto finxit præcordia Titan,

are better content, to suppresse the out-flowing of their wit, then by publishing them to bee accounted Knights of the same order. But I that, before ever I durst aspire unto the dignitie, am admitted into the company of the Paper-blurrers, doe finde the very true cause of our wanting estimation is want of desert : taking upon us to be Poets in despight of *Pallas.* Nowe, wherein we want desert were a thanke-worthy labour to expresse : but if I knew, I should have mended my selfe. But I, as I never desired the title,

so have I neglected the meanes to come by it. Onely,
over-mastred by some thoughts, I yeelded an inckie tribute
unto them.   Mary, they that delight in Poesie it selfe
should seeke to knowe what they doe, and how they doe;
5 and, especially, looke themselves in an unflattering Glasse of
reason, if they bee inclinable unto it.

For Poesie, must not be drawne by the eares, it must
But poetry re- bee gently led, or, rather, it must lead.   Which
quires a natu- was partly the cause, that made the auncient-
ral faculty,
10   learned affirme, it was a divine gift, and no
humaine skill: sith all other knowledges lie ready for any
that hath strength of witte; a Poet no industrie can make,
if his owne *Genius* bee not carried unto it; and therefore is
it an old Proverbe, *Orator fit, Poeta nascitur.*   Yet confesse
15   I alwayes that, as the firtilest ground must bee
scientific
training, and manured, so must the highest flying wit have a
practice.
           Dedalus to guide him.   That *Dedalus*, they say,
both in this and in other, hath three wings to beare it selfe
up into the ayre of due commendation: that is, Arte, Imita-
20 tion, and Exercise.   But these, neyther artificiall rules nor
imitative patternes, we much cumber our selves withall.
Exercise indeede wee doe, but that very fore-backwardly:
for where we should exercise to know, wee exercise as
having knowne: and so is oure braine delivered of much
25 matter which never was begotten by knowledge.   For, there
being two principal parts, matter to be expressed by wordes,
and words to expresse the matter, in neyther wee use Arte
or Imitation rightly.   Our matter is *Quodlibet* indeed,
though wrongly perfourming *Ovids* verse

30   *Quicquid conabar dicere versus erat:*[1]

---

[1] The 1st edition (1595) has *conabor...erit*, but corrects to *conabar*
in an erratum, leaving *erit* however uncorrected. I think that Sidney
wrote both in the imperfect. The quotation is from memory and is

never marshalling it into an assured rancke, that almost the readers cannot tell where to finde themselves.

Chaucer undoubtedly did excellently in hys *Troylus* and *Cresseid;* of whom, truly I know not, whether to mervaile more, either that he, in that mistie time, could see so clearely, or that wee, in this cleare age, walke so stumblingly after him. Yet had he great wants, fitte to be forgiven in so reverent antiquity. I account the *Mirrour of Magistrates* meetely furnished of beautiful parts; and in the Earle of Surries *Liricks* many things tasting of a noble birth, and worthy of a noble minde. The *Sheapheards Kalender* hath much Poetrie in his Eglogues: indeede worthy the reading if I be not deceived. That same framing of his stile to an old rustick language I dare not alowe, sith neyther *Theocritus* in Greeke, *Virgill* in Latine, nor *Sanazar* in Italian, did affect it. Besides these, doe I not remember to have seene but fewe (to speake boldely) printed, that have poeticall sinnewes in them. For proofe whereof let but most of the verses bee put in Prose, and then aske the meaning; and it will be found, that one verse did but beget another, without ordering at the first what should be at the last: which becomes a confused masse of words, with a tingling sound of ryme, barely accompanied with reason.

Our Tragedies, and Comedies (not without cause cried out against) observing rules neyther of honest civilitie nor of skilfull Poetrie, excepting *Gorboduck* (againe, I say, of those that I have seene,) which notwithstanding, as it is full of stately speeches and well sounding Phrases, clyming

incorrect: Ovid's line (Trist. 4, 10, 25) is *Et quod tentabam dicere versus erat.*

to the height of *Seneca* his stile, and as full of notable moralitie, which it doth most delightfully teach, and so obtayne the very end of Poesie; yet in troth it is very defectious in the circumstances: which greeveth mee, be-
5 cause it might not remaine as an exact model of all Tragedies. For it is faulty both in place and time, the two necessary companions of all corporall actions. For where the stage should alwaies represent but one place, and the uttermost time presupposed in it should be, both by *Aris-*
10 *totles* precept and common reason, but one day: there is both many dayes, and many places, inartificially imagined.

Place. But if it be so in *Gorboduck*[1], how much more in al the rest? where you shal have *Asia* of the one side, and *Affrick* of the other, and so many other
15 under-kingdoms, that the Player, when he commeth in, must ever begin with telling where he is; or els, the tale wil not be conceived. Now ye shal have three Ladies walke to gather flowers, and then we must beleeve the stage to be a Garden. By and by, we heare newes of shipwracke in the
20 same place, and then wee are to blame, if we accept it not for a Rock. Upon the backe of that, comes out a hidious Monster, with fire and smoke, and then the miserable beholders are bounde to take it for a Cave. While in the mean-time, two Armies flye in, represented with foure
25 swords and bucklers, and then what harde heart will not receive it for a pitched fielde?

Now, of time they are much more liberall. For ordinary it is that two young Princes fall in love: after
Time. many traverces, she is got with childe, delivered
30 of a faire boy; he is lost, groweth a man, falls in love, and is ready to get another child, and all this in two hours space: which how absurd it is in sense, even sense may

---

[1] *Gorboduc* in editions after 1598.

imagine, and Arte hath taught, and all auncient examples iustified : and at this day, the ordinary Players in Italie wil not erre in. Yet wil some bring in an example of *Eunuchus* in *Terence*, that containeth matter of two dayes, yet far short of twenty yeeres. True it is, and so was it to be 5 playd in two daies, and so fitted to the time it set forth. And though *Plautus* hath in one place done amisse, let us hit with him, and not misse with him.

But they wil say, how then shal we set forth a story, which containeth both many places, and many 10 times? And doe they not knowe, that a Tra-gedie is tied to the lawes of Poesie, and not of Historie? not bound to follow the storie, but having liberty, either to faine a quite newe matter, or to frame the history to the most tragicall conveniencie. Againe, many things 15 may be told which cannot be shewed, if they knowe the difference betwixt reporting and representing. As for example, I may speake (though I am heere) of *Peru*, and in speech digresse from that to the description of *Calicut :* but in action, I cannot represent it without *Pacolets* horse : 20 and so was the manner the Auncients tooke, by some *Nuncius* to recount thinges done in former time, or other place.

How the ancients overcame the difficulty.

Lastly, if they wil represent an history, they must not (as *Horace* saith) beginne *Ab ovo :* but they 25 must come to the principall poynt of that one action, which they wil represent. By example this wil be best expressed. I have a story of young *Polidorus* delivered for safeties sake, with great riches, by his Father *Priamus* to *Polimnestor* king of *Thrace*, in 30 the Troyan war time. Hee after some yeeres, hearing the over-throwe of *Priamus*, for to make the treasure his owne, murthereth the child : the body of the child is taken up by

Another mistake is to go too far back in a story.

Hecuba; shee the same day findeth a slight to bee revenged most cruelly of the Tyrant. Where nowe would one of our Tragedy writers begin, but with the delivery of the childe? Then should he sayle over into *Thrace,* and so spend I know not how many yeeres and travaile numbers of places. But where dooth *Euripides?* Even with the finding of the body, leaving the rest to be tolde by the spirit of *Polidorus.* This need no further to be inlarged, the dullest wit may conceive it.

But besides these grosse absurdities, how all theyr Playes be neither right Tragedies, nor right Comedies : mingling Kings and Clownes, not because the matter so carrieth it : but thrust in Clownes by head and shoulders, to play a part in maiesticall matters, with neither decencie nor discretion. So as neither the admiration and commiseration, nor the right sportfulnes, is by their mungrell Tragy-comedie obtained. I know *Apuleius* did some-what so, but that is a thing recounted with space of time, not represented in one moment : and I knowe, the Auncients have one or two examples of Tragy-comedies, as *Plautus* hath *Amphitrio.* But if we marke them well, we shall find that they never, or very daintily, match Horn-pypes and Funeralls. So falleth it out, that, having indeed no right Comedy, in that comicall part of our Tragedy we have nothing but scurrility, unwoorthy of any chast eares : or some extreame shew of doltishnes, indeed fit to lift up a loude laughter and nothing els : where the whole tract of a Comedy shoulde be full of delight, as the Tragedy shoulde be still maintained in a well raised admiration.

But our Comedians thinke there is no delight without laughter : which is very wrong, for though laughter may come with delight, yet commeth it not of delight, as though delight should be

the cause of laughter.   But well may one thing breed both
together.   Nay, rather in themselves they have as it were
a kind of contrarietie : for delight we scarcely doe, but in
things that have a conveniencie to our selves or to the
generall nature : laughter almost ever commeth of things 5
most disproportioned to our selves and nature.   Delight
hath a ioy in it, either permanent or present.   Laughter
hath cnely a scornful tickling.   For example, we are ravished
with delight to see a faire woman, and yet are
far from being moved to laughter.   We laugh *Distinction* 10
at deformed creatures, wherein certainely we *between things*
which move
cannot delight.   We delight in good chaunces, *laughter and*
those that give
we laugh at mischaunces; we delight to heare *pleasure.*
the happines of our friends or Country, at which he were
worthy to be laughed at, that would laugh ; wee shall con-15
trarily laugh sometimes, to finde a matter quite mistaken and
goe downe the hill agaynst the byas, in the mouth of some
such men, as for the respect of them, one shalbe hartely
sorry, yet he cannot chuse but laugh ; and so is rather
pained, then delighted with laughter.   Yet deny I not, but 20
that they may goe well together; for as in *Alexanders* picture
well set out, wee delight without laughter, and in twenty
mad Anticks we laugh without delight : so in *Hercules,*
painted with his great beard and furious countenance, in
womans attire, spinning at *Omphales* commaundement, it 25
breedeth both delight and laughter.   For the representing
of so strange a power in love procureth delight : and the
scornefulnes of the action stirreth laughter.

But I speake to this purpose, that all the end of the
comicall part bee not upon such scornefull 30
matters, as stirreth laughter onely: but, mixt with *Comedy should*
have both.
it, that delightful teaching which is the end of
Poesie.   And the great fault even in that point of laughter,

and forbidden plainely by *Aristotle*, is, that they styrre
laughter in sinfull things; which are rather execrable then
ridiculous: or in miserable, which are rather to be pittied than
scorned.   For what is it to make folkes gape at a wretched
5 Begger, or a beggerly Clowne; or, against lawe of hospita-
lity, to iest at straungers, because they speake not English
so well as wee doe?   What do we learne?   Sith it is cer-
taine

   Nil habet infelix paupertas durius in se,
10   *Quam quod ridiculos homines facit.*

But rather a busy loving Courtier, a hartles threatening
Thraso; a selfe-wise-seeming schoolemaster; a awry-trans-
formed Traveller: these if we sawe walke in stage names,
which wee play naturally, therein were delightfull laughter,
15 and teaching delightfulnes: as in the other, the Tragedies
of *Buchanan* doe iustly bring forth a divine admiration.
But I have lavished out too many wordes of this play
matter.   I doe it because, as they are excelling parts of
Poesie, so is there none so much used in England, and
20 none can be more pittifully abused.   Which like an unman-
nerly Daughter, shewing a bad education, causeth her
mother Poesies honesty to bee called in question.
  Other sorts of Poetry almost have we none, but that
     Lyricall kind of Songs and Sonnets: which, if
EnglishLyrics
25 *are tame and* the Lord gave us[1] so good mindes, how well it
forced.
    might be imployed, and with howe heavenly
fruite, both private and publique, in singing the prayses of
the immortall beauty, the immortall goodnes of that God,
who gyveth us hands to write, and wits to conceive! of
30 which we might well want words, but never matter; of
which we could turne our eies to nothing but we should

   [1] Ed. 1595 has 'Which, Lord, if he gave us etc.'

ever have new budding occasions. But truely many of such writings, as come under the banner of unresistable love, if I were a Mistres, would never perswade mee they were in love : so coldely they apply fiery speeches, as men that had rather red Lovers writings, and so caught up certaine swell- 5 ing phrases, which hang together, like a man which once tolde mee, the winde was at North West, and by South, because he would be sure to name windes enowe,—then that in truth they feele those passions : which easily (as I think) may be bewrayed by that same forciblenes or 10 *Energia* (as the Greekes cal it) of the writer. But let this bee a sufficient, though short note, that wee misse the right use of the materiall point of Poesie.

Now, for the out-side of it, which is words, or (as I may tearme it) *Diction*, it is even well worse. So is 15 that honny-flowing Matron Eloquence appa- relled, or rather disguised, in a Curtizan-like painted affectation: one time with so farre fette words, they may seeme Monsters, but must seeme straun- gers, to any poore English man ; another tyme, with cours- 20 ing of a Letter, as if they were bound to followe the method of a Dictionary: an other tyme, with figures and flowers, extreamelie winter-starved. But I would this fault were only peculier to Versifiers, and had not as large possession among Prose-printers; and (which is to be mervailed) 25 among many Schollers ; and (which is to be pittied) among some Preachers. Truly I could wish, if at least I might be so bold to wish in a thing beyond the reach of my capacity, the diligent imitators of *Tullie* and *Demosthenes* (most worthy to be imitated) did not so much keep *Nizolian* Paper- 30 bookes of their figures and phrases, as by attentive transla- tion (as it were) devoure them whole, and make them wholly theirs. For nowe they cast Sugar and Spice upon every

The style of
both verse and
prose is too
artificial.

dish that is served to the table; like those Indians, not
content to weare eare-rings at the fit and naturall place of
the eares, but they will thrust Iewels through their nose and
lippes, because they will be sure to be fine. *Tullie,* when
5 he was to drive out *Cateline,* as it were with a Thunder-bolt
of eloquence, often used that figure of repitition, *Vivit vivit?
imo in Senatum venit &c.* Indeed, inflamed with a well-
grounded rage, hee would have his words (as it were)
double out of his mouth : and so doe that artificially, which
10 we see men doe in choller naturally. And wee, having
noted the grace of those words, hale them in sometime to a
familier Epistle, when it were to too much choller to be
chollerick. [Howe well store of *Similiter Cadences* doth
sound with the gravity of the pulpit, I would but invoke
15 Demosthenes' soul to tell, who with a rare dainteness useth
them. Truly, they have made me think of the *Sophister,*
that with too much subtlety would prove two eggs three;
and, though he might be counted a *Sophister,* had none for
his labour. So these men bringing in such a kind of
20 eloquence, well may they obtain an opinion of a seeming
fineness, but persuade few, which should be the end of their
fineness[1].]

Now for similitudes, in certaine printed discourses, I
thinke all Herbarists, all stories of Beasts, Foules,
And their metaphors too far fetched.
25 and Fishes, are rifled up, that they come in
multitudes to waite upon any of our conceits;
which certainly is as absurd a surfet to the eares, as is
possible. For the force of a similitude, not being to proove
anything to a contrary Disputer, but onely to explane to a
30 willing hearer, when that is done, the rest is a most tedious
pratling : rather over-swaying the memory from the purpose
whereto they were applied, then any whit informing the

---

[1] This clause is not in the edition of 1595.

iudgement, already eyther satisfied, or by similitudes not to be satisfied. For my part, I doe not doubt, when *Antonius* and *Crassus*, the great forefathers of *Cicero* in eloquence, the one (as *Cicero* testifieth of them) pretended not to know Arte, the other not to set by it: because with a playne 5 sensiblenes they might win credit of popular eares; which credit is the neerest step to perswasion: which perswasion is the chiefe marke of Oratory;—I doe not doubt (I say) but that they used these knacks very sparingly, which who doth generally use, any man may see doth daunce to his owne 10 musick: and so be noted by the audience, more careful to speake curiously, then to speake truly.

Undoubtedly (at least to my opinion undoubtedly) I have found in divers smally learned Courtiers, a more sounde stile, then in some professors of learning: of which 15 I can gesse no other cause, but that the Courtier following that which by practise hee findeth fittest to nature, therein (though he know it not) doth according to Art, though not by Art: where the other, using Art to shew Art, and not to hide Art (as in these cases he should doe), flyeth from 20 nature, and indeede abuseth Art.

But what? me thinkes I deserve to be pounded, for straying from Poetrie to Oratorie: but both have such an affinity in this wordish consideration, that I thinke this digression will make my meaning receive the fuller understanding: which *These remarks on 'style' in oratory apply very closely to poetry.* 25 is not to take upon me to teach Poets howe they should doe, but onely finding my selfe sick among the rest, to shewe some one or two spots of the common infection, growne among the most part of Writers: that acknow- 30 ledging our selves somewhat awry, we may bend to the right use both of matter and manner; whereto our language gyveth us great occasion, beeing indeed capable of any

excellent exercising of it. I know, some will say it is a
mingled language.   And why not so much the
The capabili-
ties of the   better, taking the best of both the other?
English Lan-
guage.   Another will say it wanteth Grammer. Nay
5   truly, it hath that prayse, that it wanteth not
Grammer: for Grammer it might have, but it needes it not;
beeing so easie of it selfe, and so voyd of those cumbersome
differences of Cases, Genders, Moodes, and Tenses, which
I thinke was a peece of the Tower of *Babilons* curse, that
10 a man should be put to schoole to learne his mother-tongue.
But for the uttering sweetly and properly the conceits of the
minde, which is the end of speech, that hath it equally with
any other tongue in the world : and is particulerly happy in
compositions of two or three words together, neere the
15 Greeke, far beyond the Latine: which is one of the greatest
beauties can be in a language.

Now, of versifying there are two sorts, the one Auncient,
the other Moderne : the Auncient marked the
Versification
(1) Ancient by   quantitie of each silable, and according to that,
quantity. *(2)*
20 *Modern by*   framed his verse: the Moderne, observing onely
rhyme and
accent.   number (with some regarde of the accent), the
chiefe life of it standeth in that lyke sounding
of the words, which wee call Ryme. Whether of these be
the most excellent, would beare many speeches. The Aun-
25 cient (no doubt) more fit for Musick, both words and tune
observing quantity, and more fit lively to expresse divers
passions, by the low and lofty sounde of the well-weyed
silable. The latter likewise, with hys Ryme, striketh a
certaine musick to the eare : and in fine, sith it dooth
30 delight, though by another way, it obtaines the same pur-
pose : there beeing in eyther sweetnes, and wanting in
neither maiestie. Truely the English, before any other
vulgar language I know, is fit for both sorts : for, for the

Ancient, the Italian is so full of Vowels, that it must ever be cumbred with *Elisions.* The Dutch, so of the other side with Consonants, that they cannot yeeld the sweet slyding, fit for a Verse. The French, in his whole language, hath not one word, that hath his accent in the last silable saving two, called *Antepenultima;* and little more hath the Spanish: and therefore, very gracelesly may they use *Dactiles.* The English is subiect to none of these defects.

Nowe, for the ryme, though wee doe not observe quantity, yet wee observe the accent very precisely; which other languages, eyther cannot doe, or will not doe so absolutely. That *Cæsura,* or breathing place in the middest of the verse, neither Italian nor Spanish have, the French and we never almost fayle of. Lastly, even the very ryme it selfe the Italian cannot put in the last silable, by the French named the Masculine ryme, but still in the next to the last, which the French call the Female; or the next before that, which the Italians terme *Sdrucciola.* The example of the former, is *Buono, Suono,* of the *Sdrucciola, Femina, Semina.* The French, of the other side, hath both the Male, as *Bon, Son,* and the Female, as *Plaise, Taise.* But the *Sdrucciola* hee hath not: where the English hath all three, as *Due, True, Father, Rather, Motion, Potion;* with much more which might be sayd, but that I finde already the triflingnes of this discourse is much too much enlarged.

So that sith the ever-praise-worthy Poesie, is full of vertue-breeding delightfulnes, and voyde of no gyfte, that ought to be in the noble name of learning: sith the blames laid against it are either false or feeble: sith the cause why it is not esteemed in Englande is the fault of Poet-apes, not Poets: sith lastly, our tongue is most fit to honor Poesie,

and to bee honored by Poesie, I coniure you all, that have
had the evill lucke to reade this incke-wasting toy of mine,
even in the name of the nyne Muses, no more to scorne the
sacred mysteries of Poesie: no more to laugh at the name
5 of Poets, as though they were next inheritours to Fooles:
no more to iest at the reverent title of a Rymer.   But to
beleeve with *Aristotle*, that they were the auncient Trea-
surers of the Græcians Divinity.   To beleeve with *Bembus*,
that they were first bringers in of all civilitie.   To beleeve
10 with *Scaliger*, that no Philosophers precepts can sooner
make you an honest man, then the reading of *Virgill*.   To
beleeve with *Clauserus*, the Translator of *Cornutus*, that it
pleased the heavenly Deitie, by *Hesiod* and *Homer*, under
the vayle of fables, to give us all knowledge, Logick, Retho-
15 rick, Philosophy naturall and morall; and *Quid non?*   To
beleeve with me, that there are many mysteries contained
in Poetrie, which of purpose were written darkely, least by
prophane wits it should bee abused.   To beleeve with *Landin*,
that they are so beloved of the Gods, that whatsoever they
20 write proceeds of a divine fury.   Lastly, to beleeve them-
selves, when they tell you they will make you immortall by
their verses.

Thus doing, your name shal florish in the Printers
shoppes; thus doing, you shall bee of kinne to
25 *A blessing and a curse.*   many a poeticall Preface; thus doing, you shall
be most fayre, most ritch, most wise, most all.
You shall dwell upon Superlatives.   Thus dooing, though
you be *Libertino patre natus*, you shall suddenly grow *Her-
culea proles:*

30   *Si quid mea carmina possunt.*

Thus doing, your soule shal be placed with *Dantes Beatrix*,
or *Virgils Anchises*.   But if (fie of such a but) you be borne

so neere the dull making *Cataract* of *Nilus*, that you cannot heare the Plannet-like Musick of Poetrie; if you have so earth-creeping a mind, that it cannot lift it selfe up to looke to the sky of Poetry; or rather, by a certaine rusticall disdaine, will become such a Mome, as to be a *Momus* of 5 Poetry: then, though I will not wish unto you the Asses eares of *Midas*, nor to bee driven by a Poets verses (as *Bubonax* was) to hang himselfe, nor to be rimed to death, as is sayd to be doone in Ireland: yet thus much curse I must send you in the behalfe of all Poets, that while you live, you 10 live in love, and never get favour for lacking skill of a *Sonnet:* and when you die, your memory die from the earth for want of an *Epitaph.*

FINIS.

NOTES.

1. *Edward Wotton*, the elder brother of Sir Henry Wotton: son 1
of Thomas Wotton of Bocton Malherbe. See Walton's *Life of Sir
Henry Wotton*, p. 92 (ed. 1825).

'Sir Edward was knighted by Queen Elizabeth, and made Comptroller
of her Majesty's Household. He was—saith Camden—a man remarkable
for many and great employments in the State, during her reign, and
sent several times *Ambassador* into foreign nations. After her death, he
was by king James made comptroller of his Household, and called to
be of his Privy Council, and by him advanced to be Lord Wotton,
Baron of Merley in Kent, and made Lord Lieutenant of that County.'

2. *at the Emperors Court.* This was in the autumn of 1573.
Sidney left Paris after the Bartholomew Massacre (Aug. 24, 1572), and
went to Heidelberg and Frankfort. At the latter town he made the
acquaintance of Hubert Languet, whom in November 1573 he accom-
panied to Vienna, whither Languet was going as envoy of the Elector
of Saxony to the Emperor Maximilian II. (1564—1576).

4. *Iohn Pietro Pugliano*, an Italian Equerry of the Emperor,
famous in his day as a teacher of those elaborate evolutions and feats of
horsemanship which were thought not only necessary for soldiers, but
an important part of the education of a gentleman.

Sir Thomas Elyot, *The Governour* (ed. Croft), vol. i. p. 181.

'But the most honorable exercise, in myne opinion, and that
besemeth the astate of every noble persone, is to ryde suerly and cleue on
a great horse and a roughe, which undoubtedly nat only importeth a
majestie and drede to inferior persones, beholding him above the
common course of other men, dauntyng a fierce and cruell beaste, but
also is no little socour, as well in pursuete of enemies and confoundyng

them, as in escapyng imminent daunger, whan wisdome therto ex-
horteth.'

For particulars of the art we may consult Lord Herbert of Cher-
bury's *Autobiography*, p. 74 (ed. 1809) who gives minute particulars of
the method of graceful riding, guiding the horse by a touch of the foot
without reins, causing it to execute courbettes, cabrioes, demivoltes etc.
Lord Herbert affirms finally that 'a good rider on a good horse is as
much above himself and others as this world can make him.' But per-
haps the best description of this kind of horsemanship is that given by
Sidney himself in the second book of the *Arcadia*:

'But he, as if Centaur-like he had been on a piece with the horse,
was no more moved than one is with the going of his own legs; and in
effect so did he command him, as his own limbs: for tho' he had both
spurs and wand, they seemed rather marks of sovereignty than instru-
ments of punishment, his hand and leg, with most pleasing grace, com-
manding without threatening, and rather remembering than chastising;
at least, if sometimes he did, it was so stollen as neither our eyes could
discern it, nor the horse with any change did complain of it: he ever
going so just with the horse, either forthright or turning, that it seemed,
as he borrowed the horse's body, so he lent the horse his mind. In the
turning one might perceive the bridle-hand something gently stir: but
indeed so gently, as it did rather distil virtue than use violence. Him-
self, which methinks is strange, shewing at one instant, both steadiness
and nimbleness; sometimes making him turn close to the ground, like a
cat, when scratchingly she wheels about after a mouse: sometimes with
a little more rising before, now like a raven leaping from ridge to ridge,
then like one of Dametas' kids bound over the hillocks: and all so done,
as neither the lusty kind showed any roughness, nor the easier any
idleness; but still like a well-obeyed master, whose beck is enough for
a discipline, ever concluding each thing he did to me-wards, as if thence
came not only the beginning but ending of his motions.'

Sidney had studied the theory as well as practice of horsemanship:
in a letter to his brother Robert then in Italy, written 18 October 1580,
he says (tr. by Pears) 'At horsemanship when you exercise it, read
Crison Claudio and a book called 'la gloria del Cavallo' withal,
that you join the thorough contemplation of it with the exercise; and
so shall you profit more in a month than others in a year; and mark the
bitting, saddling, and curing of horses.'

9. *contemplations* 'theoretical studies' as in Sidney's letter quoted
above and written about the time at which he was writing this essay.

13. *admiration*, 'amazement' or 'wonder,' *Hamlet*, 1, 2, 192, 'Season your *admiration* for a while.'

15. *estate*, 'order of men,' cp. p. 40, l. 16. Elyot's *Governour* (ed. Croft 1882), vol. I. p. 254 'Every *estate* and degree of men.' So we speak of 'the three *estates* of the realm.'

16. *Maisters of warre*, 'best skilled in war.' Cp. Shakespeare, *Merry Wives*, 1, 1, 259 '*Masters* of fence.' II *Henry IV*. 3, 2 'He is not his craft's *master*.' The spelling *maister*, common at this time, is from the French *maistre* (magister).

17. *strong abiders*, 'courageous in holding their ground,' cp. Chaucer, *Troylus and Cresseyde*, 1, 473

> 'And yet was he, wher-so men went or riden
> Founde oon the best, and lengest tyme *abiden*
> Ther peril was.'

Shakespeare, *Cymb*. 3, 4, 186 'This attempt I'm soldier to, And will *abide* it with a prince's courage.'

18. *unbeleeved*, 'incredible.'

19. *bred such wonder to a Prince*, 'caused a Prince to be so much admired.'

21. *Pedanteria*, Ital. 'superficial' or 'school learning.' Cp. pedant, pedantry, pedagogue (παῖς).

PAGE 2.

1. *the onely serviceable Courtier without flattery*, 'the only attentive and useful Courtier,' cp. *Arcadia*, Book I. p. 12 (ed. 1725) 'The servants not so many in number as cleanly in apparel and *serviceable* in behaviour.' Shakespeare, *Cymb*. 3, 2, 15 'If it be so to do good service never let me be counted *serviceable*.'

Chaucer, *Prol*. 79

> 'Curteys he was, lowly, and *servysable*
> And carf byforn his fadur at the table.'

In adding 'without flattery,' Sidney is putting into Pugliano's mouth an ancient thought. See Plutarch, *de adulatione et amicitia*, c. 16, which is thus translated by Elyot [the *Governour*, vol. II. p. 181] 'Carneades was wont to saye that the sonnes of noble men lerned nothing well but onely to ryde. For whiles they lerned lettres their maisters flatered them, praysinge every worde that they spake; in wrastlynge their teachers and companions also flatered them, submittyng them selfes and fallinge downe to their fete; but the horse or courser not understandynge who rydeth him, ne whether he be a gentyll man or yoman, a ryche man or poore, if he sitte nat suerly and can skill of ridynge, the horse casteth him quickly.'

3.   *a peece of a Logician*, 'a considerable logician,' cp. p. 49, l. 7; p. 60, l. 9. Puttenham, *Arte of English Poesie* (ed. Arber), p. 61 'yet it is *a peece* of joy to be able to lament with ease'; p. 301 'that is a figure of little reverence and is *a peece* of a contempt.' Latimer *Sermons* p. 36 'The other imputed a *pese* of reproach to hym for hys such counsel given.' It is used at this period to indicate anything eminent or special. Though Sidney took no degree at Oxford, he was well trained in the logic of the day, and held a formal disputation there in the presence of his uncles Lord Warwick and Lord Leicester. He was at Christ Church, 1568—1571.

8.   *Pugliano his strong affection.* The substitution of *his* for the A. S. genitive in *-es* is common in Shakespeare and the writers of the 16th and 17th centuries. Sidney uses it in this essay only with foreign names, see p. 10, l. 24; p. 22, l. 22; p. 44, l. 9; p. 52, l. 1. Modern usage has recurred to the older form, though the *e* is represented by an apostrophe, as 'Pugliano's strong affection,' and so it appears in later editions of the 'Apologie.'

affection, 'prejudice in favour of,' cp. the common phrase 'without fear or affection.'

10.   *of my selfe.* See Index 'of.'

13.   *provoked*, 'challenged.' He may refer especially to the attack upon dramatic poetry by Gosson in his 'School of Abuse' published in 1579 and dedicated to Sidney himself; but, as we shall see, Gosson only represented a growing feeling of suspicion of poetry, especially dramatic poetry, which towards the end of the century was openly and violently expressed by the Puritans.

14.   *my unelected vocation*, 'which I did not choose for myself,' referring to his phrase in l. 12 that he had 'slipt into the title of poet.'

15.   *sith*, 'since,' from A. S. *sið* = 'a time.' Wycliffe, St Luke 17, 4 'And if sevene *sithis* in the dai he do sinne aȝens thee, and seven *sithis* in the dai he be convertid to thee.' In the 1st edition this form is always used, the later editions have 'since.'

16.   *that foloweth the steppes of his Maister.* Sidney seems to have in his mind the text 'The disciple is not greater than his master: it is sufficient for the disciple that he be as his master.' But it is not clear whether there is any definite reference to any one as his 'master' in poetry. For the spelling 'maister' see p. 1, l. 16.

18. *a pittiful defence,* 'a defence appealing to pity.'

19. *is fallen to be the laughing-stocke of children.* The low reputation into which poetry had fallen is often alluded to by writers of the age.

Elyot's *Governour,* 1, p. 120 (about 1536) 'For the name of a poete, wherat nowe, (specially in this realme) men have such indignation, that they use onely poetes and poetry in the contempte of eloquence, was in auncient tyme in hygh estimation: in so moche that all wysdome was supposed to be therein included, and poetry was the first philosophy that ever was knowen.' 2, 380 'Marcus Antoninus the Emperour was in every kynde of lernynge so excellent, that he was therfore openly named the philosopher, not in reproche (as men nowe a dayes *in despyte call them philosophers and poetes whom they perceyve studious in sundry good discipline*) but to the augmentation of his honour.'

Puttenham, *Arte of English Poesie,* 1589 (ed. Arber) p. 33 'But in these days (though some learned Princes may take delight in them) yet universally it is not so. For as well Poets as Poesie are despised, and the name become of honorable infamous, subject to scorne and derision, and rather a reproch than a prayse to any that use it: for commonly who is studious in th' Arte or shewes himselfe excellent in it, they call him in disdayne a phantasticall: and a light-headed or phantasticall man (by conversion) they call a poet.'

21. *the former,* i.e. 'learning.' And yet, according to Puttenham and others, learning generally was in equal disrepute with poetry. Elyot, 1, p. 92 'There be some, which, without shame, dare affirme that to a great gentilman it is a notable reproche to be wel lerned and to be called a great clerke: whiche name they accounte to be of so bas estymation, that they never have it in their mouthes but whan they speke anything in derision.' With which we may compare the mediaeval Latin proverb, which Chapman expressed so neatly, 'The greatest Clerks are not the wisest men,' *Caesar and Pompey,* Act II. Sc. I.

Roger Ascham (1570) is equally severe on contemners of learning. *Scholemaster* (ed. Mayor), p. 534 'I heare saie, some younge Gentlemen of oures count it their shame to be counted learned: and perchance they count it their shame to be counted honest also; for I heare saie they medle as litle with the one as with the other. A mervelouse case, that Gentlemen shold be ashamed of good learning and never a whit ashamed of ill maners.'

22. *silly,* 'simple.' The word has gone through a process of deterioration in meaning similar to that of *innocent.* A.S. *sælig*

'timely' 'happy,' Germ. *selig* 'happy' [Lat. sollers, salvus]. In Chaucer 'sely,' gentle or innocent.

even the names of Philosophers. He refers especially to the usual instance of Plato's adverse sentence on poetry, to which he recurs more than once, and undertakes to answer formally in pp. 44—46.

23. *defacing,* 'defaming,' 'dishonouring.' Thus 'any worde defacid' means 'any unseemly **word,**' Skelton, *Garlande of Laurell,* v. 1581.

30. *first lightgiver to ignorance, etc.* The same point is laboured by Puttenham in his *Arte of English Poesie,* ch. IV., which is headed 'How poets were the first Philosophers, the first Astronomers and Historiographers and Oratours and Musitiens of the World.' See also p. 62, l. 12.

whose milk...tougher knowledges. Sidney is thinking of St Paul's words, 1 Cor. 3, 2; Hebrews 5, 12—14.

PAGE 3.

3   1. *play the Hedghog.* The hedgehog hibernates in any hole, such as the burrow of a rabbit. Sidney seems to be referring to some fable or tale, which I cannot identify. See p. 58, l. 24 n.

3. *Vipers that with theyr birth kill their Parents.* Another piece of that fanciful or mythological natural history which is so common in the Elizabethan writers. Thus Lord Brooke (Sidney's friend and biographer) in his poem of *Humane Learning,* 'Else viper-like their parents they devour.' Lyly's *Euphues* (ed. Arber) p. 215 'Glad I was to send them both abroad, least making a wanton of my first, with a blind conceipt, I should resemble the ape, and kill it by cullying it, and, not able to rule the second, I should with the viper loose my bloud with my own brood.' Gosson, *Schole of Abuse* (ed. Arber) p. 46 'The adder's death is her own broode.' It is from Herodotus 3, 109.

5. *Musaeus, Homer, Hesiodus.* Sidney is quite justified in appealing to the works of Homer and Hesiod as preceding any prose literature in Greek. The dates of the poems that go by their names [Homer: *Iliad, Odyssey, Hymns.* Hesiod: *Works and Days, Shield of Hercules,* and *Theogonia*] are involved in such dispute that it is not worth the while to venture on definite figures; but they certainly may be considered the earliest Greek Literature. In mentioning Musaeus he is following the common opinion of his day which confounded the author of *Hero and Leander,* a late grammarian, with the Orphic poet whose verses were current as early as B.C. 520 and are referred to by Herodotus.

8. *Orpheus, Linus* are mythical personages representing various forms of poetry; but in the time of the Alexandrian grammarians [3rd and 2nd centuries B.C.] they had come to be regarded as historical persons, and a number of poems written by various authors were ascribed to them. Orpheus, Musaeus, Hesiod and Homer were regarded by the Greeks themselves as their earliest writers [see the end of Plato's *Apology of Socrates,* and Aristoph. *Ran.* 1032]. *Orpheus* was the teacher of religious rites and mysteries, he was the bard who accompanied the Argo, and the poems ascribed to him are often referred to by Plato. He was said to be the son of Aeagrius and the muse Calliope, and to have lived in Thrace. *Linus* was son of Apollo and one of the Muses. Cp. W. Webbe, *Discourse of English Poetrie,* 1586 (ed. Arber) p. 25 'To begin therefore with the first that was first worthelye memorable in the excellent gyft of Poetrye, the best writers agree that it was *Orpheus* who by the sweete gyft of his heavenly poetry withdrew men from raunging uncertainly, and wandring brutishly about, and made them gather together and keepe company, made houses, and kept fellowshippe together, who therefore is reported (as Horace sayth) to assuage the fiercenesse of Tygers, and moove the harde Flynts.'

11. *challenge to bee* 'claim to be.' The word generally has a substantive as object; but Shakespeare once uses it with a subordinate sentence. *Othello,* 1, 3, 188 'So much (duty) I *challenge* that I may profess due to the Moor my lord.'

14. *charming sweetnes* 'the sweet music which charmed' or 'enchanted.' See the passage of Webbe quoted above. Cp. Milton, *Lycidas*

> 'What could the Muse herself that Orpheus bore,
> The Muse herself, for her *enchanting* son?'

15. *wild* 'in a state of nature,' 'uncivilized.' Cp. Bacon, *Essay IV.* 'Revenge is a kind of *wild* justice.'

16. *Amphion,* son of Zeus and Antiope, received a lyre from Hermes, on which he played with such skill that the stones moved of their own accord to form the walls of Thebes.

18. *indeed stony and beastly people. beastly,* i.e. 'beastlike,' like wild animals. The word was used more where we should use 'animal,' and had not come to have the vulgar modern sound or meaning.

Wycliff, 1 Cor. 2, 14 'For a *beestli* man perseyveth not the thingis that ben of the spirit of God.' 1 Cor. 15, 44 'it is sowun a *beestly* bodi, it shal rise a spiritual bodi' [spelt '*beestlich*' in v. 46].

Lyly's *Euphues* (ed. Arber) p. 320 'I see thou art come from thy booke to *beestliness*' i.e. to an unintellectual way of life.

Arcadia, Bk. I. p. 20 'His silence grew wit, his bluntness integrity, his *beastly* ignorance virtuous simplicity.' id. p. 38 'and that though at the first they fought rather with *beastly* fury than soldiery discipline.'

Puttenham, *Arte of English Poesie* (ed. Arber) p. 206 'the Poet...by good and pleasant perswasion first reduced the wilde and *beastly* people into public societies and civility of life.'

19. *Livius Andronicus*, a Greek slave who received the name of Livius from the master who manumitted him. He was the first to introduce at Rome Latin translations of Greek plays, about B.C. 240.

Ennius b. B.C. 239 in Calabria, d. B.C. 169. He was the author of a famous Epic on the History of Rome which he called *Annales*, as well as of Tragedies and Comedies. He was looked upon as the father of Latin poetry, and Virgil and other poets borrowed largely from him. No complete work of his is extant.

21. *Science* 'knowledge,' not according to the modern usage, in which it has come to be confined almost exclusively to the natural sciences, but in the wider sense of Gray's *Elegy* 'Fair *Science* frowned not on his humble birth.'

Dante (Durante Alighieri) b. at Florence 1265; banished from Florence 1300; d. at Ravenna Sept. 1321. His earliest work was the *Vita Nuova*. About 1309—11 he wrote *de Monarchia* in support of the Imperial authority as against the Papal power. During the period of his banishment he wrote the *Divina Commedia*, which not only served more than anything else to fix and settle the Italian language, but contained a vast treasure of all the knowledge of the day. Of its rank among the great poems of the world this is not the place to speak. It was immediately recognised by his countrymen as their great classic, and numerous copies of the MS. were made and still exist. The first printed edition is said to be that of Foligno 1472. No English translation appears to have been made until the 18th century.

Boccaccio (Giovanni) b. at Certaldo near Florence 1313, d. at Certaldo December 1375. Boccaccio is chiefly known now for his Romances in the collection called *Il Decamerone*, first printed in 1471. But besides this, and various Latin treatises, he wrote several Italian poems *La Teseide, Il Filostrato, Amorosa Visione, Nimfale Fiesolano*, and *Rime;* as well as commentaries on Dante and other prose works.

22. *Petrarch* (Francesco) b. at Arezzo 1306, d. at Vaucluse near Avignon 18 July 1374. His writings both in Latin and Italian are very

numerous: but of his poetry it is chiefly his Sonnets to Laura that are now read. In 1340 he was publicly crowned with laurel at Rome. He was an ardent lover of learning and the ancient literature, and it was he that re-discovered the *Epistulae ad Familiares* of Cicero. The *editio princeps* of his works is that of Jenson 1470.

Sidney has mentioned the three men who more than any others influenced the form of literature, not only in England but throughout Europe, in the 15th and 16th centuries. He then goes on to mention the English poets who first received and transmitted that influence.

Gower, John, d. 1408. The year of his birth is not known, but he was about contemporary with Chaucer [1328—1400], who dedicated his *Troylus and Cresseid* to him:

> 'O moral Gower, this boke I directe
> To the, and to the, philosophical Strode,
> To vouchen-sauf, ther nede is, to correcte,
> Of youre benignites and zeles goode.'

while Gower dedicated his *Confessio Amantis* (1393) to Chaucer. He was born of a gentleman's family in Kent, was late in life patronised by Richard II., and seems always to have been in easy circumstances. From 1400 he was blind, but lived on in safety and comfort in the Priory of St Marie Overies in Southwark, to which he had been a liberal benefactor. His first work *Speculum Meditantis* was written in French, and is lost; his second *Vox Clamantis* (about 1382—4) in Latin Elegiacs; his third *Confessio Amantis* (about 1392—3) in English. French was the language of the Court and Chivalry, and Latin of the learned and the Ecclesiastics: but the time was come for the common language of the people to produce a literature. Sir John Mandeville in 1356 translated his travels into English: about 1380 Wycliffe's translation of the Bible was completed: in 1387 Trevisa's translation of the Polychronicon was finished. Thus a prose style was forming; and at the same time Chaucer was proving that the English language was capable of being used nobly for poetry. Gower therefore comes at a point of transition, and the fact of his having used all three languages in producing his poems marks this well. It must not however be supposed that nothing had been written in English before. From about 1216 (Henry III.) books of devotion, and ballads political or social were not uncommon: and in 1258 a Royal proclamation was for the first time issued in English. Still the chronicles were all in Latin or French, until Robert of Gloucester produced in common English a rhymed Chronicle of England from the siege of Troy to the death of Henry III. (1272). In the beginning of the 14th century certain other books in English were produced, among which may be mentioned the Northumbrian Psalter, and miracle plays which now began to be acted,—first it is said at Chester in 1327. But nothing of importance preceded the group above mentioned, Mandeville, Wycliffe, Trevisa, Chaucer and Gower. Sidney's meaning in speaking of the works of Gower and Chaucer as, like the Italian books, 'treasure houses of learning' will be apparent, if we consider that both embodied in their works tales and histories drawn from a great variety of writers of all ages, especially from the classical authors and from Boccaccio and Petrarch. For the position of Gower and Chaucer as the fathers of English poetry, cp. Skelton, *Garlande of Laurell* 386:

> 'And as I thus sadly among them avysid,
>   I saw Gower, that first garnisshed our English rude,
> And maister Chaucer, that nobly enterprysed
>   How that our Englysshe might fresshely be ennewed;
> The Monk of Bury then after them ensuyd,
>   Dane Johnn Lydgate: theis Englysshe poets thre,
> As I ymagenyd, repayrid unto me.

24. *fore-going* 'example' 'precedent.'

29. *Thales* flor. about B.C. 636 to 546, a native of Miletus. The first of the physical philosophers, whose leading doctrine in Physics was that water was the beginning of all things.

Empedocles of Agrigentum flourished about B.C. 444. According to the popular story he put an end to his life by throwing himself down the crater of Mt. Etna. His doctrines touched both on religion and physics. In regard to the former he taught the spiritual nature of God; in regard to the latter he taught four primary elements of all things,— earth, air, fire, water.

Parmenides of Elea, b. about B.C. 536. "His work on 'Nature' was divided into two parts: in the first is expounded the absolute Truth, as reason proclaims it; in the second human opinion, accustomed to *Follow the rash eye, and ears with singing sounds confused, and tongue*" (Lewes). These three philosophers appear to have delivered their doctrines in hexameter verses.

30. *Pythagoras,* the date of whose birth is uncertain, is generally said to have arrived in Italy between B.C. 520 and 510, and to have settled at Croton. Nearly every branch of learning and philosophy is attributed to him, and a great mass of miraculous fable attaches to his name.   He was, in the eyes of his disciples, divinely inspired and the founder of ascetic mysteries.   None of his genuine works remain; but a poem containing moral maxims and called 'the Golden Verses' exists, which has been attributed to him, and of this Sidney was probably thinking.

31. *Phocylides* of Miletus (about B.C. 560—500), and *Tyrtaeus* of Aphidna in Attica (about B.C. 668) were what were called gnomic poets, who put moral or political maxims into verse for the purpose of practical exhortation or instruction.   Tyrtaeus was also famous for his warlike songs. *Solon* (about B.C. 638—558), the famous Athenian lawgiver, wrote verses in the same way on political subjects.   In fact in these early times verse occupied the ground afterwards taken by Oratory; for verse was more easily remembered in times when writing was rare: and Sidney is quite justified in claiming for it a priority in use over prose composition.   But of course, if this were the only function of poetry, it would be rendered useless or unnecessary when writing became general and prose composition frequent.

33. *their delightful vaine*, 'their natural talent for producing that which gives pleasure.'   From the Latin *vena* for poetic talent (Horace *Od.* 2, 18, 10 ingeni benigna *vena* est).

PAGE 4.

4. *Atlantick Iland.*   If Solon ever described this fabulous island 4 his poem is lost; and all we know of it is from Plato [*Timaeus* 21—24], who represents Critias as telling Socrates that he had heard from his grandfather of an unfinished poem of Solon's in which he described his visit to the Egyptian priests.   They told him, among other things, of the former existence of a great island beyond the Pillars of Hercules, which had once governed from Egypt to Etruria, and which on one stormy night suddenly disappeared beneath the sea.   An elaborate account of the formation of this island and its original settlement is given in the fragmentary dialogue *Critias*, but the tract comes to an end just as Plato is beginning the description of the constitution.   It was this that gave Bacon the name of his imaginary state 'the New Atlantis.'

Iland, notice Sidney's spelling of this word.   It is derived from A.S. *ea-land*, *ig-land* [ea = water], Germ. *eiland*.   Our spelling *island* is from a false analogy with *isle*, which comes from *insula* through the French *isle* (île).

8. *depended most of Poetrie* 'depended on.' The 'of' [=Lat. *de*] is used where we should write 'from' or 'on.' Cp. Ps. 99, 8 'thou tookest vengeance *of* their inventions.' Acts 8, 11 '*of* long time.' Bacon, *Essays* 56 'It proceedeth not always *of* moderation, but *of* a trueness to a man's self.' Cp. p. 58, l. 28. W. A. Wright, *Bible Word-Book*, p. 431.

9. *standeth upon* 'depends upon,' see Index. Cp. Shakespeare, *Mids.* 1, 1, 139 or else it *stood upon* the choice of friends.

10. *Burgesses* 'citizens.' [L. L. *burgenses* members of a *burg* 'fortress' 'town']. *honest* 'respectable,' conveying a notion of commonplace or inferior intellect.

11. *that if they had been sette on the racke.* Sidney means that the language put in the mouths of the speakers in Plato's dialogues was such as they could not have used, and that therefore the whole is a creation of the author's, and as such a species of poetry. See p. 7.

14. *the well ordering of a banquet* as in the *Symposium.*

the delicacie of a walke 'the loveliness of a walk.' He is referring to a passage in the *Phaedrus*, 230 B 'By Herè, 'tis a lovely spot ! for this plane is umbrageous and lofty, and the height of the Agnus tree and its shadiness is quite beautiful: it is in full flower too and makes the whole place perfectly fragrant. Then the beck is very pleasant to look at, as it flows under the plane with water, to judge from dipping my foot in it, exceedingly cool. It would seem from those little puppets and statuettes that it is sacred to some Nymphs. Then notice, please, how delightful and sweet the air is; and how summer-like and musical with the chorus of cicades. But the most delicious thing of all is the grass, growing thick on a gentle slope, and offering a delightful pillow for the head as one lies down.'

15. *Giges Ring.* Plato, *de Rep.* II. 359—360. It is the story of the Lydian shepherd and his ring, which being turned one way made him invisible, and the other way visible. Whereupon he contrived to be sent to the king on a message, intrigued with the queen, and, conspiring with her, killed the king and seized the crown.

17. *walke into Apollo's Garden*, i.e. take delight in poetry, Apollo being the god of poets. Thus a collection of poetry of the day was called 'Apollo's garland.'

18. *Historiographer* [ἱστορία, γράφειν]. Sidney uses both the longer Greek term, as well as the shorter 'historian' which eventually supplanted it. Cp. Puttenham, *Arte of English Poesie* [ed. Arber] p. 25 'as the Poet was also the first *historiographer*.'

21. *fashion* 'form' [facere, Fr. façon]. Shakespeare, 2 *Henry VI.* 2, 4, 76 ' I scorn thee and thy *fashion* ' (the putting on of the red rose).

22. *Herodotus* [B.C. 484—408(?)] calls each of the nine books of his history by the name of one of the nine muses.

24. *of* = 'from.' See Index.

passionate 'moving,' from the sense of the *passions* = 'the feelings.' Cp. Puttenham, *Arte of English Poesie* (ed. Arber) p. 77 'I find Sir Walter Rawleygh's vayne most lofty, insolent, and *passionate.*' id. p. 98 'situation...doth alter the nature of Poesie, and make it lighter or graver, or more merry or mournfull, and many ways *passionate* to the ear and hart of the hearer.' Shakespeare, *Haml.* 2, 2, 452 'Come, a *passionate* speech !'

30. *into the gates of populer iudgements* 'into popular approval.' The whole metaphor, as shown by *pasport* below, is from a walled and garrisoned town. The *pasport* [Fr. *passer, porte;* though the modern word is said to be from *portus* 'harbour'] in Sidney's mind probably means what we should call a pass-word.

33. *Turky.* By *lawe-giving Divines* Sidney means the Turkish Doctcrs or Muftis, who wrote in a mixture of Turkish and Arabic.

' They have a few poets as they are called, whose compositions are mostly little songs and ballads,...the language is a barbarous mixture of the Turkish with the Persian and Arabic, not unlike that ' Babylonish dialect' of our Puritans, which Butler compares to 'Fustian cut on Satin.'' Eton's *Turkey* p. 194.

<h2 style="text-align:center">PAGE 5.</h2>

2. *Ireland.* See Spenser, *A view of the present state of Ireland* **5** (Globe edition) p. 640.

'There is amongst the Irish a certain kind of people called Bards, which are to them insteede of poetts, whose profession is to sett foorth the prayses and disprayses of men in theyr poems and rimes; the which are had in soe high request and estimation amongest them, that none dare to displease them for feare of running into reproche through theyr offence, and to be made infamous of all men. For theyr verses are taken up with a general applause, and usually songe at all feasts and meetinges, by certayne other persons, whose proper function that is, which also receave for the same greate rewardes and reputation besides.' See also ib. pp. 635, 678.

Sir William Temple, *Works* (ed. 1720) vol. I. p. 244 :

'There were, not longer since than thirty or forty years, some re-mainders of Runick poetry among the Irish. The great men of their *Scepts*, among the many officers of their family, which continued always in the same races, had not only a *Physician*, a *Huntsman*, a *Smith*, and such like, but a *Poet* and a *Tale-teller;* the first recorded and sung the Actions of their Ancestors, and entertained the company at Feasts; the latter amused them with tales when they were melancholy and could not sleep: and a very gallant Gentleman of the *North* of *Ireland* has told me, of his own experience, that in his wolf-huntings there, when he used to be abroad in the mountains three or four days together, and lay very ill a-nights, so as he could not well sleep; they would bring him one of these *Tale-tellers*, that when he lay down would begin a story of a king, or a Gyant, a Duarf and a Damsel, and such rambling stuff, and continue it all night long in such an Even Tone that you heard it going on, whenever you waked; and he believed nothing any Physicians give could have so good and so innocent effect, to make men sleep, in any Pains or Distempers of Body or Mind.'

Warton, *History of English Poetry*, vol. I. p. 129 (ed. 1871) :

'The songs of the Irish bards are by some conceived to be strongly marked with the traces of Scaldic imagination; and these traces are believed still to survive among a species of poetical historians, whom they call Tale-tellers, supposed to be the descendants of the original Irish bards. We are informed by the Irish historians, that Saint Pa-trick, when he converted Ireland to the Christian faith, destroyed three hundred volumes of the songs of the Irish bards. Such was their dignity in this country, that they were permitted to wear a robe of the same colour with that of the royal family. They were constantly sum-moned to a triennial festival ; and the most approved songs delivered at this assembly were ordered to be preserved in the custody of the king's historian or antiquary.' See also Keating's *History of Ireland* (ed. O'Mahony) Introd. p. xxxix, pp. 349, 446. Walker, *Irish Bards.* Bunting Hardiman, *Irish Minstrelsy.*

5—7. *simple Indians...Areytos.* The word *Aréito* is defined in Minsheu's Spanish Dictionary [1623] as 'a kinde of dance among the Indians': it seems to be a West-Indian word adopted and modified by the Spaniards.

Natural and Moral History of the Indies by Father Jos. de Acosta, translated (1604) by E. Guniston [ed. C. R. Markham 1880] vol. II. p. 445:

' In these dances they use sundry sorts of instruments, whereof some are like flutes or little lutes, others like drummes, and others like shells: but commonly they sing all with the voyce ; and first one or two sing the song, then all the rest answer them.   Some of these songs were very wittily composed, contayning histories, and others were full of superstitions, and some were meere follies... In Peru they commonly called dances *Taqui*, in other provinces *Areytos*, in Mexico *Mitotes.*'

Puttenham, *Arte of English Poesie* (ed. Arber) p. 26:

' This is proved by certificate of Marchaunts and travellers who by late navigation have surveyed the whole world, and have discovered large countries and strange peoples, wild and savage, affirming that the Americans, the Perusines, and the very Canniball do singe and also say their highest and holiest matters in certain riming versicles and not in prose.'

Hakluyt's *Voyages*, p. 306 (ed. 1600) of Florida: 'Being returned home from the warre they assemble all their subjects, and for joy three days and three nights they make good cheere ; they dance and sing ; likewise they make the most ancient men of the country to dance, holding the haires of their enemies in their hands; and in dauncing they sing praises to the sunne, ascribing to him the honour of the victory.'

14.   *Wales, the true remnant of the aunctient Brittons.*

'The men whom our forefathers found in the Isle of Britain were not men of their own nation or their own speech.   They were men who had lived in the land for many ages, and they were called by the same name as the land itself, for they were called the Britons.   But our forefathers called them by another name, for they spoke a tongue which our forefathers did not understand, and in Old-English those who spoke a tongue which could not be understood were called *Welsh*.' E. A. Freeman.

17.   *Bardes.*   For an account of the Welsh Bards see Warton, *History of English Poetry*, vol. 1. p. 130 sqq.

'But so strong was the attachment of the Celtic nations, among which we reckon Britain, to poetry that, amidst all the changes of government and manners, even long after the order of Druids was extinct and the national religion altered, the bards, acquiring a sort of civil capacity and a new establishment, still continued to flourish.'

23.   *stand upon their authorities*, 'stay to consider,' cp. Shakespeare, *Macbeth* 3, 4, 119 '*stand* not *upon* the order of your going.'

but even so farre, 'if only so far.'

26.   *Vates* [a 'teller' or 'speaker']. Sidney refers to the meaning

of 'seer' or 'prophet' attaching to this word, and assumes, not quite correctly, that it was the common word in Latin for a poet. W. Webbe, *Discourse of English Poetry* (ed. Arber) p. 22, distinguishes more accurately the use of the two words in Latin: 'They which handled in the audience of the people grave and necessary matters, were called wise men or eloquent men, which they meant by *Vates;* and the rest which sange of love matters, or other lighter devises alluring unto pleasure and delight were called *Poetae* or makers.' Sir W. Temple, *Essay on Poetry*, takes the same line as Sidney: 'The Greek signifying makers or creators, such as raise admirable Frames and Fabricks out of nothing, which strike with wonder and with pleasure the eyes and imaginations of those who behold them; the Latin makes the same word common to Poets and to Prophets.'

32. *chaunceable* 'chance' [Lat. cadentia, cadere].

PAGE 6.

6   3. *Sortes Virgilianae.* The word *sortes* was applied to oracular responses, as one of the methods of obtaining them was by drawing lots. The use of *sortes Virgilianae* was a plan for obtaining a quasi-oracular response by opening a book of Virgil and regarding the first verse which met the eyes as containing an intimation of fate. Thus when Alexander Severus was advised by his parents to leave philosophy for practical life, he opened his Virgil and read (*Aen.* 6, 848) *Excudent alii spirantia mollius aera.* And previously at Praeneste when in danger of his life from Heliogabalus he read (*Aen.* 6, 882) *Si qua fata aspera rumpas Tu Marcellus eris.* See *Vita Severi* by Aelius Lampridius cc. 4 and 14.

6. *Albinus.* This is Clodius Albinus, born at Adrumetum in Africa about A.D. 160. He served in Bithynia, under Marcus Aurelius in A.D. 175. Under Commodus (A.D. 180—192) he had a command first in Gaul and then in Britain. Whilst in Britain he was offered the title of Caesar by Commodus, but on a rumour of the death of that Emperor he harangued his soldiers, declaring that he would not accept the title, and urging that the old Senatorial government should be restored. His biographer Julius Capito says that he was in the habit of quoting the line of Virgil which Sidney here quotes (*Aen.* 2, 314). See the life in the *Augustan History* c. 5, where another Sors Virgiliana of his is given. To call him 'Governour of our Iland' is rather misleading.

9. *and in his age performed it.* When Septimius Severus [A.D. 193—211] was proclaimed Emperor by the troops in Illyricum and Pannonia Albinus resisted, and with an army of 150,000 men met Severus at Lugdunum (Lyons) on the 19th Feb. 197, and was eventually defeated and killed.

12. *charmes derived of Carmina,* through O. F. *charme.*

15. *Oracles of Delphos.* Strabo tells us that at Delphi the priestess gave out the oracular reply, which the *prophetes* then caused to be reduced to verse by some 'poets' kept on the premises for that purpose. At any rate most of the answers from Delphi preserved by Herodotus are in verse. The name of the place is Delphi (Δελφοί) not Delphos; but Sidney always writes Delphos, see *Arcadia,* Bk. 1. p. 18, and so do other writers of the age.

Sibillas prophecies. There were many Sibyllae or wise-women in various places; but Sidney is thinking of the Sibylla of Cumae in Campania, who was said to have given the remains of her book of prophecies (after sundry refusals) to Tarquinius king of Rome. At any rate a collection of oracular lines was preserved in historical times at Rome, under the charge of certain commissioners, which were consulted on occasions of difficulty or danger, probably by the method of shuffling the loose leaves, and drawing one out by hazard.

25. *the name Psalmes,* from the Greek *psallein* (ψάλλειν) 'to sing.'

27. *fully written in meeter, as all learned Hebricians agree.* See Tremilius, *Introduction to Latin Bible* (1575), vol. II. p. 4, 'Itaque hos libros omnes communiter vocamus Psalmos, quia sunt rythmici, non prosa oratione scripti, ut omnes alii...sed numeris adstricti ad commoditatem memoriae et cantus.'

Puttenham, *Art of English Poesie* (ed. Arber), p. 25:

'King David also and Solomon his sonne and many others of the holy Prophets wrote in meeters, and used to sing them to the harpe, although to many of us ignorant of the Hebrue language and phrase, and not observing it, the same seems but prose...but the Hebrues and Chaldees, who were more ancient than the Greekes, did not only use a metricall Poesie, but also with the same maner of rime, as hath bene of late observed by learned men.'

29. *meerely poetical,* 'entirely poetical,' from Lat. *merus* 'pure,' 'unmixed.'

30. *awaking his musicall instruments.* In such verses as Ps. 57, 8 'Awake up my glory; awake psaltery and harp: I myself will awake

right early: 108, 2 'Awake, psaltery and harp: I myself will awake early.'   See among other similar passages especially Ps. 81, 2—3.

31. *changing of persons*, i.e. putting the words dramatically now into the mouth of one person and now in that of another.   Thus in Ps. 81, 6 the speaker is suddenly changed from the Psalmist to Jehovah.   Cp. 89, 19.   So in Ps. 81, 11 the words of the enemy are given dramatically, cp. Ps. 109, 132.

32. *Prosopopeias* (πρόσωπον, ποιεῖν) 'personifications,' representing things as living persons.   Cp. Puttenham, *Arte of English Poesie* (ed. Arber), p. 246: 'But if ye will faine any person with such features, qualities, and conditions, or if ye will attribute any humane quality, as reason or speech, to dumb creatures or other insensible things, and do study (as one may say) to give them a humane person, it is not *prosopographia*, but *prosopopeia*.'

<h3 style="text-align:center">PAGE 7.</h3>

7   1.   *the Beastes ioyfulnes, and hills leaping.* Pss. 65, 3; 68, 6; 114, 4—5.

14.   *a Poet*, 'a maker,' ποιητής.   In subsequent editions the word is printed in Greek type.   In Latin and its derivative languages 'poet' is a loan word from the Greek.

18.   *have mette with the Greekes in calling him a maker*, 'have agreed with,' 'have coincided with.'   Cp. Shakespeare, *Timon*, 4, 3, 472,

> 'How rarely does it *meet with* this world's guise
> When man was wished to love his enemies.'

For 'maker,' which was still in use for 'a poet,' cp. p. 9, l. 17. Skelton, *Against Garnesde*, v. 108

> 'Ye wolde be called a *maker*,
> And *make* moche lyke Jake Rakor;
> Ye ar a comly crakar,
> Ye lernyd of sum py-bakar.'

Drayton, *Polyolbion*

> 'expert being grown
> In music, and besides a curious *maker* grown.'

N. Udal, *Royster Doyster*, Act 2, Sc. 1

> 'Of songs and balardes also he is a *maker*.'

Vision of Piers Ploughman, 7470

> 'And thow medlest thee with *makynges*.'

Ben Jonson, *Discoveries*, 'A *Poet* is that which by the Greeks is called κατ' ἐξοχὴν, ὁ Ποιητής, a *maker* or *feigner*.'

The Scotch called a poet a *makkar*, the Saxons *scóp* from *sceapan* 'to make' or 'create.'

20. *scope*, 'aim' 'object' (σκοπός). See Index.

23. *his* where we should use 'its.' The latter is seldom used in writers of this age, and does not occur in the A.V. of the Bible (1611); though it occurs ten times in Shakespeare. See W. A. Wright, *Bible Word-book*, p. 347.

28. *by that*, 'by that which.'

what order Nature hath taken therein. 'To take order' is 'to take measures,' 'to make arrangements.' Shakespeare, *Richard III.* 4, 4, 539 'Some one *take order* Buckingham be brought to Salisbury.' *Othello*, 5, 2, 72 'Honest Iago hath *ta'en order* for it.' 2 Maccab. 4. 27 'as for the money he promised unto the king he *took* no good *order* for it.'

30. *quantities*, 'things measurable' either by Geometry or Arithmetic.

PAGE 8.

3. *standeth upon the naturall vertues, vices*, 'is engaged in study-ing,' see p. 5, l. 23 and Index. **8**

4. *followe Nature.* The Stoic definition of the *summum bonum* in Ethics was to 'live according to Nature' or, as it was sometimes expressed, to 'follow Nature.' See Cicero, *de Senectute*, § 5 'natura optima dux.'

10. *which still are compassed within the circle of a question, according to the proposed matter.* Sidney (who is here following Julius Scaliger, *Poeticè*, p. 3) means that the orator must confine himself to subjects on which he is required to speak, the historian to the facts as he finds them; neither *create*, they only deal with what they find existing: their rules therefore are not of universal application or absolute, but are limited to the matter with which they are dealing. The poet, on the other hand, creating his own matter, is unconfined. Lord Brooke, in his poem on *Humane Learning*, classifies the Arts in the same order as Sidney and also expresses nearly the same thought,

> 'Now for these instrumental following arts,
>   Which in the traffick of humanity
> Afford not matters, but limme out the parts
>   And forms of speaking with authority:
>   I say who too long in their cobwebs lurks
>   Doth like him that buyes tooles, but never works.'

15. *supernaturall*, referring to the meaning of the word metaphysics (μετα-φυσικά 'beyond nature').

18. *growe*, transitive 'cause to grow.'

21. *Heroes*, a Greek word (ἥρως) for a deified man; *Demigods* gives the same idea (Lat. *dimidius* 'half'). *Cyclops*, 'round-eyed' [κύκλος, ὄψ] the one-eyed giants in Sicily described in the Odyssey. *Chimera* (χίμαιρα she-goat) a monster half goat and half woman.

23. *not inclosed within the narrow warrant of her guifts*, 'not confined to things or powers really existing in nature,' i.e. he can invent forms, powers and qualities as he chooses.

26. *tapistry* [Fr. *tapisserie*: Lat. *tapete*: Gr. τάπης], with embroideries, rich colours. Tapestries and hangings of rich embroidery had long been used in the houses; and the Eastern works of this kind were beginning now to be better known in England through the Turkey Company. Shakespeare, *Comedy of Errors*, 4, 1, 104 'The deed that's covered o'er with *Turkish tapestry*.' *Cymb.* 2, 4, 69 a bedchamber is 'hanged with *tapestry* of silk and silver.' For the simile cp. Sackville's *Induction* (to the *Mirrour for Magistrates*):

> 'The gladsome groves which now lay overthrown
> The *tapets* torne, and every blome blown down.'

30. *brasen...golden*, referring to the gold, silver, and bronze ages of the poets.

31. *deliver*, 'describe.'   See p. 3, l. 10; p. 14, l. 24.

32. *for whom*, 'for whose advantage' or 'use.'

PAGE 9.

9   1. *Theagines.*   See note on Heliodorus, p. 12, l. 17.

2. *Pilades.*   Pylades is the friend of Aeneas in Virgil's *Aeneid*.

Orlando, the hero of Ariosto's *Orlando Furioso*, the model of a valiant knight.   The work of Ariosto [1474—1533] was very popular at this time, though it does not appear to have been translated into English until 1591 (by Sir John Harrington).

3. *so right a Prince*, 'so true a prince.' Cp. p. 11, l. 8, and Index. Xenophon's 'Education of Cyrus' is an ideal account of the elder Cyrus, founder of the Medo-Persian Empire (about B.C. 560); written in the 4th century B.C. it is the earliest specimen of political romance.

4—5. *iestingly conceived*, 'taken as said in jest.' For *conceive* = 'understand' see Index.

5.   *essensiall* [L. *essentia* 'a being' from *esse*] here means 'founded on truth.'   Sidney regards Xenophon's work as partly historical.   Cp. Shakespeare, *Othello*, 4, 1, 62

> 'One that excels the quirks of blazoning pens
> And in the *essential* vesture of creation
> Does tire the ingener.'

6.   *any understanding*, 'anyone who is intelligent.'   Cp. Shakespeare, *Winter's Tale*, 1, 2, 223

> 'Was this taken
> By any *understanding* pate but thine?'

any = 'anyone.'   St James, 5, 19, 'Brethren, if *any* of you do err from the truth, and one convert him.'   Shakespeare, *As you like it*, 1, 2, 149 'But is there *any* else longs to see this broken music in his sides?'

7.   *standeth in*, 'consists in.'   Cp. p. 13, l. 32.   Cp. P. B. Collect for Peace, '*In* knowledge of whom *standeth* our eternal life.'   Chaucer, *Parson's Tale*, 'And this (penitence) *stondith* in thre thinges, contricion of hert, confessioun of mouth, and satisfaccioun.'

18.   *sawcie* [L. *salsa*, Fr. *sauce*] 'pungent,' and so 'sprightly,' or 'impudent.'

21.   *of that maker*, i.e. 'poet,' see p. 7, l. 18.

25.   *a divine breath*, 'inspiration.'

27.   *sith*, see on p. 2, l. 15.

28.   *erected wit*, 'elevated, undebased, intelligence.'   Cp. Milton, *Paradise Lost*

> 'Glory the reward
> That sole excites to high attempts, the flame
> Of most *erected* spirits.'

Arcadia, Bk. 1. 'a piercing wit, quite void of ostentation, high *erected* thought seated in a heart of courtesy.'

29.   *infected will*, 'corrupted and weakened will.'   Cf. Lord Brooke, *Of Humane learning*

> 'But these vaine idols of humanity
> As they *infect* our wits, so do they stain
> Or bind our inclinations borne more free.'

32.   *the name above all names*, i.e. the maker.

PAGE 10.

6.   *for so Aristotle termeth it.*   Aristotle, *Poet.* c. 1 ἐποποιΐα δὴ **10** καὶ ἡ τῆς τραγῳδίας ποίησις...πᾶσαι τυγχάνουσιν οὖσαι μιμήσεις τὸ

σύνολον. Sidney follows Aristotle both in his definitions and in his divisions of the various kinds of poetry: but his immediate authority appears rather to have been the *Poeticè* of J. C. Scaliger (published in 1561), in which much the same method of arrangement is followed. In the first page of his treatise Scaliger says '*quamobrem tota in imitatione* (*poesis*) *sita fuit.*'

9. *a speaking picture.* See Ben Jonson's *Discoveries*, ' Poetry and Picture are arts of a like nature; and both are busy about imitation. It was excellently said of Plutarch, *Poetry* was a speaking picture, and Picture a mute poesy.' The passage of Plutarch referred to, and which was doubtless in Sidney's mind, is *de Audiendis Poetis*, c. 3 ζωγραφίαν μὲν εἶναι φθεγγομένην ποίησιν, ποίησιν δὲ σιγῶσαν τὴν ζωγραφίαν. Plutarch however does not pretend to be the author of it; he speaks of it as a common saying. Cp. G. Puttenham, *Arte of English Poesie* (ed. Arber), p. 218

> 'If Poesie be, as some have said,
> A speaking picture to the eye,
> Then is a picture not denaid,
> To be a muet Poesie.'

Scaliger, *Poeticè*, c. 1 applies the metaphor rather to other arts as opposed to the creative function of poetry, 'ceterae artes res ipsas, uti sunt, representant, *veluti aurium quandam picturam.*' Cp. p. 18, l. 6.

10. *with this end, to teach and delight.* Sidney is again following Scaliger (*Poet.* p. 1): 'hic enim finis est, medius ad illam ultimam, qui est *docendi cum delectatione.* Nam Poeta etiam docet, non solum delectat.'

17. *Emanuell Tremilius and Franciscus Junius.* Two learned Hebraists, whose Latin translation of the Bible, first published at Frankfort in 1575—1580, was widely used.

John Emmanuel Tremilius (or Tremellius), a Jew, born in Ferrara in Italy about 1510, was converted to Christianity first as a Catholic by Reginald Pole. He afterwards became a Protestant principally under the influence of Peter Martyr, and resided both in Germany and England. In Germany he had a prebend at Strasburg. He came to England in the reign of Edward VI. and, after residing in the family of Cranmer, was in 1549 sent to Cambridge to teach Hebrew, being supported by a canonry of Carlisle. In the reign of Mary I. he retired from England, and resided first in Brussels, and, afterwards as Hebrew

Professor at Heidelberg. He afterwards retired to France and died at Sedan 9 Oct. 1580. Besides the Latin Bible he was the author of numerous other works on Hebrew and Syriac. Cooper's *Athenae Cantabrig.* 1, p. 425.

Francis Junius (du Jon) a French Protestant, born at Bourges (1545). He was minister of the Walloon Church in Antwerp in 1568, Theological Professor successively at Neustadt, Heidelberg, and Leyden (1592). In 1573 he went to Heidelberg, at the invitation of the Elector Palatine, to assist Tremellius in translating the O. T. into Latin. He died of the plague at Leyden in 1602. Hallam's *Literature*, 2, p. 343.

18. *doe entitle the poeticall part of the Scripture.* The 2nd volume of Tremellius' Latin Bible, which begins with Job, has on the title page 'Bibliorum pars tertia *id est* quinque libri *poetici*, Latini recens ex Hebraeo facti.' And the dedication to the Prince Palatine begins, 'edituri *poeticos* sacrae scripturae *libros*.' Cp. Puttenham, *Arte of English Poesie* (ed. Arber), p. 25, quoted on p. 6, l. 27.

21. *Orpheus, Amphion, Homer,* see p. 3, l. 16. Here again Sidney is following Scaliger, who counts after Apollo the first class of poets as that from which came *theologia et mysteria*, among whom are 'Orpheus, Musaeus, and Linus.' p. 3—5 'primum genus est Theologorum, cujusmodi Orpheus et Amphion.'

24. *S. Iames his counsell.* See Epistle of S. James, 5, 13. For *his* see on p. 2, l. 8.

26, 27. *death-bringing...never-leaving.* See Index under 'Compound epithets.'

30. *Tirteus,* p. 3, l. 31. Tyrtaeus is classed as a *moral* poet, as being political; and political science is a branch of moral philosophy, according to Scaliger, *Poeticè*, p. 5.

Phocilides, p. 3, l. 31.

Lucretius. Titus Lucretius Carus (B.C. 95—55) whose philosophical poem *de rerum natura* survives.

31. *Cato.* Dionysius Cato is the reputed author of a small volume consisting of four books of *disticha* or couplets of Latin hexameters, containing moral precepts epigrammatically expressed. It was very popular in the middle ages: and numerous editions appeared after the invention of printing. Erasmus published it as a school-book in 1523, and Joseph Scaliger even took the trouble to edit it with a dissertation, notes, and a Greek version [1646 Amsterdam]. Nothing is known of the supposed author, or of the time at which the book

was produced, except that it must apparently have been before A.D. 300. Some have thought that *Cato* is a mere title of the book like the 'Laelius' of Cicero. Others have attributed it to a variety of people, Seneca, Ausonius, Boethius and others. It was translated from a French version into English and printed by Caxton in 1483. See p. 37, l. 4.

32. *Georgicks* (γῆ, ἔργειν) *georgica*, poems on farming: published by Virgil, about B.C. 30.

Manilius, who probably flourished in the reign of Tiberius, was the author of a poem on astronomy in five books called *Astronomica*.

PAGE 11.

11   1. *Pontanus*, John Jovius Pontanus [1420—1503], born at Cerreto, was one of the best of the mediaeval Latin poets of Italy. Among his numerous works both prose and verse was an astronomical poem called *Urania*. Scaliger has a lengthy criticism of his poems, praising his skill in verse and the gracefulness of his style, but censuring his want of self-restraint, and the exuberance of his language [*Poetice*, lib. 6, p. 311 sq. ed. 1561]. He was tutor, and afterwards secretary, to Alphonso king of Arragon. See Hallam's *Literature*, vol. 1, pp. 228, 270; vol. 2, p. 302.

Lucan. Marcus Annaeus Lucanus [A.D. 39—65] the Roman poet put to death by Nero. His poem the *Pharsalia* is an account of the civil war of Caesar and Pompey.

which who mislike, 'which those who mislike.' Sidney frequently uses the relative *who* without an antecedent expressed. See p. 17, l. 21; p. 32, l. 33; p. 45, l. 33. Cp. Shakespeare, *Othello*, 3, 3, 157 '*Who* steals my purse steals trash.' *mislike* where we should say 'dislike,' cp. Shakespeare *Merchant*, 2, 1, 1 '*Mislike* me not for my complexion.'

4. *thys second sorte*, i.e. the philosophical poets.

is wrapped within the folde of the proposed subiect, i.e. they are confined to the facts of the subject of which they are treating. Cp. p. 8, l. 10.

8. *indeed right Poets*, 'who are without doubt real poets,' i.e. imaginative poets, who are not tied to any particular class of facts. For *right* see Index.

13. *wit*, 'genius' or 'imagination,' see Index.

15. *Lucrecia.* Lucretia, wife of L. Tarquinius Collatinus, who killed herself after the violence done her by Sextus. Sidney seems to be referring to some picture he had seen in Italy.

20. *onely rayned with learned discretion*, 'restrained by nothing but cultivated taste.' Sidney uses *with* where we should use 'by,' cp. p. 17, l. 24, 26; p. 27, l. 10; p. 31, l. 3.

23. *iustly bee termed Vates*, see p. 5, l. 26. Sidney alludes to the two meanings of *vates*, (1) a seer or prophet, (2) poet.

24. *are waited on* 'are greeted.' Thus in Shakespeare, *Tempest*, 1, 2, 388 music '*waits upon* some god of the island.'

26. *make*, 'compose poetry,' see on p. 7, l. 18.

31. *scope*, 'aim' or 'object,' see Index.

PAGE 12.

8. *numbrous*, 'metrical' [formed from Fr. *nombre*, Engl. 'number,' **12** instead of 'numerous' from Lat. numerosus].

12. *versifiers*, cp. Puttenham, *Arte of English Poesie* (ed. Arber), 'Even so the very poet makes and contrives out of his owne braine, both the verse and matter of his poeme, and not by any foreine copie or example, as doth the translator, who therefore may well be sayd a *versifyer* but not a poet.' Elyot's *Governour* (ed. Croft, vol. 1, p. 120), 'Semblably they that make verses, expressynge thereby none other learnyrge but the craft of versifying, be not of auncient writers named poetes, but only called *versifyers*.'

15. *Cyrus*, see p. 9, l. 3.

as Cicero sayth of him. See *Epist. ad Quintum Fratrem*, 1, 1, 8 'Cyrus ille a Xenophonte non ad historiae fidem scriptus est, sed ad effigiem justi imperii.'

16. *absolute*, 'perfect' (L. *absolutus*), *Euphues* (ed. Arber), p. 151 'I hope, if Tully confesse any to be an *absolute* orator, it will be my youth.'

17. *Heliodorus in his sugred invention.* Heliodorus, Bishop of Tricca in Thessaly, about A.D. 400, wrote a romance in Greek called Aethiopica, of which Theagines and Chariclea are the hero and heroine. It was first printed at Basle in 1534. A Latin translation was published in 1552, but none in English till 1792.

sugred, 'sweet,' a favourite word in writers of the age, especially in regard to love matters. Cp. *Euphues* (ed. Arber), p. 422 'the

Nightingale which is saide, with continual strayning to singe, to perish in his sweete lays as they do in their *sugred* lives.'

20. *riming*, the M.E. rime is from the A.S. rím 'number': but the modern spelling 'rhyme' is a mistake from the false analogy of 'rhythm' ($\rho\upsilon\theta\mu\delta s$).

21. *long gowne.* The long gown, usually fringed with fur, which was the regular dress of lawyers, civil magistrates, graduates, and generally of men of a certain age and dignity. It has partially survived in the distinctive dress of University graduates. Cp. Elyot's *Governour* (ed. Croft), vol. 2, p. 18 'And what enormitie shoulde it be thought, a thinge to laugh at, to see a juge or sergent at the lawe in a short cote, garded and pounced after the galyade facion.'

24. *the right describing note,* 'the true distinctive sign' or 'mark,' in the sense in which '*a note* of the Church' is used [Lat. *nota* 'a mark'].

26. *the Senate of Poets.* The word *Senate* is here wrongly used for 'the general body' or 'corporation.' Cp. Skelton, *Garlande of Laurell*, 224

> 'I am contente that he be not exylide
> Frome the laureat *senate* by force of proscripcyon.'

27. *as in matter they passed all in all, so in maner to goe beyond them*, i.e. as the subjects of which poets treat are the highest, so their manner of expressing themselves is to be the best. We may remember the definition of Coleridge: 'prose=words in their best order;—poetry=the *best* words in the best order.' *Table Talk*, p. 48.

28. *table talke fashion*, i.e. in careless language, p. 15, l. 10. Shakespeare, *Merchant*, 3, 5, 92

> 'No, pray thee, let it serve for *table-talk:*
> Then howsoe'er thou speak'st, 'mong other things
> I shall digest it.'

30. *peyzing*, 'weighing' [Fr. *peser*, L. *pensare*].

PAGE 13.

13   1. *his*, for 'its,' see p. 7, l. 23.

5. *enabling*, 'making able' or 'strong.' Cp. *Arcadia*, Bk. 1, ' Fear breedeth wit, anger is the cradle of courage, joy openeth and *enableth* the heart.'

6. *conceyt*, 'imagination,' see Index.

12. *many formed*, 'manifold,' 'various.'

16. *if they knewe the causes of things.*   Cp. Elyot's *Governour* (ed. Croft), vol. 2, p. 351 'The noble philosopher and moste excellent oratour *Tullius Cicero*, in the IV boke of his Tusculane questions saieth in this wise, Sapience is the science of things divine and humaine, which considereth *the cause of everything*.   See Cicero, *Tusc.* 4, c. 26, Virg. *Georg.* 2, 490 'Felix qui potuit rerum cognoscere causas.'

17. *supernaturall* 'metaphysical,' p. 8, l. 15.

19. *the Mathematickes*, the definite article was commonly used with this word, cp. Mulcaster's *Positions*, p. 242 'Which bookes (Xenophon) he caused to be red in the same house, and gave them to the studentes, to encourage as wel to the Greek tongue, as he did to *the Mathematicks*.'

20. *scope*, p. 7, l. 20 and Index.

21. *dungeon of the body.*   Cicero (*de Amic.* § 17) speaks of the escape of the soul *tanquam e custodia vinculisque corporis*.   Cp. Words-worth's

> 'Shades of the *prison-house* begin to close
>   About the growing boy.'

22. *his*, see Index.   *his owne divine essence*, the spiritual elements of which the soul itself is composed.   *essence=essentia* 'real being.' Cp. p. 45, l. 26; p. 9, l. 5.

23. *ballance*, 'test,' that which weighs every thing as in scales. For the *Astronomer* falling into a ditch, cp. Chaucer, *Miller's Tale*, 269

> ' Ye! blessed be alway a lewed man,
>   That nat but oonly his bileeve can.
>   So ferde another clerk with astronomye;
>   He walked in the feeldes for to prye
>   Upon the sterres, what ther schulde bifalle,
>   Til he was in a marle pit i-falle.'

28. *serving Sciences*, 'subordinate sciences,' only ministering to the chief science (Architectonike) greater than themselves : what Lord Brooke calls 'instrumental following arts.'   See on p. 8, l. 11.

29. *a private end*, 'a separate end' or 'object' (τέλος).   Thus the 'end' of oratory is persuasion, the 'end' of Geometry is the measure-ment of dimensions : but the end of all sciences alike is the supreme one of KNOWLEDGE.

31. *Arkitecktonike* (ἀρχιτεκτονικὴ), Aristot. *Eth.* 1, 1.   The master-knowledge, that namely which leads to and makes possible the highest

end or aim—right action; for the end is action not mere knowing (πρᾶξις not γνῶσις).

32. *stands in*, 'consists in,' see Index.

33. *in the Ethicke and politick consideration*, 'in regard to his moral and social duties,' or 'considered as a moral and social being.'

PAGE 14.

14 3. *facultie*, 'art' or 'profession,' see p. 1, l. 14.

6. *ending end*, 'final' or 'supreme end,' the summum bonum of ethics. See on p. 13, l. 31.

19. *larges* ('largesse,' L. *largitio*), a word used at tournaments and still employed in various parts of the country by labourers after harvest. Cp. Puttenham, *Arte of English Poesie*, p. 36 (ed. Arber), 'For that liberality is come to fayle in Princes, who for their *largesse* were wont to be accompted the only patrons of learning and first founders of all excellent artificers.'

21. *soberly*, 'gravely.'

24. *delivering forth*, see Index.   *his* = 'its,' see Index.

26. *combersome*, 'embarrassing.'   To cumber is 'to impede,' from L. L. *cumbrus* 'a pile of timber for blocking up the way,' L. *cumulus*, Ger. *Kummer*.   The transition in the formation of the word is shewn in the form *comerous* used by Skelton, *The Bowge of Courte*, v. 294 'Dysdayne, I wene, this *comerous* crabes hyghte.'

27. *the generalities that contayneth it, and the specialities that are derived from it*, i.e. the general category under which virtue or vice come, such as 'the good' or 'the bad,' 'the profitable' or 'the unprofitable': and the specific results of the two, such as 'pleasure,' 'pain,' 'honour,' 'disgrace.'   The plural 'contayn*eth*' is not usual in English of this age, though in the Old English Southern dialects it was the ordinary inflexion for all persons; and is occasionally found in MSS. of Chaucer, e.g. *Knightes Tale*, 1185 'And over his head ther *schyneth* two figures.'   Morris' Chaucer p. xxxvii.

PAGE 15.

15 1. *old Mouse-eaten records.*   Sidney was perhaps thinking of the line of Juvenal (3, 207) et divina opici rodebant carmina mures.   But it is possible that what he really wrote was *mought-eaten* (i.e. moth-eaten), cp. More's *Utopia* (ed. Arber), p. 25 '*moughteaten* terms,' p. 59 'old *mought-eaten* laws.'   Skelton, *Colin Clout*, v. 53

> 'For though my rhyme be ragged
>   Tattered and jagged,
>   Rudely rayne-beaten
>   Rusty and *mought-eaten*.'

2. *authorising himselfe upon*, 'using as his sole authorities,' i.e. without any independent knowledge.

5. *to accord*, 'to reconcile.'

10. *table talke*, p. 12, l. 28.

11. *chafe*, 'irritation.' Shakespeare, *Antony*, 1, 3, 85 'How this great Roman does become the carriage of his *chafe*.'

12. *I am Lux*, etc. Sidney appears to have quoted from memory and not quite accurately. Cicero, *de Orat*. 2, 9, 36 'Historia vero testis temporum, lux veritatis, vita memoriae, magistra vitae, nuntia veritatis.'

15. *a disputative vertue*, 'a theoretical virtue,' such as is defined in philosophical discussion.

18. *Marathon* (B.C. 490), *Pharsalia* (B.C. 48), *Poitiers* (1356), *Agincourt* (1415).

21. *goeth beyond*, 'excels.' *fine-witted*, 'subtle.'

28. *Brutus*. Marcus Brutus, the assassin of Julius Caesar [B.C. 85—42], was a great student of history, and is said by Plutarch to have been engaged on his compendium of Polybius in his tent on the evening before the battle of Pharsalia.

Alphonsus of Aragon. Alphonso V. of Aragon and I. of Sicily reigned from 1416 to 1458. He was called the 'magnanimous,' and enjoyed a great reputation for warlike prowess and generosity of temper among his contemporaries. His romantic career was described by Antonio of Palermo in his work *de dictis et factis Alphonsi;* but Sidney refers to him here because of his patronage of letters and love of learning, especially of history. He caused the Florentine Poggio to translate the Cyropaedia of Xenophon, rewarding him, as he did other writers, with great munificence. He took as his device an open book; encouraged his soldiers in all his sieges and expeditions to collect and bring to him all books they could lay hands upon; always had some volumes at the head of his bed; and never travelled without the *Commentaries* of Caesar, part of which he read every day.

30. *maketh a poynt*, 'comes to a stop.' Shakespeare, 2 *Henry IV.* 2, 4, 199 'come we to full *points* here; and are etceteras nothing?'

PAGE 16.

1. *Moderator*, a technical word (still in use) for the umpire or 16

arbitrator in disputations in the Universities between the challenger and defender. For its metaphorical use cp. Sir T. Browne, *Religio Medici* (ed. Greenhill) p. 62, 'When I take a full view and circle of myself without this reasonable *moderator*, and equal piece of justice, Death, I do conceive myself the miserablest person extant.'

2.   *to carrie the title*, 'to win the title.'

4.   *serving Sciences*, see p. 13, l. 28.

9.   *scope.* See Index.

14.   *Formidine pœnæ…Virtutis amore.* Horace, *Ep.* 1, 16, 52

> 'Oderunt peccare boni virtutis amore,
>   tu nihil admittes in te formidine poenae.'

20.   *naughtines*, 'wickedness.' S. James 1, 21 'filthiness and superfluity of *naughtiness*.' More's *Utopia* (ed. Arber), p. 64 'Evil opinions and *naughty* persuasions.'

21.   *cabinet*, 'chamber.' Shakespeare, *Lucrece*

> 'They (the veins) mustering to the quiet *cabinet*
> Where their dear governess and lady lies.'

23.   *manners*, 'morals.'

31.   *to bee conceived*, 'to be understood.'

PAGE 17.

17   1.   *standeth so upon*, 'deals so much with,' see Index.

7.   *not to the general reason of things.* What is called 'philosophical history' was perhaps unknown in English, the chronicles dealing almost exclusively in a record of facts; but ancient historians, especially Polybius, had made a great point of discovering and setting forth the ultimate causes of events (αἱ αἰτίαι).

14.   *So as*, 'so that,' see Index.

15.   *picture*, see on p. 10, l. 9.

18.   *woordish*, 'consisting of words,' cp. *Arcadia*, Bk. 1 'a sheepish squadron.'

21.   *who* = 'he who,' p. 11, l. 1.

22.   *most exquisitely*, 'most minutely.'

24.   *with* = 'by,' see Index.

30.   *a iudicial comprehending*, 'such a conception as enables the mind to form a judgment.' Cp. p. 18, l. 5 'the iudging powre.' He is using more or less scientific terms: the senses receive 'impressions,' the intellect forms a 'judgment' or as others called it a 'notion.'

PAGE 18.

6. *speaking picture*, p. 10, l. 9.   **18**

8. *Tullie taketh much paynes.* See such passages as 3 *de Fin.* 64, 'decet cariorem esse patriam nobis quam nosmet ipsos.' 4 *Catil.* 16 'patriae solum cum omnibus est carum tum vero dulce et jucundum.' 1 *de Orat.* § 196 'ac nos, id quod maxime debet, patria nostra delectat: cujus rei tanta est vis, ut Ithacam illam in asperrimis saxulis tanquam nidulum affixam sapientissimus vir immortalitati anteponeret.'

11. *Anchises speaking in the middest of Troyes flames,* Virg. *Aen.* 2, 638—649.

middest, formed, with added *t,* from M.E. *middes,* Skeat.

12. *Ulisses, in the fulnes of all Calipso's delights.* Homer, *Odyss.* 5, 215 'Myself I know it well, how wise Penelope is meaner to look upon than thou in comeliness and stature...Yet even so, I wish and long day by day to fare homeward and see the day of my returning.'

14. *Anger...a short maddnes.* Horace, *Epp.* 1, 2, 62 'ira furor brevis est.' Seneca, who professed Stoicism, wrote a treatise on anger, in which he shows how it has all the external marks of madness, 'the brow is bold and lowering, the expression fierce, the step quickened, its hands restless, the colour changed, the breath drawn frequently and rapidly' (*de Ira* 1, 1, 3).

15. *let but Sophocles bring you Aiax on a stage, killing.* In the play of Sophocles Ajax is only brought on the stage *after* the slaughter of the sheep and oxen. His violence is described by his wife. But Sidney is thinking of the play as a Poem rather than of its actual representation on the stage.

19. *his,* 'its,' see Index.

20. *temperance in Ulisses.* In the Iliad and Odyssey Ulysses is the embodiment of caution and wisdom. *Diomedes* and *Achilles* are the bravest warriors in the Iliad.

The story of the devoted friendship of *Nisus* and *Euryalus* is in Virgil *Aeneid* 9, 175 sqq.

22. *an apparent shyning,* 'a brilliant light' or 'illustration.' For this use of *apparent* 'evident,' cp. *Arcadia,* Bk 1 'he took him to his Court with *apparent* (i.e. evident) show of his good opinion.'

23—26. *Oedipus...Agamemnon...Atreus...the two Theban brothers.* Sidney is evidently referring not to the plays of Sophocles and Aeschylus, but to those of Seneca, one of which, called *Thyestes,* is concerned with the horrible story of Atreus serving up to his brother Thyestes a banquet of Thyestes' own sons. The other plays of Seneca referred to are the 'Agamemnon,' the 'Oedipus' and the 'Thebais.' Atreus is called *self-devouring* apparently as equivalent to 'cannibal.'

27. *the sowre-sweetnes of revenge in Medæa.* Here again Sidney probably knew the Medea of Seneca rather than that of Euripides. Medea kills her children to punish her husband Jason for deserting her and marrying a Greek wife, and also secures the death of the bride.

sowre-sweet, a combination of contradictory adjectives producing the figure called by Grammarians an *oxymoron.* Sowre is used as = 'sad,' 'terrible.' Cp. Shakespeare, *Richard II.* 3, 2, 193 'Speak *sweetly,* although thy looks be *sour.*'

27. *Terentian Gnato.* Gnatho is a parasite and flatterer in the *Eunuchus* of Terence. His name is used as synonymous for the qualities of such persons by Cicero and others. See Cic. 2 *Phil.* § 15, cp. p. 30, l. 19.

28. *Chaucers Pandar.* In the 'Troylus and Cresseyde' (about 1382) which was taken from the *Filostrato* of Boccaccio. Though Shakespeare's *Troilus and Cressida* has made the name of Pandar familiar to modern readers, it had become a byword before that play. See *Merry Wives,* 1, 3, 83; *Twelfth Night,* 3, 1, 58.

PAGE 19.

19   1. *the fayned Cyrus in Xenophon.* See p. 9, l. 3.

3. *Sir Thomas Moore's Eutopia.* Though the variety in spelling names was at this time and long afterwards extraordinarily great, yet I believe the undoubtedly correct form is More and not Moore. Still Puttenham, *Arte of English Poesie* (ed. Arber), p. 55 writes Moore; and so does Burton, *Anatomy of Melancholy,* p. 300 (ed. 1651), though at p. 617 he has the Latin form *Morus.*

As to *Eutopia* for *Utopia,* this mistake is not altogether without warrant or excuse. In the Latin editions of the Utopia [Basle 1518] the following Hexastichon is prefixed, professing to be by Anemolius poet-laureate of the Island:

> 'Utopia priscis dicta ob infrequentiam,
> Nunc civitatis aemula Platonicae,
> Fortasse victrix (nam quod illa literis
> Deliniavit, hoc ego una praestiti
> Viris et opibus optimisque legibus)
> *Eutopia* merito sum vocanda nomine.'

The author therefore at least contemplated a play on the words *Utopia* 'nowhere' (οὐ, τόπος)—which in a letter to Erasmus he calls *Nusquama*—and *Eutopia* 'well-place' (εὖ, τόπος).

The *Utopia* was first printed at Louvain in 1516. The first edition actually corrected by More was that of Basle (1518). The first English Version of it was by Raphe Robynson (London 1551). The Utopia contains the description of an ideal commonwealth, with its laws, usages, religion and manners, meant of course as a satire on the state of things then existing in England and other European countries at the time; and this satiric motive somewhat excludes it from the category of prose poems in which Sidney classes it, as he seems indeed to feel.

7. *absolute*, p. 12, l. 16.

14. *Mediocribus esse*, etc. Horace *A. P.* 372.

18. *common places* (*communes loci*), sentences or longer passages kept in readiness by orators or philosophical writers as universally applicable to certain subjects such as 'virtue,' 'patriotism,' 'anger,' etc. See Cic. *de Invent.* 2, 15 'haec ergo argumenta, quae transferri in multas causas possunt, *locos communes* nominamus.' Hence it is applied to stock instances or tales, as here, illustrating certain general truths. Cp. Latimer, *Sermons* (ed. Arber) p. 135 'I might have dylated this matter at large. But I am honestly prevented of this *common place*, and I am verye glad of it.' Ib. p. 101 'And so I have a *commune place* to the ende, yf my memory serve me, beati qui audiunt verba Dei et custodiunt illud.' Roger Ascham, *Scholemaster* (ed. Mayor) p. 126 'Indeede bookes of *common places* be verie necessary to induce a man into an orderlie generall knowledge, how to referre orderlie all that he readeth *ad certa rerum Capita*, and not wander in Studie. And to that end did P. Lombardus, the master of Sentences, and Ph. Melancthon in our daies, write two notable bookes of common places.'

20. *Dives and Lazarus.* St Luke 16, 19—31.

21. *the lost Child.* St Luke 15, 11—32.

22. *gratious*, 'merciful,' 'forgiving.'

PAGE 20.

1. *right*, 'real,' p. 9, l. 3.

Esops tales. Aesop is believed to have lived about B.C. 570, and to **20** have been a Phrygian slave in Samos. The collection of fables that go by his name are probably none of them really his, though they may be founded on some that were genuine. The standard edition in Sidney's day was that of R. Stephanus, Paris, 1546 : but there were also numerous editions printed in London in the 16th century, as well as English translations, beginning with that of Caxton in 1484. It was in fact one of the most popular of books, both for entertainment and purposes of education. See Elyot's *Governour* (ed. Croft), pp. 55, 56, 'Nowe to folowe my purpose: after a fewe and quicke rules of grammer, immediately, or interlasynge hit therwith wolde be redde to the Childe Esopes fables in greke: in whiche argument children moche do delite.'

2. *formall tales of Beastes*, 'tales of persons in the form or shape of beasts.' Cp. Shakespeare, *Antony and Cleop.* 2, 5, 41 'Thou should'st come like a Fury crowned with snakes, not like a *formal* man,' i.e. in the ordinary shape of a man. *Comedy of Errors*, 5, 105 'to make of him a *formal* man again.'

3. *beastly*, see on p. 3, l. 18. Cp. Latimer's *Sermons* (ed. Arber), p. 27 'But because thou art stiffe-necked, wilde, and art given to walk without brydell and lyne; therefore now I wyll prevent thy evyl and *beastly* manners.' Elyot's *Governour*, vol. 1, p. 85 'contrarye wise whan he was ones vanquished with voluptie and pride his tiranny and *beastly* crueltie abhorreth all reders.'

9. *fantastically*, 'from fancy' or 'imagination.'

10. *Truely Aristotle...plainely determineth*. See Aristotle, *Poet*. c. 9 διὸ καὶ φιλοσοφώτερον καὶ σπουδαιότερον ποίησις ἱστορίας ἐστίν· ἡ μὲν γὰρ ποίησις μᾶλλον τὸ καθόλου, ἡ δὲ ἱστορία τὰ καθ' ἕκαστον λέγει. ἔστι δὲ καθόλου μὲν, τῷ ποίῳ τὰ ποῖ ἄττα συμβαίνει λέγειν ἢ πράττειν κατὰ τὸ εἰκὸς ἢ τὸ ἀνάγκαιον οὗ στοχάζεται ἡ ποίησις ὀνόματα ἐπιτιθεμένη· τὰ δὲ καθ' ἕκαστόν τι Ἀλκιβιάδης ἔπραξεν ἢ τί ἔπαθεν. 'Wherefore poetry is more philosophical and more elevated than history: for poetry delivers rather the universal, history the particular. Now by "delivering the universal" we mean that it attributes certain words or actions to certain characteristic classes of people, such as they would probably or necessarily use: and this is what poetry aims at representing, merely adding distinctive names. An example of "the particular" is such a phrase as "Alcibiades did so-and-so," or, "So-and-so happened to Alcibiades."'

26. *Vespasians picture*. Vespasian was a square-built man with an expression of intense effort in his face (*quasi intendentis*). Sueton. *Vesp*. c. 20.

30. *doctrinable*, 'instructive.' *Cyrus of Xenophon*, see p. 9, l. 3.

31. *Cyrus in Iustine*. Justinus (of uncertain date, probably in the 4th century A.D.) wrote a Latin epitome of the *Historiae Philippicae* of

Trogus (who wrote in Greek in the time of Augustus).   His account of the elder Cyrus is contained in Book I. cc. 4—8; II. c. 3.

32.   *the right Aeneas in Dares Phrygius*, i.e. the historical Aeneas as described in the history of the Trojan war by Dares Phrygius.   The name of Dares the Phrygian is connected with a curious literary forgery. There was an ancient tradition of the existence of an Iliad, earlier than that of Homer: it was called the Phrygian Iliad (Φρυγία 'Ιλιάς) and was believed to have been the work of Dares, who in Homer's *Iliad* (5, 9) is mentioned as a priest of Hephaestus in Troy.   This, if it ever existed, has entirely perished; but a Latin work purporting to be a translation of it exists.   The author of the translation professes to be Cornelius Nepos, and says that he had found and read the original at Athens. From internal evidence it can be shewn to be a late forgery, and it is never heard of until the 14th century.   It was believed however, both before and after Sidney's time, to be genuine, and is referred to as such here.   Thus Chaucer refers to Dares as his ultimate authority: *Troylus and Cresseyd*, 145

> 'But the Troyanes gestes, as thei felle
> In Omer or in *Dares* or in Dite
> Whoso that kan may rede hem as thai write.'

Ib. 5, 1784

> 'His worthy deedes whoso list him here
> Rede *Dares;* he kan telle him alle ifeere.'

In the 'House of Fame' Chaucer places him with Homer and Livy (3, 377)

> 'Ful wonder hye on a pilere
> Of yren, he, the great Omere;
> And with him Dares and Titus
> Before, and eke he Lollius,
> And Guydo eke de Columpnis
> And Englyssh Gaunfride eke I wis.'

PAGE 21.

2.   *Canidia...who Horace sweareth was...ill favoured.*   Canidia is the old witch of Horace's *Epodes*, 3, 5, and 17.   Cp. also *Satires*, 1, 8, 23.

3.   *ill favoured*, 'ugly,' from the use of *favour* for 'face.'   Shakespeare, *Tr. and Cress.* 4, 5, 213

> 'I know your *favour*, Lord Ulysses, well.'

See Ps. 45, 12; 119, 58.   W. A. Wright, *Bible Word-book.*

5.   Tantalus served up the flesh of his son Pelops to the gods.   He was punished in the lower world by a perpetual hunger and thirst in the sight of food and water, which always retreated from his lips; and by having a huge rock above his head always on the point of falling.

Atreus, see p. 18, l. 25.

9.   *without*, 'unless,' see Index, and compare *Arcadia*, Bk. I. 'O, said he, you will never live to my age, *without* you keep yourselves in breath with exercise and in heart with joyfulness.'

10.   *Alexander*, the Great (B.C. 356—323).

Scipio may mean either Scipio Africanus the elder, the conqueror of Hannibal (B.C. 234—183), or his nephew and adoptive grandson the younger Africanus (ob. B.C. 129), who destroyed Carthage in B.C. 146.

14.   *Quintus Curtius.*   Nothing is certainly known of the age of Q. Curtius Rufus, who wrote a history of Alexander the Great founded on the accounts of that king's contemporaries.

15.   *in universall consideration of doctrine*, 'if we regard its power of giving lessons of general application.'

17.   *doth warrant a man more in that hee shall follow*, 'makes a man feel more certain as to what step he is to take.'   *To warrant*, 'to give a feeling of security,' the root of the word is seen in 'ware.'

18.   *if hee stande upon that was*, 'if he dwells upon,' 'deals only with what has been.'   *that* = 'that which.'

21.   *a grose conceite*, 'a dull imagination.'

23.   *as hee is to frame*, 'inasmuch as it is his business to suit his example to general principles of probability.'   That is, the poet can conduct his story according to the rules of right and wrong, and can indulge in 'poetic justice,' while in history this regular course of events is interrupted by good or ill luck.

25.   *where*, 'whereas.'

31.   *sith*, see Index.

PAGE 22.

22   1.   *Herodotus*, 3, 153—8.   *Iustine*, 1, 10, 15—22.

8.   *Livie*, 1, 53—4.   *Tarquinius*, that is, Tarquinius Superbus, the last of the Roman kings, whose son Sextus pretended to desert his father and take refuge in Gabii, where after obtaining great influence he surrendered the town to his father.

9.   *Xenophon*, in the *Cyropaedia*, 6, 1, 31.   But Sidney quotes from memory and has mistaken the name; it is not *Abradates* but *Araspes* of whom the story is told.

22. *Dante*, p. 3, l. **21**. *his*, p. **10**, l. 24 and Index.
23. *Which*, 'as to which.'
24. *as*, 'although.'

PAGE 23.

1. *Well may you see*, 'certainly you may see.' **23**

6. *as the Tragedie Writer answered.* Plutarch, *de Audiendis Poetis*, c. 4 'As Euripides is said to have replied to some one who found fault with his Ixion as an impious and abominable character, "Yes, but I did not take him off the stage until I had riveted him to his wheel."'

11. *valiant Milciades rot in his fetters.* The year after the battle of Marathon (B.C. 490) Miltiades obtained the command of 70 ships, with which he besieged Paros. There he was wounded in the thigh by a stake as he was leaping over the fence round the temple of Demeter. When he returned unsuccessful to Athens he was impeached, fined, and imprisoned. 'Soon after this,' says Herodotus, 'his thigh mortified and he died.' There is some doubt however as to whether he did really die in prison, Herod. 6, 136.

The spelling *Milciades* seems to have been a common mistake: see Sackville's *Complaynt of the Duke of Buckingham,* in the 'Mirror for Magistrates' :

> '*Milciades*, O happy hadst thou ben
> And well rewarded of thy countrymen,
> If in the field, wher thou hadst forc'd to fly
> By thy prowess three hundred thousand men,
> Content they had been to exile thee then :
> And not to cast thee in depth of prison, so
> Laden with gyves to end thy life in wo.'

12. *Phocion*, a famous Athenian statesman, was put to death as a traitor in B.C. 319 by a popular vote, on the ground of his having helped Nicanor to seize the Peiraeus in the interests of Cassander. 'But,' says Plutarch, 'after a short interval, taught by facts what a master and champion of virtue and justice the people had lost, they set up a bronze statue of him, and gave his bones a public funeral, while they condemned his accusers to death,' Plutarch, *Phocion*, c. 38.

Socrates was condemned and executed B.C. 399 on the charges of corrupting the Athenian youth and teaching disbelief in the national gods.

accomplished, 'finished,' 'perfect,' not quite in the modern sense. Cp. Shakespeare, *Henry V.* Chorus, 12, 'The armourers *accomplishing* the knights.'

13. *The cruell Severus. L. Septimius Severus*, Roman emperor A.D. 193—211, was born at Leptis in Africa A.D. 146, and died at York, 4 February, A.D. 211. He was a man of great ability, and, when not irritated by personal opposition, a good and moderate ruler; but he was merciless to all whom he suspected of opposition, and his biographer (Aelius Spartianus, c. 12) calls him *crudelissimus.*

The excellent Severus. M. Aurelius Alexander Severus, Roman emperor, A.D. 222—235. He was born about A.D. 205 at Arce, in Phoenicia, and was murdered with his mother by some mutinous soldiers on his way to Gaul in A.D. 235, at the instigation of his successor Maximinus.   His character for virtue and clemency endeared him to the people and army, and his death was regarded with profound sorrow.   Life by Aelius Lampridius, c. 63.

15. *Sylla. L. Cornelius Sylla* died B.C. 78, having the year before resigned his dictatorship and retired to his villa at Puteoli.   Sidney in noticing his dying peacefully in his bed is thinking of his cruel proscriptions in B.C. 81—80.

Marius. Caius Marius had also been the author of terrible proscriptions, whereby the partisans of Sylla were put to death in B.C. 87. He too died a natural death in B.C. 86, aged 71, while he was actually consul.

Pompey. Cnaeus Pompeius Magnus, b. B.C. 106, was murdered in the boat in which he was trying to land in Egypt in his flight after being defeated by Caesar at Pharsalus, B.C. 48.

16. *Cicero. M. Tullius Cicero*, the famous orator, b. B.C. 106, was killed near his villa at Puteoli by the soldiers of M. Antonius, his name having been put in the list of the proscribed by the Triumvirs, Nov. B.C. 43.

Sidney means that, in spite of their virtuous lives, these men were reduced to such straits that they would have been thankful if they could only have been allowed to live in exile, but that they had not even that good fortune.

17. *Cato. M. Porcius Cato*, usually called *Uticensis*, because he killed himself at Utica in Africa, where, after the battle of Thapsus, he and the remains of the Pompeian party had taken refuge, rather than fall into the hands of Caesar, B.C. 46.

18. *rebell Cæsar. C. Julius Caesar*, the Dictator (B.C. 100—44),

is called 'rebell,' because by entering Italy at the head of troops in B.C. 49 he broke the law, which forbade a Proconsul to leave his province, and thus put himself into hostility to the Senate.

his name, that is, 'Kaiser,' still used as the title of the emperor.

21. *to put downe his dishonest tyrannie*, i.e. when he resigned his dictatorship. See note on l. 15: cp. Byron's *Ode to Napoleon Buonaparte*

> 'The Roman, when his burning heart
>   Was slaked with blood of Rome,
> Threw down the dagger—dared depart,
>   In savage grandeur, home.
> He dared depart in utter scorn
> Of men that such a yoke had borne,
>   Yet left him such a doom!
> His only glory was that hour
> Of self-upheld abandon'd power.'

22. *Literas nescivit:* Sueton. *Jul.* 77 'Sullam nescivisse literas qui dictaturam deposuerit' 'that Sulla showed ignorance of literature in laying down his dictatorship.'

23. *Hee meant it not by Poetrie*, 'against poetry.' Cp. Shakespeare, *Love's Labour Lost*, 4, 3, 150 'I would not have him know so much *by* me.' *Merchant*, 2, 9, 26 'That many may be meant *by* the fool multitude that choose by show.' G. Gascoine, *Steel Glas* (ed. Arber), p. 71

> 'For whom no word appeareth fine enough
> (I speak not this *by* English courtiers,
> Since English wool was ever thought most fine).'

Latimer's *Sermons* 'I think S. Paul spake these words *by* the Clergymen that will take upon them the spiritual office of preaching and yet meddle in worldly matters too, contrary to their calling.'

24. *new punishments in hel for Tyrants.* Sidney may have been thinking of Virgil (*Aen.* 6, 621) who places among the damned the establishers of tyranny:

> 'Vendidit hic patriam auro dominumque potentem
>   imposuit';

or of Dante, *Inferno*, 12, 104 (tr. Longfellow)

> 'Tyrants are these
> Who dealt in bloodshed and in pillaging.
> Here they lament their pitiless mischief; here

Is Alexander, and fierce Dionysius
Who upon Sicily brought dolorous years.'

25. *Occidendos esse.* Perhaps Sidney is referring to Seneca, *de Beneficiis*, 7, 20, 3, who says that if every other method of converting tyrants fails the only remedy is death (quoniam ingeniis talibus exitus remedium est). His friend Hugh Languet wrote a tract *Vindiciae contra Tyrannos* under the pseudonym of *Junius Brutus Celta*, and professing to be printed at Edinburgh 1579, though really produced at Paris, in which occurs the same counsel, though not directly expressed. He labours (p. 193) to shew that tyrants are worse than ordinary felons, and deserve the punishment of felony, i.e. death. 'Kings receive their power from the people; the people is the king's superior; the king is only the highest servant and agent (*supremum tantum ministrum et actorem*) of the people: the people is the lord. It follows therefore that a tyrant is guilty of felony against the people as his feudal lord, is guilty of treason to the realm (*regni imperii majestatem caedere*), is a rebel; and therefore falls under the laws of treason, and deserves still heavier penalties.' A bold doctrine for the 16th century.

27. *Cipselus, Periander, Phalaris, Dionisius.* *Cypselus*, tyrant of Corinth, so called from having been hidden in a chest (κυψέλη) when an infant to save him from being put to death by his mother's family, the Bacchiadae, oligarchs of Corinth. He was succeeded about B.C. 620 by his son *Periander*, who reigned 40 years (Herod. 5, 92). Though Sidney adopts the common account of their cruelty, Aristotle asserts that their reigns were notable for their law-abiding and popular character.

Phalaris, tyrant of Agrigentum, in Sicily, about B.C. 570, proverbial for his cruelties, especially for the brazen bull in which his victims were roasted.

Dionysius, tyrant of Syracuse from about B.C. 406 to 367. His son, the younger Dionysius, reigned from 367 to 343 B.C., when he was driven out and retired to Corinth.

PAGE 24.

24   9. *Philophilosophos*, 'fond of philosophers.'

10. *in mooving*, 'in respect of their power of affecting the mind.'

17. *as Aristotle sayth, Eth.* 1, 1 ἐπειδὴ τὸ τέλος ἐστὶν οὐ γνῶσις ἀλλὰ πρᾶξις 'since the ultimate object is not knowing but acting.'

23. *by-turnings*, 'wrong roads.' Hence the term 'by-walkers' for sinners or dishonest persons. Latimer, *Sermons* (ed. Arber), p. 57 'he was a stoute stomaked chyld, a *bi-walker*, of an ambitious mynde.' Ib. p. 61 'I have ript the matter now to the pyll, and have tolde you of playne walkers and of *bi-walkers*.' Ib. p. 36 'And therefore let us not take any *biwalkers*, but let god's word direct us.'

26. *painfulnes*, 'diligence,' 'the taking of pains.' Elyot's *Gover-nour* (ed. Croft), vol. 1, p. 275 'than folowe the furye or rage, whiche they calle courage; amonge them cometh inordinate watch, which they call *painfulness*.' Id. vol. 2, p. 273, chapter x. is headed 'Of *paynfulness* the first companion of fortitude.' Hooker, *Ecclesiastical Polity*, v. 22, § 7 '*Painfulness* by feeble means shall be able to gain that, which in the plenty of more forcible instruments is through sloth and negligence lost.' *Sidney Papers*, I. p. 280 'Be suer of a juste and *painful* man to be gentleman of your horse.' Bishop Hall's *Defence*, 'Can they say that I barred the free course of religious exercises by the suppression of *painful* and peaceable preachers?'

28. *beholding*. Shakespeare, *M. of Venice*, 1, 3, 106 'Shall we be *beholding* to you?' and so generally in Shakespeare, not *beholden*.

PAGE 25.

2. *out of naturall conceit*, 'from ideas implanted by nature.' For 25 *conceit*, see Index.

5. *Hoc opus*, etc. Virg. *Aen.* 6, 128

> 'Sed revocare gradum, superasque evadere ad auras,
>   hoc opus, hic labor est.'

14. *margent*, 'margin,' on which glosses, notes, and explanations were commonly written; cp. Hall's *Satires*, Bk. 1. Sat. 6, 6

> 'Which who reads thrice, and rubbs his rugged brow,
>   And deep indenteth every doubtful row,
>   Scoring the *margent* with his blazing stars,
>   And hundred crooked interlinears.'

Shakespeare's *Haml.* 5, 2, 162 'I knew you must be edified by the *margent* ere you had done.' *Love's Labour*, 5, 2, 85 'Write o' both sides the leaf, *margent* and all.'

22. *even as the childe is often brought to take most wholsom things.* Cp. *Euphues* (ed. Arber), p. 328 'The admonition of a true friend should be like the practise of a wise Physition, who wrapped his sharpe pils in

fine sugar...or as mothers deale with their children, who put their bitter seedes into sweet reasons' (raisins). Gosson, *School of Abuse* (ed. Arber), p. 20 'The deceitfull Physition giveth sweet syrropes to make his poyson goe down the smoother.' Sidney we know studied Tremellius' Latin Bible, in the preface to the 2nd volume of which we have 'quemadmodum periti medici faciunt, qui potanda austeriora pharmaca praebentes aegris saepe os poculi melle circumlinunt.'

25. *Rubarb.* Subsequent editions have *Rubarbarum*, Gk. ῥῆον βάρβαρον from Rha (ῥὰ), a name of the Volga. The plant was also called *Rha Ponticum.* For its use as a medicine, cp. *Euphues* (ed. Arber), p. 411 'It falleth out sundry times that company is the cause to shake off love, working the effects of the roote *Rubarbe,* which being full of choler purgeth choler.'

31. *valure.* This spelling arises from the O. F. *valor, valur* 'worth.'

PAGE 26.

26 4. *wherof Poetry is,* 'to which Poetry belongs.' See p. 10, l. 6.
hath the most conveniency to Nature, 'best harmonises with nature' (L. convenientia, convenienter).

6. *as Aristotle sayth.* See *Poet.* c. 4 ἃ γὰρ αὐτὰ λυπηρῶς ὁρῶμεν, τούτων τὰς εἰκόνας τὰς μάλιστα ἠκριβωμένας χαίρομεν θεωροῦντες, οἷον θηρίων τε μορφὰς τῶν ἀτιμοτάτων καὶ νεκρῶν. 'These are things which are disagreeable to us to see in real life, and yet their likenesses presented with the utmost exactness give us pleasure to look at; as, for instance, shapes of the lowest animals and of dead bodies.'

9. *Amadis de Gaule.* 'A new era of romance began with Amadis de Gaul, derived as some have thought, but upon insufficient evidence, from a French metrical original, but certainly written in Portugal, though in the Castilian languagè, by Vasco de Lobeyra, whose death is generally fixed in 1325.' Hallam's *Literature,* vol. 1, p. 135. An English version of part of it called 'The Treasurie of Amadis of France' from the French of Nicholas de Herberay, was published by Thomas Peynel in 1567. Many English translations have appeared since, especially one by Southey in 1803. It is a prose romance, but metrical versions of it have been made.

17. *Fugientem,* etc., Virgil, *Aen.* 12, 645.

20. *whether Vertue bee the chiefe or the onely good,* etc. Some of the stock paradoxes of the Stoics, ὅτι μόνον ἀγαθὸν τὸ καλόν, *quod honestum*

est id solum bonum est; cp. Seneca, *Vit. beat.* 4, 3 'solum bonum honestas, solum malum turpitudo.'

21. *whether the contemplative or the active life.* The Stoics recommended an active life. See Cicero, *Tusc.* 4, 23, 51. Aristotle (*Ethics,* 1, 3) distinguishes three kinds of lives: (1) the life of pleasure (βίος ἀπολαυστικός), (2) the life of social activity (βίος πολιτικός), (3) the life of contemplation (βίος θεωρητικός).

22. *Which Plato and Boethius well knew.* He has before said that Plato borrowed from poetry the plan of casting his philosophical discussions in the form of dramatic dialogues; as well as the introduction of poetical tales or myths. See p. 4, ll. 5—17.

23. *Boethius. Manlius Severinus Boethius,* b. about A.D. 470, d. A.D. 524, the last of the Classical Latin writers, held high office under Theodoric, king of the Ostrogoths, and was famed for his beneficence and learning, especially his learning in Greek philosophy. His honesty, and particularly his boldness in defending the Provincials from oppression, gained him enmity in the king's Court. He was charged with a plot against the life of Theodoric, as well as with the practice of magic, was imprisoned at Ticinum, and after about a year's captivity—during which he wrote his *Consolatio*—was executed.

His chief work was this *Consolatio Philosophiae,* in alternate sections of prose and verse, which King Alfred translated into Saxon, and Chaucer imitated in his 'Testament of Love.' It was perhaps the most popular book of any in the middle ages ; and Boethius himself, though never canonised, and indeed of very doubtful Christianity, was regarded as a saint and martyr. He is the 8th Light in Dante's *Paradiso* (X. 125 Longfellow)

> 'The sainted soul, which the fallacious world
>   Makes manifest to him who listeneth well ;
> The body, whence 'twas hunted forth, is lying
>   Down in Cieldauro, and from martyrdom
>   And banishment it came unto this peace.'

25. *who thinke vertue a schoole name,* 'merely a subject for discussion in the schools of the philosophers.' Horace, *Epp.* 1, 6, 32 ' virtutem verba putas.'

26. *indulgere genio.* Persius, 5, 151. To indulge one's genius or birth-god is to indulge oneself.

28. *the inward reason they stand upon,* ' the operations of the intellect or conscience on which the philosophers dilate.'

29. *the good felow Poet*, 'the good-natured poet.' Cp. *Arcadia*, Bk. I. 'Fortune (that belike was bad to the banquet, and meant to play the *good felow*) brought a pleasant adventure among them.'

The spelling 'felow' is in accordance with the etymology of the word,—A.S. *felaw*, Icelandic *félag*.

30. *and so steale to see*, 'and so come insensibly to see.'

the forme of goodnes, cp. p. 33, l. 1, and Tennyson, *Guinevere* 'We needs must love the highest when we see it.'

PAGE 27.

27   4. *Menenius Agrippa's* address to the Plebs on the Sacred Mount is given in Livy 2, 32.

7. *apparant*, 'clear,' see Index.

8. *upon trust of figurative speeches*, 'trusting to rhetorical phrases.' For 'figures' in this sense cp. Nicholas Breton (Bulien's *Lyrics from Elizabethan Romances*, p. 104)

> 'But if he get a benefice of worth
> That may maintain good hospitality,
> And in the pulpit bring a *figure* forth,
> Of faith and works with a formality,
> And tell a knave of an ill quality,
> If with his preaching he can fill the purse
> He is a good man : God send ne'er a worse.'

10. *farre fet*, 'far-fetched.' Ben Jonson, *Silent Woman*, Prol.

> 'Though there be more *far-fet*, these will deare-bought
> Be fit for ladies.'

Andrewes' *Sermons*, XCVI (ed. 1661), p. 417 'They are all here, and they are not *far fet*, they have no curious speculation in them.' Roger Ascham, *Toxophilus* (ed. Arber, p. 145) 'In drawing (the bow) some *fet* such a Compasse, as though they woulde tourne about and blysse all the feelde.' Shakespeare, 2 *Henry VI.* 2, 4, 33

> 'And followed with a rabble that rejoice
> To see my tears, and hear my *deep-fet* groans.'

The present indicative was written *fette.* *Royster Doyster* (ed. Arber), p. 54 'Nay, if ye will kyl him, I will not *fette* him.' (M.E. *fecchen*, pt. t. *fehte.* A.S. *feccan, fetian.*)

11. *they must have learned Geometrie.*

To Plato mathematical science was not philosophy, but a necessary preliminary education, without which no one could ever attain to philosophy, 'for it tends to draw the soul towards truth and give the finishing stroke to the philosophic spirit' (*de Rep.* 7, 527). Therefore on the Portico of his school there was said to be inscribed μηδεὶς ἀγεωμέτρητος εἰσίτω, 'Let no one enter who has not learned Geometry.' See Thompson's edition of Butler's *Sermons*, vol. 1, p. 341.

12. *conceived*, 'apprehended,' see Index. Cp. *Sidney Papers* (ed. Collins), vol. 1, p. 237 'So large a matter cannot be delyvered in few woordes, nor the thinge well *conceived*, but by a declaration of some circumstance, which I have in as fewe conteined as I could.'

19. *with punishing*, 'by punishing,' cp. p. 17, l. 24 and Index.

23. *a perfect reconcilement.* Liv. 2, 33 'Thereupon negociations for a reconcilement were begun, and it was conceded that the plebs should have their own magistrates whose persons should be inviolable, and who should have the right of helping them against the Consuls. So Tribunes were appointed.'

24. *Nathan*, 2 Samuel xii. 1—7.

30. *ungratefullie* seems to mean 'unkindly,' as there is no question of gratitude in the Bible story. Thus 'grateful' = 'agreeable,' 'gratifying': cp. Shakespeare, *Shrew*, 2, 76 'Neighbour, this is a gift very *grateful*.'

PAGE 28.

1. *as that heavenly Psalme of mercie wel testifieth*, i.e. the *Miserere*, **28** Ps. li.

8. *to make his end of*, 'to adopt as its end or object' (τέλος). For *his*, see Index.

18. *defectious peece*, 'defective part.' (Fr. pièce, L. L. petium, 'a piece of land,' whence the derivation from *pes* 'a foot,' has been suggested).

23. *Sanazzar.* *Giacopo Sannazaro*, b. at Naples, 28 July, 1458, d. April, 1530, was a famous Italian poet. His chief works were *Arcadia*, a pastoral romance of mixed prose and verse, besides *Sonnetti e Canzoni*. He also wrote several Latin poems, *de Partu Virginis*, *Eclogae*, etc.

'The Pastoral Romance began a little before this time in Portugal. An Italian writer of fine genius, Sannazaro, adopted it in his Arcadia, of which the first edition was in 1502. Harmonious prose intermingled with graceful poetry, and with a fable just capable of keeping awake the attention, though it could never excite emotion, communicate a tone of pleasing sweetness to this volume.' Hallam, *Literature*, vol. 1,

p. 265. His Latin poems (under the name of *Actius Sincerus*) are criticised by Scaliger, *Poet.* lib. VI. p. 315.

Boetius, or Boethius, see p. 26, l. 23.

PAGE 29.

29   1. *the poore pype*, the pipe or flute of the shepherd, hence, 'pastoral poetry.' Cp. Virg. *Ecl.* 1, 2 'silvestrem tenui musam meditamur avena.' *Arcadia*, Bk. 1.

> 'But you, *my pype*, whilom my chief delight,
> Till strange delight delight to nothing wear.'

Barnaby Googe, *Eclogues* (1563), 1 ad fin.

> 'Yet for thy payne (no recompence) a small reward have here
> A whistle framèd long ago, wherewith my father dear
> His joyful beasts was wont to kepe, no *Pype* for tune so swete
> Might shepharde ever yet posses, a thing for thee most mete.'

3. *ravening Souldiours*. The first Eclogue of Virgil refers especially to loss of lands which were given to the soldiers as their retiring pensions. For the description of the subjects of pastoral poetry, cp. *Arcadia*, Bk. I. 'And then truly it would delight you under some tree, or by some river side (when two or three of them meet together) to hear their rural muse, how prettily it will deliver out, sometimes joys, sometimes lamentations, sometimes challengings one of the other, sometimes under hidden forms, uttering such matters as otherwise they durst not deal with.'

4. *Titirus*, Virg. *Ecl.* 1, 6

> 'O Meliboee, deus nobis haec otia fecit.
> Namque erit ille mihi semper deus.'

10. *Darius*, the last Persian king, *Darius Codomannus*, conquered by Alexander the Great B.C. 330.

13. *Hæc memini et...*, Virg. *Eclog.* 7, 69.

17. *Heraclitus*, of Ephesus, a philosopher of what is called the Ionian School. He flourished about B.C. 513, and, refusing the chief magistracy of Ephesus, lived in the mountains as a recluse. He has been called 'the weeping philosopher,' because he wept over the follies of mankind, as opposed to Democritus (about B.C. 460), who laughed at them. Juvenal, X. 28

> 'Jamne igitur laudas, quod de sapientibus alter
> ridebat, quotiens a limine moverat unum
> protuleratque pedem, flebat contrarius alter?'

19. *who surely*, i.e. the elegiac poet.

for compassionate accompanying iust causes of lamentation, 'for producing verses in sympathy with sorrow that is thoroughly justified.'

21. *paynting out*, 'displaying as in a picture'; cp. Shakespeare, *Much Ado*, 3, 2, 112 'The word is too good to *paint out* her wickedness.' Latimer, *Sermons*, p. 39 'The honour of a king...is *painted forth* in the Scriptures.' Cp. *to set out*, p. 33, l. 2.

25. *naughtines*, cp. p. 16, l. 20.

26—30. *omne vafer*, etc. Sidney has slightly altered the words of Persius (:, 116) who is referring to Horace:

> 'Omne vafer vitium ridenti Flaccus amico
>   tangit, et admissus circum praecordia ludit.'

Gosson quotes the same lines as being put forward to justify comedy, *Schoole of Abuse* (ed. Arber), p. 31.

PAGE 30.

1. *a passionate life*, 'a life under the dominion of the passions.' For other uses of the word 'passionate' see Index. In Shakespeare it is used of a man under influence of strong emotion, especially sorrow. *Two Gent.* 1, 2, 124 'Poor forlorn Proteus, *passionate* Proteus.' Or for that which expresses emotion, as 'a *passionate* speech,' *Ham.* 2, 2, 452.

3. *Est Ulubris*, etc. Horace, *Epp.* 1, 11, 30

> 'Est Ulubris, animus si te non deficit aequus.'

4. *the Comick.* We have now come to the point in the 'Apology' at which Sidney is answering not general impressions only or common talk, but a definite attack. It was against plays, and especially against comedies, that Gosson's 'Schoole of Abuse' was directly written. Other kinds of poetry are scarcely touched by him at all. He says in his 'Apologie for his Schoole of Abuse,' p. 65 (ed. Arber) 'They that are greeved are Poets, Pipers, and players: the first thinke that I banishe poetrie, wherein they dreame; the second judge that I condemne Musique, wherein they dote; the last proclaime, that I forbid recreation to man, wherein you may see they are starke blinde. He that readeth with advise the booke which I wrote shal perceive that I touche but the abuses of all these.' And further on (p. 69) he explains that the special 'abuse' which he was attacking was the 'bringing their cunning into Theaters.'

Sidney's defence of comedy had in substance been made by Elyot, *Governour* (ed. Croft), vol. 1, p. 124

'First comedies, which they suppose to be a doctrinall of rybaudrie, they be undoubtedly a picture or as it were a mirrour of man's life, wherin ivell is nat taught but discovered; to the intent that men beholdynge the promptnes of youth unto vice, the snares of harlots and baudes laide for yonge myndes, the disceipte of servantes, the chaunces of fortune contrary to mennes expectation, they being therof warned may prepare them selfe to resist or prevente occasion.'

This defence is referred to satirically by Gosson, *Schoole of Abuse* (ed. Arber), p. 31 'Nowe are the abuses of the worlde revealed, every man in a play may see his owne faultes, and learne by this glasse to amende his manners. *Curculio* may chatte til his hearte ake, ere any be offended with his gyrdes. Deformities are checked in jeast, and mated in earnest. The sweetnesse of musicke and pleasure of sportes temper the bitternesse of rebuke and mitigate the tartness.'

The growing puritanism would have no such excuse. Stubbes in the *Anatomie of Abuses* 1582 (ed. Furnivall, p. 145) says: 'And wheras you say there are good Examples to be learned in them, Truly so there are: if you will learne falshood; if you will learne cosenage; if you will learne to deceive; if you will learne to play the Hipocrite, to cogge, lye and falsifie; if you will learn to jest, laugh, and fleer, to grin, to nod, to mow; if you will learn to play the vice, to swear, tear and blaspheme both Heaven and Earth;.. If you will learne to murther, slaie, kill, picke, steal, robbe and roue; if you will learne to rebel against Princes, to commit treasons, to consume treasures, to practise ydleness, to sing and talk of love and venery: if you will learne to deride, scoffe, mock, and flowt, to flatter and smooth: if you will learne to play the glutton Drunkard or incestuous person: if you will learne to become prowde hawtie and arrogant; and finally, if you will learne to contemne God and al his lawes, to care neither for heaven nor hel, and to commit all kinde of sinne and mischief, you need goe to no other schoole, for al these good examples may you see painted before your eyes in enterludes and playes.'

See also on p. 40, l. 7.

18. *Demea*, a 'heavy father' in the *Adelphi* of Terence. *Davus* a slave in the *Phormio* of Terence.

19. *Gnato*, p. 18, l. 28. *Thraso*, a braggart captain in the *Eunuchus* of Terence. These names are frequently employed in the literature of the age as synonyms for the qualities which they represent. Terence was much used in schools for the sake of his colloquial Latin, and all men of education were familiar with him. Cp. Barnaby Googe, *Sonnettes* (ed. Arber), p. 85

'In Countrye
Thraso hath no Grace;
In Countrye
few of *Gnatoes* secte.'

Stubbes' *Anatomie of Abuses* (ed. Furnivall), p. 141 'and doo these Mockers and Flowters of his majesty, these dissembling Hipocrites, and flattering *Gnatoes* think to escape unpunished?' Latimer's *Sermons* (ed. Arber), p. 68 'Take hede of these claubacks, these venemous people that wyll come to you, that wyll folewe lyke *gnatoes* and Parasites; if you folowe theym, you are oute of youre boke.'

21. *signifying badge.* It seems to have been the practice for each of the players to wear some badge or cognizance, by which the nature of the part he had to play might be known,—character-dresses being scarce. See Stubbes' description of the Lord of Misrule in the *Anatomie of Abuses* (ed. Furnivall), p. 148:

'They have also certain papers, wherin is painted some babblerie or other of imagery woork, and these they call 'my Lord of misrules *badges*'; these they give to every one that wil give money for them to maintain them in their heathenrie, divelrie, whordom, drunkennes, pride and what not. And who will not be buxom to them, and give them money for these their devilish cognizances, they are mocked at and flowted not a little. And so assotted are some, that they not only give them monie to maintain their abomination with all, but also were their *badges* and cognizances in their hats or caps openly.' [*Badge* is the same word as Fr. *bague*, 'a ring,' hence 'signet' or badge of distinction, from L. L. *baga*, L. *bacca* or *baca*. Cp. Bacon, *Advancement of Learning* (ed. W. A. Wright) p. 31 'For he assigneth two marks or *badges* of suspected and falsified science.']

26. *Pistrinum*, 'mill,' used as a place of punishment for criminal or unruly slaves.

sack of his owne faults. Referring to the well-known fable of the two wallets which each man carries, the one in front for his neighbour's faults, the one behind for his own. Phaedrus, 4, 9

'Peras imposuit Jupiter nobis duas:
propriis repletam vitiis post tergum dedit;
alienis ante pectus suspendit gravem.'

PAGE 31.

2. *fcare to be Tyrants.* Cp. Elyot's *Governour* (ed. Croft), vol. 1, 31 p. 71 'And whan a man is comen to mature yeres, and that reason in

him is confirmed with serious lerning and large experience, than shall he, *in redyng tragoedies, execrate and abhorre the intollerable life of* tyrantes.'

4. *affects,* 'feelings.' Shakespeare uses it as = 'inclinations': *L. L. L.* 1, 1, 152 'For every man with his *affects* is born.'

8. *Qui sceptra,* etc. Seneca, *Oedipus,* 705. Sidney quotes the same in his *Defence of Lord Leicester, Sidn. Papers,* vol. 1, p. 291. The tragedies attributed to Seneca were much read in the middle ages. They were translated by Thomas Marsh, 1581.

10. *Plutarch yeeldeth,* etc., in the *Life of Pelopidas,* c. 29.

11. *Alexander,* tyrant of Pherae in Thessaly, from about B.C. 369 to 357, ruled with great cruelty, and was at length assassinated by the brothers of his wife Thebe, at her instigation.

Sidney knew Plutarch well, as we can see by his frequent references. In a letter to Languet, dated from Venice 19 Dec., 1573, he says, ' I wish you would send me Plutarch's works in French, if they are to be bought in Vienna; I would gladly give five times their value for them, and you will be able to send them no doubt by the hand of some trader.' The first English translation, by Thomas North, appeared in 1579.

24. *giveth praise, the reward of vertue, to vertuous acts.* Cp. Puttenham, p. 50, ' But as the bad and illawdable parts of all estates and degrees were taxed by the Poets in one sort or another, and those of great Princes by Tragedie in especial,.......So was it great reason that all good and vertuous persons should for their well-doings be rewarded with commendation, and the great Princes above all others with honours and praises, being for many respects of greater moment to have them good and vertuous than any inferior sort of men. Wherefore the Poets being indeed the trumpetters of all praise and also of slaunder (not slaunder, but well-deserved reproch), were in conscience and credit bound next after the divine praises of the immortal gods, to yield a like ratable honour to all such amongst men, as most resembled the gods by excellencie of function, and had a certaine affinitie with them, by more then humane and ordinarie vertues shewed in their actions here upon earth. They were therfore praised by a second degree of laude: shewing their high estates, their Princely genealogies and pedegrees, mariages, aliances, and such noble exploites, as they had done in th' affaires of peace and of warre to the benefit of their people and countries, by the invention of any noble science or profitable Art, or by making wholsome lawes or enlarging of their dominions by honorable and just conquests, and many other wayes.'

26. *naturall Problemes*, 'tropes founded on points of natural history.' A problem ($\pi\rho\grave{o}$, $\beta\acute{a}\lambda\lambda\omega$) is any question proposed for discussion and answer. But it was used especially of such as referred to points of natural history. Hence the title of one of the dialogues of Erasmus, *Problema*, which deals with such subjects as the meaning of 'hot' and 'cold,' 'heavy' and 'light,' etc. Accordingly it is applied to illustrations drawn from natural history in poetry. See Sidney's own Sonnet, *Atrophel to Stella*, III:

> 'Let dainty wits cry on the sisters nine,
> That, bravely masked, their fancies may be told:
>   Or, Pindar's apes, flaunt they in phrases fine,
> Enam'ling with py'd flowers their thoughts of gold.
>   Or else let them in statlier glory shine,
> Ennobling new found tropes with *problemes* old:
>   Or with strange similes enrich each line,
> Of herbs or beasts which Ind or Africk hold.
> For me, in sooth, no muse but one I know,
> Phrases and *problems* from my reach do grow,
>   And strange things cost too dear for my poor sp'rits.
> How then? even thus, In Stella's face I read
> What love and beauty be, then all my deed
>   But copying is, what in her Nature writes.'

30. *the olde song of Percy and Duglas.* The ballad of Chevy Chase. The old version of it, to which Sidney doubtless refers, is given in Percy's *Reliques*, vol. I, p. 4 (ed. 1857), beginning:

> 'The Percie out of Northumberland
>   And a vowe to God made he,
> That he woulde hunte in the mountayns
>   Off Cheyviat within dayes three,
> In the mauger of doughte Douglas
>   And all that ever with him be.
> The fattest hartes in all Cheviat
>   He sayd he wold kill, and carry them away:
> Be my feth, sayd the doughetie Duglas agayn,
>   I wyll let that hontyng yf that I may.'

PAGE 32.

1. *some blinde Crouder* 'fiddler' [Welsh, *crwth*, 'a fiddle']. Wyc- **32** liffe's *Bible*, Luke xv. 25, 'But his eldere sone was in the field; and

whanne he cam and neiȝed to the hous, he herde a symfone and a *croude.*' Lily's *Mother Bombie,* Act 5, Sc. 3, 'What *crowding* knaves have we here? case up your fiddles.'

Bullen's *Lyrics* (from Friar Bacon), p. 59

> 'The fair is oft unconstant
>   The black is often proud,
> I'll chuse a lovely brown;
>   Come, fiddler, scrape your *crowd.*
> Come, fiddler, scrape your *crowd,*
>   For Peggy the brown is she
> Must be my bride: God guide
>   That Peggy and I agree.'

For such minstrels as Sidney here refers to see Jusserand's charming *English Wayfaring Life in the Middle Ages,* pp. 189—211.

4. *Pindar* (about B.C. 518 to 442). He mentions Pindar in this connexion, not only as the chief lyric poet of Greece, but also because his Odes are all *epinikian,* i.e. in honour of victories in the Great Games, and in them the famous deeds of the victors' ancestors are celebrated.

In Hungary. Sidney was in Hungary in 1572—3, going thither with Languet from Vienna.

8—13. *The incomparable Lacedemonians...what they wold doe.* He is referring to Plutarch's *Lycurgus,* c. 21 'Their education in regard to songs and singing was also carefully attended to...and these songs had a powerful influence in raising courage and promoting enthusiasm in action. Their language was simple and without affectation; the themes lofty and moral: for they consisted for the most part of praises of those who had died for Sparta, and taunts against those who had shewn fear,—asserting that these last led a bitter and miserable life; while they held forth high-sounding promises suited to the various ages, and calculated to entice to manliness. For instance, at their feasts there were three choruses, each of different ages. That composed of old men began their song with, "Time *was* when we were young and brave." That composed of men in their prime began, "But we *are* so e'en now: say, will ye try?" That composed of boys sang, "But we *shall* be: nay, better far than ye."'

18. *toyes,* 'trifles.' Bullen's *Lyrics* (Nicholas Breton, 1577), p. 89

> 'In court what pretty *toys,* what fine and pleasant joys
>   To pass the time away.'

Stubbes' *Anatomie of Abuses* (ed. Furnivall), p. 80 (in regard to new-fangled dresses, &c.) 'It cannot be but the Inventors of these new *toyes* are in great danger before God, as they who shall render accounts to God, not only for the invention of them, but also for the evil committed by them.' So Sidney calls his own writings '*toyfull* books,' *Sidn. Pap.* vol. 1, p. 285.

19. *Phillip of Macedon*, that is, Philip II. (B.C. 359—336), father of Alexander the Great.

20. *Olympus*, mistake for *Olympia*.

among hys three fearefull felicities. See Plutarch, *Alexander*, c. 3 'Just after Philip had taken Potidaea (B.C. 356) he received these three messages at one time: that Parmenio had overthrown the Illyrians in a great battle; that his racehorse had won at the Olympic games; and that his wife had given birth to Alexander: with which being naturally well-pleased, as an addition to his satisfaction, he was assured by the diviners that a son, whose birth was accompanied with three such successes, could not fail of being invincible.'

Sidney calls these felicities 'fearefull' (too good to be safe), partly, it would seem, because of the sentence in Plutarch immediately preceding this, in which he narrates that the temple of Artemis at Ephesus was burnt on the same day, and the soothsayers 'ran about the town, beating their faces, and crying that this day had brought forth something that would prove fatal and destructive to Asia.'

24. *Heroicall*, cp. Puttenham, *Arte of English Poesie* (ed. Arber), p. 40 'Such therefore as gave themselves to write long histories of the noble gests of kings and great Princes, entermedling the dealings of the gods, half-gods or Heroes of the gentiles, and the great weighty consequences of peace and warre, they called *Poets Heroick*, whereof Homer was chief and most auncient among the Greeks, Virgill among the Latines.'

25. *conceit*, 'idea,' see Index.

28. *Achilles…Tydeus*, see p. 18, l. 21.

29. *Rinaldo.* The chief warrior in Tasso's *Gerusalemme Liberata*, —the 'Achilles of the Christian army.'

33. *Who, if the saying of Plato and Tullie*, &c. Unless we take 'who' to stand for 'in regard to whom' the construction breaks down utterly after the parenthesis. The references are to Plato's *Phaedrus*, 25 D, where it is 'wisdom' (φρόνησις) that is spoken of, not exactly virtue. Cicero, however, seems to take this wisdom as 'the knowledge of the virtuous,' *de Fin.* 2, 52 'oculorum est in nobis sensus acerrimus,

quibus sapientiam non cernimus.   Quam illa ardentes amores excitaret
sui, si videretur!' *de Offic.* 1, 5 § 15 'formam quidem, Marce fili, et tan-
quam faciem honesti vides, quae, si oculis cerneretur, mirabiles amores,
ut ait Plato, excitaret sapientiae.'   The Platonic doctrine of the identity
of knowledge and virtue thus makes φρόνησις almost equivalent to the
'wisdom' of the Proverbs, which is constantly used as equivalent to
righteousness and piety.   'The fear of the Lord is the beginning of
wisdom.'

PAGE 33.

33   2.   *sets her out*, 'describes her,' cp. 'to paint out,' p. 29, l. 21.

14.   *religious ceremonies*, the *sacra*, which rather mean the objects
of religious worship, the Penates.

16.   *passionate kindenes*, 'lover's affection,' cp. Shakespeare's *Son-
net* 152, 9 'I have sworn deep oaths of thy deep *kindness.*'

22.   *his outward government*, 'his outward behaviour'; cp. Shake-
speare 1 *Henry IV.* 1, 2, 31 'men of good *government.*'   id. 3, 1, 184
'defect of manners, want of *government.*'

24.   *as Horace sayth.   Epp.* 1, 3, 4

'Qui, quid sit pulcrum, quid turpe, quid utile, quid non
   planius ac melius Chrysippo et Crantore dicit.'

29.   *his...him.*   See Index.

30.   *the sum that containes him*, 'the total or upshot of its value';
cp. Shakespeare, *Romeo*, 2, 6, 34 'Your *sum* of parts did not alto-
gether pluck such envy from him.'

particularities, 'particulars.'   Shakespeare, *Henry V.* 3, 2, 142
'Being as good a man as yourself both in discipline of war, and in the
derivation of my birth, and in other *particularities.*'

PAGE 34.

34   7.   *prophecying...making*, see p. 5, l. 26; p. 7, l. 14.

12.   *stuffe*, 'matter,' 'material,' cp. Shakespeare, *Antony*, 5, 2, 97
'Nature wants *stuff* to vie strange forms with fancy.'   *Merchant*, 1, 1, 4
'what *stuff* (my melancholy) 'tis made of.'   Bacon, *Adv. of Learn.* (ed.
Wright), p. 32 'The wit of man worketh according to the *stuff* and is
limited thereby.'   (Lat. *stupa* or *stuppa*, 'tow,' Germ. *stoff.*)

14.   *ende* (τέλος) 'object,' see p. 14, l. 6.

20.   *the holy scripture...whole parts in it poeticall*, p. 10, l. 18.

33.   *yeelding*, 'granting.'

PAGE 35.

1. *Misomousoi*, 'haters of the muse' (μισεῖν, μοῦσα).   **35**

4. *quips*, 'cavils,' 'taunts.' Cp. G. Puttenham, *Arte of English Poesie* (ed. Arber), p. 238 'with a like subtil speech gave a *quip* to William Gyfford.' Shakespeare, *Much Ado*, 2, 3, 249 '*Quips* and sentences and these paper bullets of the brain.' 1 *Henry VI.* 1, 2, 51 'How now, how now, mad wag! What, in thy *quips* and thy quiddities?' Milton, *L'Allegro*

> '*Quips* and cranks and wanton wiles,
> Nods and becks and wreathed smiles.'

So as a verb, Spenser *F. Q.* 7, 44

> 'and still when she complains
> The more he laughs, and does her closely *quip*,
> To see her sore lament, and bite her tender lip.'

Bullen's *Lyrics* (Rt. Greene), p. 18

> 'To *quip* fair Venus' overweening pride,
> Love's happy thoughts to jealousy were hid.'

The origin of the word may be a shortened form of *quibble*, itself a corruption of *quidlibet*, 'anything you please,' for a scholastic subtlety. Others derive it from Welsh *chwip*, 'a quick turn,' *cwipio*, 'to whip,' 'to move briskly.'

carping and taunting, two Lat. words, *carpere*, 'to pluck,' 'to detract from,' *tentare* (whence O. F. *tenter*), 'to tempt,' 'to put to proof.'

5. *Spleene*, 'ill humour,' 'anger'; of which the spleen was believed to be the seat. Shakespeare, 1 *Henry IV.* 5, 2, 19 'a hair-brained Hotspur governed by a *spleen*.'

6. *through*, 'thorough.' Shakespeare, 2 *Henry IV.* 1, 2, 45 'If a man is *through* with them.' On the other hand he uses 'thorough' for 'through,' *Midsummer N. D.* 2, 1, 3

> ' Over hill, over dale,
> *Thorough* bush, *thorough* briar.'

Marlowe, *Hero and Leander*, 'Went Hero *thorough* Sestos from her tower.' Cp. St Matt. 3, 12 'He shall *throughly* purge his floor.' They are, of course, the same word.

7. *Those kinde of obiections.* This use of the plural with 'kind' comes from 'kind' suggesting a noun of multitude. Cp. Shakespeare, *Shrew*, 1, 1, 247

'I advise
You use your manners discreetly in *all kind* of companies.'

Twelfth Night, 1, 5, 95 'I protest I take these wise men that crow so at *these* set *kind* of fools, no better than the fools' zanies.' See W. A. Wright's *Bible Word-book*. But though this use may be found in many good authors, it is nevertheless a mistake and should be avoided.

11. *a playing wit*, 'a genius for paradox.' For *playing* as an adjective cp. Chaucer, *Troylus and Cresseyde*, 1, 280 'And caughte ageyn his firste *playinge* chere.' The examples seem taken from some real jests or paradoxical arguments.

13. *iolly commoditie*, 'the excellent profit' or 'advantage.' Shakespeare, *2 Henry IV.* 1, 2, 178 'I will turn diseases to *commodities*.' *King John*, 2, 2, 573 'That smooth-faced gentleman, tickling *commodity*.' More's *Rich. III.* (ed. Lumby), p. 33 'And in good faith me thinketh it were as great *commoditie* to them both, as for yet a while, to ben in the custody of their mother.' *Arcadia*, bk. 1, p. 11 'These houses you see so scattered are of men, as we two are, that live upon the *commoditie* of their sheep.'

jolly, for 'pleasaut' or 'gay' is common in writers of the 16th and early 17th centuries. (Fr. *joli*, 'pretty'; Icel. *jol*, 'a feast'; A.S. *géola*, 'yule.') Its ironical employment here nearly approaches the modern slang.

16. *Ut lateat.* A variation of Ovid, *Ars Am.* 2, 662

'Dic habilem quaecumque brevis: quae turgida plenam:
Et lateat vitium proximitate boni.'

'Call her a neat figure if she is short: well-rounded if she is fat; and let defect be concealed under the excellence most closely allied to it.'

17. *Agrippa. Henry Cornelius Agrippa* was born at Cologne in 1486, of a noble family, and served for some years in the Imperial army. Quitting the military life while still young, he devoted himself to literature and science; became a Doctor of Law and Physic; was master of eight languages; and finally turned his attention to alchemy. Between 1507 and 1530 he published works on various subjects, 'De verbo mirifico,' 'On the excellency of women,' 'Commentaries on the Epistles of St Paul.' Besides these he lectured at Pavia, Metz, and other places, and acted as a physician at Geneva, Fribourg and Lyons. In 1530 he published his most famous work, *De incertitudine et vanitate scientiarum*, an attack not upon real learning, but upon the methods of instruction of the day, upon the monks, theologians, and universities.

This cost him the pension which he was enjoying from the Bishop of Liége, and involved him in difficulties and imprisonment. From the latter, however, he was soon released, and 1531 published another work on the 'Occult Philosophy,' i.e. on Mystical Divinity, and died at Grenoble in 1533. In 1550 his entire works were published at Leyden, and have been often reproduced. Hallam's *Literature*, 1, p. 398 sqq.

18. *Erasmus. Desiderius Erasmus* (1467—1536) the greatest scholar and most prolific writer of his age, among his numerous works, published in 1510 the *Encomium Moriae*, 'Praise of Folly.' It was composed in little more than a week in Sir Thomas More's house at Chelsea, originally to beguile some days of sickness, and was a satire on the foibles of various classes of people and branches of learning,—grammarians, philosophers, scholastic science and theology, sportsmen, monks, kings, and even the Pope.

21. *another foundation then the superficiall part would promise,* 'something more than appeared on the surface.' Sidney means that these profoundly learned men were not satirizing real but false learning.

22. *Mary*, 'by Mary,' generally written 'Marry.'

26. *commeth not of wisedom*, 'does not arise from.' Cp. 'whatsoever is more than these *cometh of* evil.'

28. *good fooles*, 'good' in the same sense of contemptuous toleration as in 'good felow,' p. 26, l. 29. Cp. Transl. of Erasmus' *Praise of Folly* (ed. 1713), p. 58 'Add to that Fools do not basely laugh and sing, and play the *good fellow* alone to themselves.' The general reference is to the professional fools or jesters formerly kept in great families, especially at Court. Cp. More's *Utopia* (ed. Arber), p. 52 'There chaunced to stande by a certain jesting parasite or scoffer, which would seem to resemble and counterfeit *the foole.*'

30. *scope*, see Index.

31. *It is already sayde*, p. 12, l. 10.

PAGE 36.

3. *as indeede it seemeth Scaliger iudgeth.* Cp. *Poeticè* 1, 2, init. **36** 'Poetae igitur nomen non a fingendo, ut putarunt, quia fictis uteretur, sed initio a *faciendo versu* ductum est.' And later on in the same chapter he points out that *verse* differentiates Lucan and Livy.

Julius Caesar Scaliger was born 23 April, 1484, at Ripa, in the territory of Verona, and of a princely family, *Della Scala*. Till he was 38 he was engaged either in the court or army of the emperor, and among other actions was present at the battle of Ravenna (1512), where he lost his father and brother.   About 1522 he left Italy and after devoting him-self for some years to the study of medicine, settled at Agen, in Guienne, as a physician.   There he married and became the father of a large family, among whom was Joseph, who became a still greater critic than his father.   At Agen he lived till his death in 1558, and there produced the first fruit of studies to which he had always been addicted, in the shape of commentaries on Theophrastus, Aristotle and Hippocrates, as well as other works, such as *De Causis Linguae Latinae*, and a treatise on Poetry, *Poetices Libri Septem.*   It is this last-named work which Sidney appears to have studied particularly.   His son Joseph wrote a biography of his father.   See also the Essay of Mark Pattison on the Scaligers.

12.   *without,* 'except,' see Index.

30.   *the Art of memory,* that is by a 'Memoria technica.'   Of such books the earliest that I find in English is '*The Art of Memorye, other-wise called the Phoenix, A boke very behovefull and profytable to all Professors of Scyences, Grammaryens, Retoryciens, Legystes, Phyloso-phers, and Theologiens.*   Translated out of French into English by Rob. Copland.   Printed by W. Middleton, 1548.   See Herbert's Ames, p. 576.

PAGE 37.

37   4.   *Cato,* Dionysius Cato, whose *Disticha de Moribus* were so popu-lar as a school book, see p. 10, l. 31.

The additional sentence here inserted in later editions, and printed at the foot of p. 37 is somewhat curious.   It contains one verse from Horace (*Epp.* 1, 18, 69) and one from Ovid (*Rem. Amor.* 686), but neither, in whole or in part, occurs in the 'Distichs' of Cato.   If the addition was in Sidney's MS. he must have been quoting, as he so often does, from memory.   If it was inserted by some one it looks as if the inserter had read *Naso* for *Cato.*

6.   *delivery,* 'exposition,' see Index.

7.   *Grammer...Logick,* &c....*compiled in verses.*   The Latin grammar most in use in the 16th century in schools was Colet's (1511), which, added to and improved by Lilly (first Master of St Paul's School) and Erasmus, was known as Lilly's Grammar.   It superseded the earlier grammars or Donates (from the grammarian Donatus).   There were, however, other grammars also.   For the other treatises, see *System of Logic and Rhetoric* published by Thomas Wilson (1553), Leonarde Cox (1532), Richard Rainolde (1567), and others.

19.   *Nurse of abuse,* 'nurse of corruption.'   This is the sense in which Gosson uses the word, as well as Stubbes in his *Anatomie of*

Abuses. So 'to abuse' is 'to corrupt.' Cp. Skelton, *Ware the Hawke,* l. 5

> 'This wyrke devysed is
> For such as do amys;
> And specially to controule
> Such as have care of soule,
> That be so far *abused,*
> They cannot be excused
> By reason or by lawe.'

Barclay, 3 *Ecloges*

> 'Be all yonge galantes of these *abused* sorte
> Which in yong age unto the court resorte?'

22. *give the largest field to ere, as Chaucer sayth,* 'give the largest field to plough,' i.e. give the greatest opportunity. The reference to Chaucer is not for the sentiment, but merely for the phrase: *Knightes Tale,* 29

> 'But at that thing I most as now forbere.
> I have, God wot, *a large feeld to ere,*
> And wayke ben the oxen in my plough,
> The remenaunt of the tale is long inough.'

The word *ere* (spelt in the 1st edition *erre;* and later *ear*) is from A.S. *erian*; L. *aro,* 'to plough.' Cp. Shakespeare, *Rich. II.* 3, 2, 212

> 'And let them go
> To *ear* the land that hath some hope to grow.'

And the numerous examples in W. A. Wright's *Bible Word-book.* Deut. 21, 4 'And the elders of that city shall bring down the heifer unto a rough valley, which is neither *eared nor sown,* and shall strike off the heifer's neck there in the valley.'

23. *howe both in other Nations.* The construction is loose; we must understand some such words as 'they allege,' 'they argue.' For the statement of the enervating influence of poetry, see Gosson's *Schoole of Abuse* (ed. Arber), p. 34, which Sidney seems to be answering here.

26. *lulled a sleepe,* seems to refer to Gosson's 'all suche delights as may win us to pleasure, or *rocke us asleep*' (p. 34).

28. *as if they out shot Robin Hood,* i.e. 'had shot their deadliest weapon,' 'had surpassed everything.' The renown of Robin Hood, the prince of outlaws of the 12th century, was still great. Large numbers of popular ballads celebrated him, and village festivals or games were called after his name.

Latimer tells us how he arrived at a certain town on a Saints' day to preach, but found the church locked, and all the people out on this festival: 'I tarried there halfe an houer and more, at last the keye was founde, and one of the parishe commes to me and sayes, Syr, this is a busye daye wyth us, we can not heare you, it is Robyn hoodes daye. The parishe are gone a brode to gather for Robyn hoode, I praye you let them not. I was fayne there to geve place to Robyn hoode, I thought my rochet shoulde have bene regarded, thoughe I were not, but it wouldne not serve, it was fayn to give place to Robyn hoodes men. It is no laughynge matter my friendes, it is a wepyng matter, a heavy matter, under the pretence for gatherynge for Robyn hoode, a trayter and a theefe, to put out a preacher, to have hys office lesse estemed, to prefer Robyn hood before the ministration of God's word, and al thys hath come of unpreachyng prelates.' *Sermons* (ed. Arber), p. 173. See also Jusserand's *English Wayfaring Life*, p. 207 sqq.

PAGE 38.

38   1. *Plato banished them out of hys Commonwealth.* In the *Republic* (Book 2) Plato does not forbid the presence of poets, but says their works must be expurgated for the use of the young. In Book 3, after criticising the stories in Homer and elsewhere, he concludes [392 A], 'On these accounts we must suppress such fables, lest they engender in our young men a great aptitude for wickedness.' In Book 10 [607 A] he says, 'Having recurred to the subject of Poetry, let this serve to shew the reasonableness of our former judgment in banishing from our State a pursuit which has the tendencies we have described. Then, Glaucon, whenever you meet with eulogists of Homer, who tell you that he has educated Greece, and that he deserves to be taken up and studied with an eye to the administration and guidance of human affairs, and that a man ought to regulate the tenour of his whole life by this poet's directions, it will be your duty to greet them affectionately as excellent men to the best of their ability, and to admit that Homer is first and greatest among tragic poets; but you must not forget, that, with the single exception of hymns to the god and panegyrics on the good, no poetry ought to be admitted into the State.' Davis and Vaughan's *Translation of the Republic.* For Sidney's answer see p. 44.

22. *to measure the height of the starres,* cp. Gosson, *Schoole of Abuse* (ed. Arber), p. 38 'The height of heaven is taken with a staffe.'

33. *The Poet never maketh any circles about your imagination,*

'does not use magic arts to take in your imagination.' Cp. a poem in *Arcadia*, Bk. 1. p. 137

> 'Teach me what *circle* may acquaint her sprite
> Affection's charms in my behalf to prove.
>   The *circle* is my round-about-her sight,
> The power I will invoke dwells in her eyes
> My charm should be, she haunt me day and night.'

Green's *Quaint dispute between velvet breeches and cloth breeches* [1592], 'He walked not as other men in the common beaten way, but came compassing circumcirca, *as if we had been divells and he would draw a circle about us.*' Tennyson's *Merlin and Vivien*, sub fin.

> 'Then, in one moment, she put forth the charm
> Of *woven paces* and of waving hands.'

PAGE 39.

3. *for hys entry*, 'as his introduction.'
7. *without*, 'unless,' see Index.
 10. *that Esope lyed.* In more recent times, however, Rousseau held that such tales weakened the regard for truth in the young;—an opinion ridiculed by Cowper:

> 'I shall not ask Jean Jacques Rousseau
> If birds confabulate or no.'

 14. *seeing Thebes written in great Letters upon an olde doore.* This refers to a state of things before the erection of public theatres in London (1575), and doubtless for some time after their first erection, when plays were generally acted in the yards of various city hostelries,—a practice apparently of very early date: for in an Act of Edward III. a company of men called vagrants, who had made masquerades through the whole city, are ordered to be whipt out of London, 'because they represented scandalous things in the little ale-houses and other places where the populace assembled.' *Biograph. Dram.* vol. 1. p. xii. Stow (*Survey of London*) says of the plays—commonly given on Sundays—'Great inns were used for the purpose, which had secret chambers and places, as well as open stages and galleries.' Gosson, *Schoole of Abuse*, p. 40 (ed. Arber) 'The two prose bookes played at the *Belsavage*, where you shall never find a word without wit, never a line without pith, never a letter placed in vaine. The Jew and Ptolomie showne at the *Bull*, etc.'

If the play was a tragedy it was notified by hanging the stage with black: Induction to *A Warning for faire women* (1599), Act I. v. 74

'*History*. Look, Comedy, I mark'd it not till now,
    The stage is hung with black, and I perceive
    The auditors prepared for tragedy.'

Also the scene, at which the tragedy was supposed to take place, had to be indicated in some rough way, as we know from Shakespeare's parody in the *Midsummer Night's Dream*. A tragedy was published in 1581 by Thos. Newton called *Thebais*, a translation of the *Thebais* of Seneca; also in the same year the *Oedipus* of Seneca translated by Alexander Neville. Either or both of these may have been presented before, and have suggested this illustration to Sidney.

29. *Iohn a stile and Iohn a noakes.* The Doe and Roe of the ancient law-courts. Cp. *The Play of Stuckey*, v. 289

'Nay hark you, father, I pray you be content,
    I've done my goodwill, but it will not do.
    John a Nokes and John a Style and I cannot cotton.
    O this law-French is worse than butter'd mackerell;
    Full o' bones, full o' bones.'

Used also for any name: cp. *Histrio Mastix*, Act 4, v. 5

                    'I am vexed,
    Stung with a viperous impatience,
    That yon nobility, yon *John-a-Stile*
    Should sole possess the throne of dignity.'

Skelton, *Colyn Clout*, v. 324 (cp. v. 857)

        'What care they though Gil sweate
        Or *Jacke of the Noke?*'

PAGE 40.

40   6. *estates*, see on p. 1, l. 15.

11. *Comedies rather teach, then reprehend, amorous conceits.* See passages quoted on p. 30, l. 4. Add Gosson, *Schoole of Abuse* (ed. Arber), p. 38 'Therefore he that will avoyde the open shame of pryvy sinne... must set hande to the sterne and eye his steppes...nor goe to theatres for being allured, nor once bee allured for feare of abuse.'

12. *larded*, 'garnished.' Shakespeare, *Troilus*, 5, 1, 63 'Wit *larded* with malice.' *Hamlet*, 4, 5, 35

> 'With his shroud as the mountain snow
>   *Larded* with sweet flowers.'

The word seems to rise from the not very savoury metaphor of the use of bacon for garnishing dishes.

19. *beastlie*, p. 3, l. 18.

26. *scurrilitie*, from Lat. *scurra*, a low wit or buffoon, here = 'indecency.'

28. *theyr sentence*, 'their decision.'

32, 33. *Eikastike, Phantastike*, εἰκαστικὴ and φανταστικὴ τέχνη. Both are, according to Plato, subdivisions of the mimetic art, or art of imitation; but whereas the former gives an exact reproduction of an object, its size, colour, and proportion preserved, the latter only produces a likeness by illusion, as a painter does by the art of perspective; thus producing an impression of size, distance etc. which do not really exist in the picture. Plato, *Sophistes*, 235—36.

PAGE 41.

8. *better hidden matters*, 'things that had better have been hidden,' **41** the *et sic melius situm* of Horace.

10. *I yeeld*, 'I admit,' p. 34, l. 33.

13. *concluding*, 'proving,' a logical term. Shakespeare, *Richard III.* 2, 2, 12 'Then, grandam, you *conclude* that he is dead.'

19. *rampire*, 'fortification,' 'defence.' It seems to be the same word as rampart, from Lat. *re-parare*. Cp. Lord Nicholas Vaux, *Assault of Cupid* (quoted by Puttenham, p. 247)

> 'Goodwill, the master of the shot,
>   Stood in the *rampire* brave and proude.'

Rainold's *Overthrow of Stage-plays*, Introd. 'So that the cause being thus wittely and Scholerlike maintained on the one side, and in defence of plaies, and yet in the end all their *rampire* of defence quite overthrown...' Shakespeare, *Timon*, 5, 1, 203 'Set but thy foot against our *rampired* gates.'

25—29. *Truely, a needle...Country.* Sidney is arguing on the principle *corruptio optimi pessima.* In proportion as poetry is a powerful instrument for good, so is it if misused powerful for evil.

PAGE 42.

1. *to be in price*, 'to be valued' (*in pretio esse*). Chaucer, *Troylus* **42** *and Cresseyde*, 1, 375 'but *in pris* and upborne of all lovers.' Roy, *Rede*

me and be not wroth (ed. Arber), p. 57 'Are soche with him *in any pryce?*' More's *Utopia* (ed. Arber), p. 67 'all things be so wel and wealthlye ordered that vertue is had *in price* and estimation.'

2. *rather doing things worthy to bee written, then writing things fitte to be done.* From Pliny, *Epist.* 6, 16, 3 'equidem beatos puto quibus deorum munere datum est *aut facere scribenda aut scribere facienda,* beatissimos vero quibus utrumque.' John Owen (ob. 1622) wrote an epigram on Sidney himself, with the same point,

> ' Qui scribenda facit scribitque legenda beatus
>   Ille; beatior es tu quod utrumque facis.
> Digna legi scribis, facis et dignissima scripto:
>   Scripta probant doctum te, tua facta probum.'

Cp. Ben Jonson, Epigram xcv (to Sir Henry Savile)

> 'Although to write be lesser than to do
>   It is the next deed and a great one too.'

Cp. also Sallust, *Cat.* 3 'Vel jam pace vel bello clarum fieri licet ; et qui fecere et qui facta aliorum scripsere multi laudantur.'

9. *the Albion Nation.* Sidney means the nation even before Roman times. 'Albion' seems probably to have been the oldest name of the Island known. See a treatise *de Mundo* c. 3 (once attributed to Aristotle) ἐν τούτῳ τῷ Ὠκεανῷ νῆσοι μέγισται τυγχάνουσιν οὖσαι δύο, Βρετavvικαὶ λεγόμεναι, Ἄλβιον καὶ Ἰέρνη. In the early Anglo-Saxon period some of the kings called themselves *Reges Albionis insulae,* but the name soon came to be used only in poetry.

11. *a chaine-shot.* Bullets or half-bullets fastened together by a chain, and formerly used principally to destroy the rigging of ships.

against all learning. See on p. 2, l. 21; and compare Bacon's *Advancement of Learning,* Book I. init. 'I think good to deliver it (learning) from the discredit and disgraces it hath received, all from ignorance, but ignorance severally disguised; appearing sometimes in the zeal and jealousy of divines; sometimes in the severity and arrogance of politiques ; and sometimes in the errors and imperfections of learned men themselves.'

bookishnes. Cp. Shakespeare, 2 *Henry VI.* 1, 1, 259 'whose *bookish* rule hath pulled fair England down.' *Winter's Tale,* 3, 3, 73 'Though I am not *bookish* I can read waiting-gentlewoman in the 'scape.'

12. *certaine Gothes.* See Gibbon, *Decline and Fall,* vol. I. p. 434, of the conduct of the Goths at Athens (in the 4th century). 'Another circumstance is related of these invasions which might deserve our

notice, were it not justly to be suspected as the fanciful conceit of a
recent sophist.   We are told, that in the sack of Athens, the Goths had
collected all the libraries, and were on the point of setting fire to
this funeral pile of Greek learning, had not one of their chiefs, of more
refined policy than his brethren, dissuaded them from the design, by the
profound observation, that, as long as the Greeks were addicted to the
study of books, they would never apply themselves to the exercise of
arms.'   Gibbon's authority is Zonaras, xvi. p. 635.   Sidney perhaps
got the anecdote from Montaigne's Essay on Pedantry, first published
1580.   (*Essays*, Bk. I. Ess. 24.)

28.   *Iubeo stultum esse libenter*, 'I bid him be a dunce to his
heart's content,' varied from Horace, *Satires*, I, 1, 63 'miserum jubeo esse
libenter.'

31.   *Orlando Furioso*, see p. 9, l. 2.

King Arthur.   The stories of King Arthur and the Round Table
were told in ballads of very early date.   The first prose book was the
Morte d'Arthur, printed by Caxton in 1485, translated from the French
by Sir Thomas Mallory, and often subsequently reprinted.

32.   *quiddity*, 'subtlety.'   From *quid?* used in scholastic disputa-
tions ; cp. Gascoigne, *The Steel Glas*, p. 77 (ed. Arber) :

> 'That Logike leape not over every stile
>   Before he came a furlong neare the hedge,
>   With curious *Quids*, to maintain argument.'

Shakespeare, *Hamlet*, 5, 1, 107 'Why may not that be the skull of a
lawyer?   Where be his *quiddities* now, his quillets, his cases, his terms
and his tricks?'   1 *Henry IV*. 1, 2, 49 'How now, mad wag! what in
thy quips and thy *quiddities?*'

PAGE 43.

1.   *Ens*, 'being' (participle of *sum, esse*), a philosophical term much **43**
used in scholastic treatises to translate the Greek τὸ ὄν or οὐσία (thus
entia = τὰ ὄντα, Quintil. 2, 14, 2).   See note on *essence*, p. 13, l. 22.

Prima materia (πρώτη ὕλη) the original 'matter' or 'substance' of
the universe, concerning which the various schools of philosophers were
widely disagreed, some maintaining it to be air, others fire, water, &c.
It frequently therefore entered into scholastic discussions.

Corslet, 'body-armour.'   (O. Fr. *cors*, L. *corpus* 'body.')

2.   *as I said in the beginning*.   He has quoted the instances of Turkey,
p. 4, l. 33, but not that of the Tartars, whom he here seems to include
in the Turkish Empire.   Montaigne, on the other hand, *Essays*, 1, 24,

says 'The most potent Empire, that appears at this day on the whole world, is that of the Turks, a People who have a great esteem for Arms, and as hearty a contempt for Literature.' Coste's Translation, vol. 1, p. 153 (ed. 1759).

9. *who by Plutarch is accounted...foote-stoole.* Sidney seems to be referring to the treatise of Plutarch *De seu Fortuna seu virtute Alexandri,* c. 3 'I think that he would say to Fortune, if she claimed the honour of his successes: Do not slander my valour, nor deprive me of my glory by your claims.'

14. *tooke deade Homer with him.* Plutarch, *Alexand.* c. 8 'Alexander was naturally a great lover of learning and reading. Onesicritus informs us that he constantly laid Homer's *Iliad,* according to the copy which he had corrected by Aristotle, called the 'casket copy,' with his dagger under his pillow, declaring it a perfect portable treasure of military virtue.' See Elyot's *Governour* (ed. Croft), vol. 1, p. 59.

15. *he put the Philosopher Calisthenes to death.* Callisthenes, of Olynthus, whose mother Hero was a niece of Aristotle, was a fellow pupil of Alexander under the great philosopher. Alexander took him with him on his Asiatic expedition in B.C. 334. He seems to have written a work on Constitutional Philosophy (Polyb. 6, 45) as well as an account of Alexander's campaign (Polyb. 12, 17). But he was a man of as little prudence as veracity, and presently offended Alexander by untimely attacks upon him for assumption of the ensigns of Oriental royalty. When the 'conspiracy of the pages' broke out, in B.C. 328—7, Callisthenes was accused of complicity in it. The result is told by Plutarch (*Alexand.* c. 55) 'Some say he was hanged by Alexander's orders; others, that he died of sickness in prison and in chains.'

17. *that Homer had been alive.* 'On one occasion a messenger coming with a joyful countenance, Alexander exclaimed, "What are you going to tell me? That Homer has come to life again?"' Plutarch, *Morals,* 101, 50. 'When Alexander was at the town of Troy he visited the antiquities and ran stripped round the tomb of Achilles, declaring how happy he esteemed him in having, while he lived, so faithful a friend, and when he was dead so famous a poet to proclaim his actions.' Plutarch, *Alexand.,* c. 15.

20. *if Cato misliked Fulvius, for carying Ennius with him to the fielde.* In B.C. 189 Ennius accompanied M. Fulvius Nobilior in his Aetolian campaign and took part in his triumph on his return. This proceeding was attacked by Cato. See Cicero, *Tusc.* 1, 1, 3 'oratio Catonis, in qua objecit ut probrum M. Nobiliori quod is in provinciam

poetas duxisset. Duxerat autem Consul ille in Aetoliam, ut scimus, Ennium.'

21. *Ennius*, see p. 3, l. 19.

22. *Cato*, that is, M. Porcius Cato the elder, called Censorius, on account of the severity with which he exercised his censorship in B.C. 184. Cato was born about B.C. 234, and is one of the most original characters in the Roman history of the time. His peculiar appearance, his rugged manners, and his opposition to all the innovations which were then beginning to be made in the habits of Rome, and still more his caustic wit and severity of denunciation, made him the theme of endless anecdotes. The sterling honesty of his character secured him considerable influence, though his contemporaries rather feared and respected than loved him. He wrote a history of Roman antiquities called *Origines*, and a tract on agriculture, which is partly extant, as well as many orations and other works intended for the education of his son.

23. *Cato Uticensis*, see p. 23, l. 17.

26. *a man that had never wel sacrificed to the Graces.* 'Xenocrates was haughty and always had a frowning expression; so that Plato frequently said to him "Xenocrates, sacrifice to the Graces."' Diog. Laert. 4, 2, 3. Plutarch, *Conjug. Praecept.* 28.

27. *and yet being* 80 *yeeres olde began to learne it.* Cato, though he knew and could speak Greek before, was vehemently opposed to the study of Greek philosophy and literature in Rome; yet late in life he gave way to the prevailing fashion and commenced studying Greek literature. Cicero, *de Sen.* § 38.

32. *his unmustered person*, 'not on the muster-roll of the army.' Roman commanders, consuls or pro-consuls, frequently took with them men not enrolled in the legions, or formally appointed as *legati* on their staff; but such men could not lawfully act as combatants. Thus Cato wrote to his son not to appear on the field after his corps had been disbanded (Cicero *de Off.* 1 § 36). *muster* from O. F. *mostre = monstre*, Lat. *moneo*, 'to warn.'

PAGE 44.

1. *Scipio Nasica, iudged by common consent the best Romaine.* Publius Cornelius Scipio Nasica was in B.C. 203 declared *optimus vir*, to receive the figure or symbol of the *Magna Mater* (Cybele) which was being brought to Rome (Livy 29, 14; Ovid, *Fast.* 4, 347). In his later life he was celebrated as a jurist. **44**

2. *Both the other Scipio Brothers.* (1) Publius Cornelius Scipio

Africanus, the elder, b. B.C. 234, the conqueror of Hannibal at Zama, B.C. 202.   Ob. B.C. 187.

(2)   Lucius Cornelius Scipio Asiaticus (or Asiagenes), brother of Africanus, under whose command king Antiochus was defeated near Mt. Sipylus in B.C. 190.   His title Asiaticus or Asiagenes was given in honour of this campaign.

4.   *caused his body to be buried in their Sepulcher.*   'Our poet Ennius was beloved by the elder Africanus, and so is even believed to be represented in marble on the tomb of the Scipios,' Cicero, *pro Arch.* § 22.   This tomb with the bust of Ennius is still extant.

5.   *So as*, 'so that,' see Index.   *Cato, his*, see index.

9.   *Plato his name*, see p. 38, l. 1.

12.   *he is the most poeticall.*   This is explained in p. 4, l. 5 sqq.

22.   *putting it in method*, 'reducing it to a system.'

29.   *seaven Cities.*   Smyrna, Chios, Colophon, Cymae, Rhodos, Argos, Athenae.   But many more (in all, it is said, nineteen) have been mentioned by various authors for this honour.

32.   *For onely repeating certaine of Euripides verses.*   The story is told by Plutarch (*Life of Nicias*, c. 29).   He is speaking of the fate of the survivors of the ill-fated Athenian expedition against Syracuse B.C. 415—413.   'Some were saved, owing to Euripides.   For it appears that of the Greeks living outside Greece the Sicilians were most especially devoted to his muse; and when merchants sailing to their shores brought specimens and fragments of his poetry they used eagerly to learn them by heart, and pass them on to each other.   At least on this occasion it is said that several of these captives, on their getting safe back to Athens, saluted Euripides with great warmth and told him, in some cases, that while serving as slaves they had been released in return for teaching their masters all they could recollect of his poems; in other cases, that while wandering about the country after the battle they had got food and water in return for singing some of his odes.'

Robert Browning has used this tale in his 'Balaustion's Adventure.'

PAGE 45.

45   2. *Certaine Poets, as Simonides, and Pindarus had so prevailed with Hiero the first.*   Hiero I. tyrant of Syracuse, B.C. 478 to B.C. 467.   He was a great patron of men of letters.   The poets Aeschylus, Pindar, Bacchylides and Simonides, as well as others, frequently resided at his court.   Pindar in the first Pythian Ode (v. 86 sq.) thus admonishes

him : 'Be not blinded, dear friend, by subtlety of gain.   Muse on the high glory that comes after the grave,—how in chronicle and song it celebrates the doings of the departed.   Not dead is the large-souled liberality of Croesus : but Phalaris,—that pitiless heart, who kindled his fires in the brazen bull,—infamy with loathing wholly compasseth; no lyre in men's houses greets his children with ditties in tender fellowship.'

The tradition of the influence of Simonides on Hiero was embalmed by Xenophon in a dialogue named Hiero.

4—6. *Plato could do so little...slave.*   The story referred to is that Plato, during his residence in Sicily (about B.C. 390), was introduced to the elder Dionysius by the philosopher Dion; and, after enjoying his favour for a time, was presently surrendered by him to the Spartan ambassador Pollis.   By this man he was sold into slavery at Aegina, when he was found and liberated by Anniceris of Cyrene.   The latter part of this story, however, rests on very doubtful authority.

14. *communitie of women.*   Plato, *de Repub.* 5, 449—462.   It is putting rather a false colour on Plato's scheme to say that he 'allows' it, as though it were an indulgence.   It is in fact part of a general plan for securing the purity and high *physique* of the people, and is rather a restraint than an indulgence.

So as, 'so that,' see Index.

18. *so as they be,* 'on condition of their being.'

19. *which is likewise stretched to Poetrie,* 'which also applies to poetry.'   Shakespeare, *Henry VIII.* 1, 2, 4 'It *stretches* beyond you, to your friends.'

20. *S. Paule himselfe...alledgeth twise two Poets.*

(1)   Aratus of Cilicia : in his speech at Athens (*Acts* 17, 28) τοῦ γὰρ γένος ἐσμέν, 'for we are his offspring.'

(2)   Epimenides of Crete : *Titus* 1, 12 Κρῆτες ἀεὶ ψεῦσται, κακὰ θηρία, γαστέρες ἀργαί, 'Cretans are ever liars, evil beasts, slow bellies.'

22. *setteth a watch-word upon Philosophy,* 'attaches a word of warning to philosophy.'   *Coloss.* 2, 8 'see that none lead you away captive by philosophy and vain deceit, according to the tradition of men, according to the elements of the world.'   1 *Tim.* 6, 20 'avoiding profane and vain babblings and oppositions of science falsely so called.'

25. *wrong opinions of the Gods.*   In the *Republic* (Book 2) Plato enumerates the stories of the Gods which are not to be admitted, and ends thus: 'when a Poet holds such language concerning the Gods we shall be angry with him, and refuse him a chorus; neither shall we allow our teachers to use his writings for the instruction of the young, if we would have our guardians grow up to be as godlike and god-fearing as it is possible for man to be.'

28. *induce*, 'introduce,' 'bring in.'

31. *the very religion*, 'the true religion.' (Fr. vrai, O. F. verai, Lat. verax.) W. A. Wright, *Bible Word-book*. 'He that holdeth himself in verray penitence.' Chaucer, *Parson's Tale*. 'We must be clothed or armed with the habergeon of *very* justice or righteousness.' Latimer's *Sermons*. Shakespeare, *R. and J.* 3, 1, 115
> 'This gentleman, the Prince's near ally,
> My *very* friend, hath got his mortal hurt
> In my behalf.'

stoode upon, 'dwelt upon,' 'was concerned with,' see Index.

PAGE 46.

46   1. Titles of some of the minor treatises of Plutarch in what are commonly called the *Moralia*. (1) περὶ Ἴσιδος καὶ Ὀσίριδος; (2) περὶ τῶν ἐκλελοιπότων χρηστηρίων; (3) περὶ τύχης.

9. *conster*, 'explain,' 'construe' (con-struere, 'to pile up,' 'to construct'), cp. *Euphues* p. 362 'with that she drew out hir Petrarke, requesting him to *conster* hir a lesson, hoping his learning would be better for a scholemaister than his lucke was for a Phisition...with that the gentlewomen clustered about them both, eyther to hear how cunningly Philanthus could *conster*, or how readily Camilla could conceive.'

11. *Iulius Scaliger. Poeticè*, lib. 1, p. 5 (ed. 1561) 'Idem Plato eos et ἑρμηνέας et ὑπηρέτας deorum vocat in Ione. Quo fit ut minus valeat ejus authoritas in libris politicis: qua authoritate barbari quidam atque hispidi abuti velint ad Poetas e republica exigendos,' 'which authority the barbarous and uncultivated would use for the expulsion of poets from the state.'

18. *Ion.* In the dialogue of Plato thus entitled Socrates is represented as congratulating Ion, a professional reciter, on the delightfulness of his calling, as it involves 'continual association with the works of Poets, and especially with those of Homer, the best and most divine of the Poets; and not only the learning by heart their verses, but thoroughly understanding their thoughts and meaning,' 530 B.

19. *So as*, 'so that,' see Index.

24. *then goe about to overthrow his authority*, 'than try to overset his authority.' Shakespeare, *Measure*, 3, 2, 215 'See how he *goes about* to abuse me.' *Much Ado*, 1, 3, 12 'I wonder that thou, being, as thou

sayest, born under Saturn, *goest about* to apply a moral medicine to a mortifying mischief.'

28.   *namely, to be a very inspiring of a divine force.* Plato, *Ion*, 534 B and C 'For all good epic poets utter their beautiful poems, not from art, but from being god-inspired and possessed; and just as those who feel the Corybantic frenzy are beyond their own control when they dance, so the lyric poets also are not under their own control when they compose these beautiful songs; but as soon as they set foot on the enchanted ground of harmony and rhythm, they feel the Bacchic furor, and are possessed like Bacchanals.'

But comparing what Socrates is made to say of poets in the *Apology* (22 C), that he found that they did not understand what they wrote themselves, and appeared to write under some instinct or inspiration (φύσει τιυί καὶ ἐνθουσιάζοντες), it seems questionable whether Plato meant in the *Ion* to compliment poets in Sidney's sense.

30.   *apparant,* 'evident.' This spelling, which is not always employed in this book (see Index), is found in the A.V. 1611. See W. A. Wright, *Bible Word-book.* Cp. Burton's *Anatomy*, p. 628 (ed. 1651) ' My last caution is that a woman do not bestow herself upon a fool, or an *apparant* melancholy person.'

PAGE 47.

1. *Lelius.* C. Laelius Sapiens the younger, the friend of the younger 47 Scipio Africanus: b. B.C. 186. He was chiefly famous for his skill in the science of augury, his study of Greek philosophy and letters, and his oratory. He is the chief speaker in Cicero's dialogue on Friendship. The ground for Sidney's remark, 'himself a poet,' is to be found in a passage in the old life of Terence: 'Nepos says that he has ascertained on unquestionable authority that Caius Laelius once upon a time at his villa at Puteoli on the first of March, when summoned by his wife somewhat earlier than usual to take his place at dinner, begged her not to interrupt him; and when he did at length come into the dining room at a late hour, he said that he had not often been so happy in composition; and then, on being asked to produce what he had composed, he recited some verses from the *Heautontimorumenos* beginning "Well, I'm sure, Syrus' promises have enticed me here in a pretty impudent manner."' Cicero (*ad Att.* 7, 3, § 10) refers to the same tradition of the assistance given by Laelius to Terence.

the Romane Socrates.   Sidney appears to be referring to Cicero *de Amicit.* § 6, where Fannius says to Laelius, ' We know that you are called wise in a peculiar sense, not only from your natural ability and character, but also from study and learning; and not as the vulgar count wisdom, but in the sense in which men of learning use the word,—a word never applied in all Greece in the highest sense except to one man, him, namely, who was declared so by the oracle of Apollo.'

3.   *Heautontimorumenon,* ' the self-tormentor,' a title of a play of Terence, in which a father is represented as doing voluntary penance by labouring in the fields, for having driven his son into exile by his severity.

6.   *in putting Esops fables into verses.*   Socrates left no written work, except perhaps a hymn to Apollo and Artemis composed in prison (Plato, *Phaedo,* 61), and a rhythmical version of one of Aesop's fables: Diogenes Laert. *Vit. Socratis,* c. 22.   But even this is doubtful; and Cicero (*de Orat.* 3, § 60) says, ' cum ipse litteram Socrates nullam reliquisset.

11.   *Plutarch teacheth the use...of them,* in his treatise *de Audiendis Poetis* (πῶς δεῖ τὸν νέον ποιημάτων ἀκούειν).

13.   *hee trymmeth both theyr garments with gards of Poesie.*   Referring to the frequent quotations from the Poets found in all Plutarch's biographies and treatises.

14.   *trymmeth,* ' ornaments,' cp. Shakespeare, *Richard II.* 3, 4, 56 ' That he had not so *trimmed* and dressed his land as we this garden.'

gards, ' ornaments,' generally on dress.   Shakespeare, *Much Ado,* 1, 1, 289 ' The *guards* are but slightly basted on neither.'   *Love's Labour,* 4, 3, 58 ' rhymes are *guards* on wanton Cupid's hose.'   Stubbes' *Anatomy of Abuses* (ed. Furnivall), p. 56 ' The *Gallye-hosen* are made very large and wide, reaching downe to their knees only, with three or foure *guardes* a peece laid down along either hose.'   id. 60 ' These clokes must be *garded,* laced, and thorowly faced.'   id. 74 ' Or if not so (as lace is not fine enough sometimes) then it must be *garded* with *gardes* of velvet.'

16.   *Historiography,* see p. 4, l. 18.

29.   *the price they ought to be had in,* see p. 42, l. 1.   Cp. *Arcadia,* 1, p. 61 ' Activity and good fellowship being nothing *in the price* it was then held in.'

the ill-favouring breath, ' the unfavourable remarks.'   Thus ' breath ' for ' words ' expressing a judgment in Shakespeare, *Measure,* 5, 122 ' permit a blasting and scandalous *breath* to fall upon him.'   *Mids. N. D.*

3, 2, 44 'Lay *breath* so bitter on your bitter foe.' *Merchant*, 2, 9, 90 'commend, and courteous *breath*.'

30. *wrong-speakers*, 'unfavourable critics.' 'To wrong,' 'to speak ill of.' Shakespeare, *Rich. III.* 4, 4, 213 ' *Wrong* not her birth, she is of royal blood.'

PAGE 48.

5. *onely proceedeth from their wit*, 'comes exclusively from their own imagination.'

6. *being indeede makers of themselves*, 'independent composers.' For *makers*, see p. 7, l. 18. For *of*, see Index.

9. *Musa mihi* etc. Virgil, *Aen.* 1, 8.

12. *Adrian.* The Emperor Hadrian (A.D. 117—138) wrote several works in prose and verse, of which a few epigrams are preserved in the Anthologies. The most famous is the address to his soul:

> 'Animula vagula, blandula,
> hospes comesque corporis,
> quae nunc abibis in loca
> pallidula rigida nudula,
> nec, ut soles, dabis jocos?'

The first line of which suggested Pope's ' Vital spark of heavenly flame.'

Sophocles. It is not quite fair to class Sophocles among 'great Captaines,' though he did once hold office as Strategus or General, and was engaged in the Samian War (B.C. 440—439). But he did not particularly distinguish himself in this capacity; and Pericles is said to have remarked of him that 'he understood the composition of poetry, but not the commanding of armies' (Athenaeus, 13, 604).

Germanicus, son of Drusus, the brother of the Emperor Tiberius (b. B.C. 15, d. A.D. 19), who served with great distinction in many parts of the world, especially in Germany, from which he took his name. He left orations and poems and Greek comedies, which once enjoyed considerable reputation, but are now lost, with the exception of some fragments of his translation of the *Phaenomena* of Aratus, and some epigrams.

Elyot's *Governour*, vol. 1, p. 109 (ed. Croft) 'Was it any reproche to the noble Germanicus (who by assignement of Augustus shulde have succeded Tiberius in the Empire, if a traitorous enemy had not in his flourysshynge youth bireft hym hys lyfe) that he was equall to the most noble poetes of his time, and, to the increase of his honour and moost worthy commendation, his image was set up at Rome, in the habite that poetes at those dayes used?'

14. *Robert, king of Sicil.* Robert d'Anjou, king of Naples 1309—1343. He was the third son of Charles II. king of Naples. His elder brother, Charles Martel, became king of Hungary, his second brother Louis retired to a monastery. On the death of Charles Martel, Hungary fell to his son Charobert; but Robert was created Duke of Calabria. He acquired reputation in the war in Sicily (1299—1300), and on the death of his father (5 May, 1309) he obtained the crown of Naples, his nephew Charobert consenting to submit their rival claims to the decision of the Pope (Clement V, at Avignon) as Suzerain of Naples. He had with Naples the Vicariate of many towns in Piedmont, and was also granted that of Ferrara and the Romagna. When freed from fear of invasion by the death of the Emperor Henry VII. (24 Aug. 1313) he set about conquering Sicily, but was repulsed (1314). Relying on the support of the Pope (John XXII.) he determined to continue the attempt in 1316. Two years later (1318) he was granted possession of Genoa, and for some time was engaged in defending it against the Ghibelines, the lords of Lombardy (1318—1323). In 1324 he renewed his attempts on Sicily. But after the unsuccessful invasion of the island and death of his son Charles (9 Nov. 1328), Robert seems to have given up schemes of conquest and to have devoted himself rather to the accumulation of wealth. Notwithstanding a life so full of struggle and activity he always shewed the greatest interest in literature. His special friends and favourites were Petrarch and Boccaccio. It was to Marie of Sicily (Robert's natural daughter) that Boccaccio dedicated *Filocopa* and *Fiammetta*. Petrarch submitted to be examined by the king before receiving his laurel crown at Rome (1340). But he also cultivated letters himself, prided himself on his Latin and Italian letters to his allies, composed poetry in Tuscan (published at Rome in 1642), and said that he 'gloried more in the title of poet and philosopher than in that of king.' He also composed an ' Office ' in honour of St Louis of Toulouse.

15. *Francis of France.* Francis I., 1515—1547, called 'the father of letters and arts,' was a munificent patron of letters, and protected Budaeus (Budè) the great Greek scholar, Rabelais, Scaliger, Robert Etienne (Stephanus) and Clement Marot, besides the great painters Leonardo da Vinci, Andrea del Sarto, Salviati and Primaticcio, as well as the famous Cellini.

King Iames of Scotland. James I. of Scotland (1405—1436) during his eighteen years of detention in England received an excellent education, and on his return to Scotland is said to have done much for the introduction of letters and polite learning there.   He was also the author of a poem called the 'King's Quair' (i.e. book), besides some *Cantilenae Scoticae* and *Rhythmi Latini*.

Such Cardinals as Bembus and Bibiena.

Peter Bembo was born at Venice in 1470 and died at Rome in 1547, having been named Cardinal by Paul III. in 1539.   From 1513 to 1521 he was secretary to Leo X., shortly before whose death he retired to Padua, and lived there in learned leisure among the best scholars of the time, until summoned to Rome on his creation as Cardinal by Paul III. in 1539.   He was celebrated not only for his splendid collection of Latin and Greek MSS., but for his own Latin and Italian style.   He wrote a Latin poem 'Azolani'(1498), 'Epistolae,' Italian Rime, 'Historia rerum Venetarum,' and other things.   See Roscoe's *Leo X.*, vol. 2, p. 113 (ed. 1876).

16. *Bibiena.* Bernardo Dovizi (1470—1520) or Bernardo da Bibbiena (the place of his birth), a private secretary of Lorenzo de Medici, and one of the instructors of his son Leo X., whose election to the Pontificate he did much to secure.   He was the author of a famous comedy called *Calandra*, represented at Venice in 1508, and published, after his death, in 1524.   'It bears only a general resemblance to the *Menaechmi* of Plautus.   Perhaps the *Calandra* may be considered the earliest modern Comedy. or at least its five acts and intricate plot exclude the competition of *Maitre Patelin.*' Hallam, *Literature*, 1, p. 263.   Roscoe, *Leo X.*, vol. 1, p. 17.

17. *Beza.* Theodore Beza was born at Vezelai in France in 1519, and died at Geneva in 1605.   In his youth he composed numerous Latin poems, which were collected and published at Paris in 1597.   His controversial works were on the side of Calvin's doctrines, with whom he was long associated.

Melancthon. Philip Melancthon (*Schwarzerdt*) was born at Bretten in the Palatinate in 1497, and died in 1560, at Wittenberg, where he had been professor of Greek from 1518.   His chief works are theological treatises on the side of the Reformation instituted by Luther, with whom he was intimate, though his moderation was regarded with suspicion by the more violent Reformers.   He also wrote commentaries on the Classics, works on history, and Latin poems; all of which were collected and published in four volumes at Wittenberg in 1580.

18. *Fracastorius.* Hieronymus Fracastorius (1483—1553) of Verona, a poet, philosopher, astronomer, and physician.   Scaliger in his *Poeticè*, 6, 4 (p. 35, ed. 1561), in his criticism of the modern Italian

Latin poets, gives him the highest praise of all,—'in quo, cum nihil soleam desiderare, admirationi potius erit locus quam castigationi.'

Scaliger, see p. 36, l. 4.

19. *Pontanus*, see p. 11, l. 1.

Muretus. Marc Antoine Muret was born at Muret, near Limoges, in 1526, and died in 1585. Till 1554 he taught languages in various parts of France, after which he was obliged by accusations of immorality to retire to Venice; thence in 1560 he went to Rome on the invitation of Cardinal d'Este, and finally became a Jesuit. Besides orations, classical criticisms, and treatises in law and jurisprudence, he published Latin poems, which he called *Carmina juvenilia.*

George Buchanan (1506—1582), one of the greatest names in Scotch literature of the 16th century. He was born at Killearn in Lennoxshire, and was early left fatherless and in poor circumstances. He was, however, sent by an uncle to Paris for education; whence, after two years' stay, he had to return, and, after serving with some French troops, went to St Andrews and studied under John Mair; with him he went to Paris again, and was tutor for five years to the Earl of Cassilis. When he returned to Scotland (having now become a Lutheran) he was tutor to the king's natural son, the Earl of Moray, and began writing Latin Satires on the monks. After being consequently imprisoned for heresy he again went abroad, and became Professor of Humanities at Bordeaux (1540—1543), where he wrote the two Latin plays of *Jephthah* and *John the Baptist,* to be acted by the students of the University there, and also translated into Latin the *Medea* and *Alcestis* of Euripides. Among his pupils here was Montaigne (see M.'s Essay on the *Education of Children*). After three years at Bordeaux he returned to Paris and taught in the College of Bourbon (1544—7); whence he was invited to Portugal by Govea, the head of the University of Coimbra. After Govea's death in the next year he was again imprisoned for heresy in a monastery, where he partly wrote a Latin metrical version of the Psalms. Obtaining his freedom he returned to England in 1551; but not finding things satisfactory there, he again went to Paris for some years as tutor to the son of the Marshal de Brissac. Returning to Scotland in 1560 he was received well at Court, and in 1566 was made Principal of St Leonard's College at St Andrews, and was tutor of James VI. (James I. of England). He afterwards attacked Queen Mary for her complicity in the murder of her husband; but the principal work of his later life was his treatise *De jure regni,* and his history of Scotland, *Rerum Scoticarum Historia* in twenty books. His Latin poetry was considered by Joseph Scaliger and other critics as superior to that of all others of his age in France, Italy, and Germany. The translation of the Psalms shews indeed a great command of language and a considerable mastery of the classical metres; but the general result is rather artificial than wholly pleasing. The plays, written on the model of Seneca's imitation of the Greek dramas, are very readable, and often full of life and point.

See Jos. Scaliger's *Epitaphium*

'Imperii fuerat Romani Scotia limes:
Romani eloquii Scotia finis erit.'

Hallam's *Literature*, 2, p. 246.

21. *Hospitall of Fraunce.* Michael de l'Hospital was born in 1505 at Aigueperre in Auvergne, and died 13 March, 1573. He was a distinguished French lawyer and statesman, who was sent by Henry II. to represent him at the Council of Trent. After that king's death (1559) he was a member of the Council of State under the Guises, and worked in favour of toleration for the Huguenots. He was principally the author of the decree of 1562, which secured them liberty of worship outside towns. At that time he was Chancellor, owing to the influence of Catherine de Medici,—a post which he continued to hold in the next reign (Charles IX. 1560—1574). He retired into the country a few years before the Bartholomew Massacre [24 Aug. 1572], was dismissed from the Chancellorship, and was in considerable danger of death. It was during this interval of retirement that he composed a considerable number of Latin poems, chiefly in the manner of Horace's *Epistles* and *Satires*. He wrote, besides these, harangues and discourses.

Hallam, *Literature*, 2, p. 244.

31. *when the trumpet of Mars did sounde loudest.* For instance, Chaucer, who lived in the warlike reign of Edward III.

32. *an over-faint quietnes.* The 25 years' peace under Queen Elizabeth was much talked of; and the queen apparently liked to have it referred to; cp. Puttenham, *Arte of English Poesie* (ed. Arber), p. 192 'So did our forefathers call Henry I. *Beauclerc*, Edmund *Ironside*, Richard *Coeur de Lion*, Edward the *Confessor*, and we her Majestie *Elizabeth the peaceable.*' However, this long peace was not wholly grateful to the more active spirits in the country, who sought a vent for their suppressed energies in the expeditions to the New World, which Sidney himself longed to join, or a little later in service against Spain in the Netherlands. For Sidney's view of the disadvantages of such 'over-faint quietness,' cp. *Arcadia*, Book 1. p. 38 'Already there were assembled between 3 and 4000 men, all well disposed, for Kalender's sake, to abide any peril: but like men *disused with a long peace* more determinate to do than skilful how to do: lusty bodies and brave armours; with such courage as rather grew of despising their enemies, whom they knew not, than of any confidence for anything which in themselves they knew: but neither cunning use of their weapons, nor art shewed in their marching, or incamping.' We seem to read here the forebodings entertained by many as to the state of preparation in the country to repel the Spanish invasion, then believed to be coming.

strew the house, a metaphor taken from the use of rushes strewn on the floors, which was still the common practice in all large halls, and in all rooms but those of the richest, who were just beginning the use of carpets; cf. Shakespeare, *Shrew*, 4, 48 'Is supper ready, the house trimmed, rushes *strewed?*' 1 *Henry IV*. 3, 1, 214 'She bids you on the wanton *rushes* lay you down.' Elyot's *Governour* (ed. Croft), 2, p. 120 'as a maiden would seeke for a small pinne in a great chamber *strawed* with rushes.' Puttenham, *Arte of English Poesie* (ed. Arber), p. 66 'For they used no matts or rushes as we do now.'

PAGE 49.

49   2. *Mountibancks at Venice.* The mountebanks (Italian montam-banco lit. *one who mounts a bench*) were the vendors of quack medicines and other nostrums; and their eloquence was like that of the cheap Jacks of our day. Of these the mountebanks of Venice were especially famous. Jusserand (*English Way-faring Life*, p. 186) quotes an English traveller in Venice in 1608—9: 'Truly I often wondered at many of these natural orators. For they would tell their tales with such admirable volubility and plausible grace, even *extempore*, and seasoned with singular variety of elegant jests and witty conceits, that they did often strike great admiration into strangers that never heard them before.' They 'sell oyles, soveraigne waters, amorous songs printed, apothecary drugs, and a common-weale of other trifles...I saw one of them holde a viper in his hand and play with his sting a quarter of an houre together, and yet receive no hurt.' Coryat's *Crudities* (ed. 1776), vol. 2, pp. 50—3.

5. *troubled in the net with Mars.* The net was forged by her jealous husband Vulcan. Homer, *Odyssey*, 8, 266—358.

7. *peece of a reason*, p. 2, l. 3.

13. *as Epaminondas is sayd.* The office was that of *Telearch*, a sort of local police office or commissionership of sewers at Thebes.

'He was appointed to it,' says Plutarch, 'in scorn, but did not neglect it.' But saying 'that not only was it true that office shews the man, but also that the man shews the office,' he raised the *Telearchy* to a great height of reputation and esteem, though of no repute before.' Plutarch, *Reipub. gerendae Praecepta*, c. 15.

20. *banckes of Helicon.* Helicon is a mountain in Boeotia, a continuation of the range of Parnassus, and regarded as a special haunt of the Muses.

23. *Queis meliore,* &c.   Juvenal 14, 36

'unus et alter

forsitan haec spernant juvenes, quibus arte benigna

et meliore luto finxit praecordia Titan.'

24. *cre better content, to suppresse the out-flowing of their wit.* 'The poets of the 16th century wrote for their own delectation and for that of their friends, and not for the general public.   They generally had the greatest aversion to their works appearing in print.' Arber, Introduction to *Tottel's Miscellany*, p. iii.

Mr Saintsbury (*Elizabethan Literature*, p. 2) comments on this: 'This aversion which continued in France till the end of the 17th century, if not later, had been somewhat broken down in England by the middle of the 16th, though vestiges of it long survived, and in the form of a reluctance to be known to write for money may be found even within the confines of the 19th.'

It was in fact not creditable to a gentleman to be known to write,—a fact dwelt on by the advocates of the strange theory of the Baconian authorship of Shakespeare's plays, to account for Bacon's supposed reserve,—and it is greatly owing to this feeling that so much of Tottel's Miscellany and of other Miscellanies is anonymous.   Cp. Puttenham (ed. Arber), p. 37 'Nowe also of such of the Nobilitie or gentrie as be very well seene in many laudable Sciences, and especially in making of Poesie, it is so come to passe that they have no courage to write, and, if they have, yet are they loathe to be knowen of their skil.   So as I knowe many notable Gentlemen in the Court that have written commendably and suppressed it agayne, or els suffered it to be publisht without their owne names to it: as if it were a discredit for a gentleman to seeme learned and to shew himselfe amorous of any good Art.'

29. *in despight of Pallas,* Horace, *Ars Poet.* 385

'Tu nihil invita facies dicesve Minerva.'

PAGE 50.

50   9. *the auncient-learned*, 'the learned among the ancients.'

10. *a divine gift.* Cicero, *de Orat.* 2, 194 'Saepe enim audivi poetam bonum neminem—id quod a Democrito et Platone in scriptis relictum esse dicunt—sine inflammatione animorum existere posse, et sine quodam afflatu quasi furoris.'

13. *carried unto it,* inclined to it by an irresistible impulse ($\phi\acute{\epsilon}\rho\epsilon\tau\alpha\iota$).

14. *an old Proverbe, Orator fit, Poeta nascitur.* Though the proverb is undoubtedly old, it does not appear to be used by any classical writer. The substance is expressed in Cicero, *pro Archia*, § 18 'atque sic a summis hominibus eruditissimis accepimus, ceterarum rerum studia et doctrina et praeceptis et arte constare, poetam natura ipsa valere et mentis viribus excitari et divino quodam spiritu inflari.' Yet in the *de Oratore* § 1, 14 he labours to prove that the orator also is formed by nature and not art. Diogenes Laertius, *Life of Xenocrates*, § 13, says 'For when Poets try to write in prose they succeed; but when prose-writers try poetry they fail. The reason is that the one is a gift of nature, the other of art.' The earliest occurrence of the proverb in printed literature appears to be in the *Lectiones Antiquae* of Coelius Rhodigenus (1450—1525), in which one chapter is headed, 'An poeta nascatur, orator fiat, sicut receptum vulgo est, neminem unum posse in multis excellere.' And further on occurs, 'vulgo certe jactatur *nasci poetam oratorem fieri.*' Cp. Ben Jonson, *Underwoods*, 'For a good poet's made as well as born.'

17. *Dedalus.* Daedalus, who invented wings for himself and his son Icarus. Ovid, *Metam.* 8, 261.

22. *fore-backwardly*, 'putting the cart before the horse,' $\ddot{\upsilon}\sigma\tau\epsilon\rho\upsilon\nu$ $\pi\rho\acute{\upsilon}\tau\epsilon\rho\upsilon\nu$, Puttenham (ed. Arber), p. 181.

28. *Quodlibet*, 'vague,' lit. 'anything you please,' a word used to express the matter of scholastic disputations. (See D'Israeli, *Curiosities of Literature* (ed. 1867), p. 22 'Scholastic questions were called *questiones quodlibeticae*; and they were generally so ridiculous that we have retained the word *quodlibet* in our vernacular language to express anything ridiculously subtile.') Sidney seems to use it in a double sense here. Though our subject-matter is catholic enough—*quodlibet* in two ways—yet we cannot follow Ovid in always producing out of it a line of poetry.

30. *Quicquid conabar dicere versus erat.* Pope's 'I lisped in numbers, for the numbers came.' The first edition (1595) has *quicquid conabor dicere versus erit*, but corrects to *conabar* in an erratum, leaving *erit* uncorrected. I think Sidney probably wrote both

imperfects: but as usual he quotes from memory and incorrectly the verse of Ovid (*Tristia*, 4, 10, 26) *et quod temptabam dicere, versus erat.*

PAGE 51.

3. *Troylus and Cresseid.* This poem Chaucer always professes to **51** be a translation and not original. It is founded on an old history written by Lollius of Urbino. In the 'House of Fame' [3, 375] Chaucer enumerates the Historians of Troy:

> 'And by him stood, withouten lees,
> Ful wonder hye on a pilere
> Of yren, he, the great Omere;
> And with him Dares and Tytus
> Before, and eke he Lollius.'

It is curious that Sidney should speak of this poem as Chaucer's obvious title to fame, without mentioning the *Canterbury Tales*, which however he knew (see p. 37, l. 23). It seems an instance of the false taste of the time that gave the superiority in poetry to everything 'classical' in subject.

9. *Mirrour of Magistrates* [properly *for*]. This was a joint work projected in 1555 or 1557 by Baldwin and Ferrers. The first edition appeared in 1559. It was framed on the plan of Boccaccio's *Fall of Princes*, which had been translated by Lydgate, and was to contain a series of legends of famous men in England who had sustained great reverses of fortune. In the 2nd edition (1563) an *Induction* and a *Complaint of the Duke of Buckingham* were added by Thomas Sackville, Lord Buckhurst, which is the only part of the work now much read. Additional contributions were afterwards made by Phayer, Higgins, Churchyard and others, and the plan was extended by the admission of characters other than English. The best modern edition is one edited by Jos. Haslewood in 1815. The subject of the book is thus stated in a stanza of Sackville's *Induction* (76)

> 'Loe here,' quoth sorrow, 'princes of renoune,
> That whilom sate on top of fortune's wheele,
> Now layde full low, like wretches whurled downe,
> Even with one frowne, that slayde but with a smyle,
> And now beholde the thing that thou, erewhile,
>   Saw onely in thought, and, what thou now shalt heere,
>   Recompt the same to kesar, king, and peere.'

Mr Saintsbury (*History of Elizabethan Literature*, p. 11) says: 'Sackville's contributions to the *Mirrour for Magistrates* contain the best poetry written in the English Language between Chaucer and Spenser, and are certainly the originals or at least the models of some of Spenser's finest work.'

11. *the Earle of Surries Liricks.* The learned and accomplished Lord Henry Howard, son of the Duke of Norfolk, and by courtesy Earl of Surrey, was born in 1516, and beheaded on a charge of High Treason (principally grounded on the allegation of having quartered the royal arms in his shield) 19 January 1547, a few days before the death of Henry VIII. He had served with distinction under Sir John Wallop in the war of 1543—4; and in defence of Boulogne in 1545—6. Surrey, like Sidney, had a real or imaginary passion for a lady, which animates most of his verse, and in whose honour, if we are to believe the common story, he travelled through Italy, asserting her charms against all comers according to the chivalrous customs of a past age. This lady he calls *Geraldine*, and she has been identified with Lady Elizabeth Fitzgerald, daughter of the 9th Earl of Kildare by Margaret d. of Thomas Gray, Marquis of Dorset.

His poems, inspired by this real or fancied passion, were circulated in MS. during his life, and were first printed in Tottel's *Miscellany* (1557), and became immediately so popular that they were reprinted four times in the same year, and republished seven times before 1587, besides being at the same time still circulated in MS., and often partially reprinted in single sheets called Garlands. Besides these he wrote a paraphrase of the 1st five chapters of Ecclesiastes, and a metrical version of some of the Psalms. More important is a translation of the 2nd and 4th books of Virgil's *Æneid* in ten syllable blank verse, as it is probably the earliest use of that metre in English. His blank verse lacks variety in pause and cæsura, but the translation is generally neat and accurate. Of his lyrical work, which did much for the improvement of English poetry in regard to correctness of form, the following is a favourable specimen:

> 'The soote season, that bud and bloom forth brings,
>   With green hath clad the hill, and eke the vale.
>   The nightingale with feathers new she sings;
>   The turtle to her mate hath told her tale.
>   Summer is come, for every spray now springs,
>   The hart hath hung his old head on the pale;
>   The buck in brake his winter coat he slings;

The fishes flete with new repaired scale;
The adder all her slough away she slings;
The swift swallow persueth her flies smale;
The busy bee her honey now she mings;
Winter is worn that was the flowers' bale.
    And thus I see among these pleasant things
    Each care decays, and yet my sorrow springs!'

12. *Sheapheards Kalender.* Spenser published 'the Shepheardes Calender' anonymously in 1579—80, dedicated 'To the noble and vertuous Gentleman, most worthy of all titles both of learning and chevalrie MAISTER *Philip Sidney.*' This series of Twelve Eclogues, one for each month of the year, with an introduction in the shape of a critical letter to Gabriel Harvey, and glosses or notes by E. K. (Edward Kirke) contains the following poetical dedication to Sidney:

'Goe, little booke! thyself present,
    As child whose parent is unkent,
    To him that is the president
    Of Noblesse and of Chevalree:
    And if that envie barke at thee,
    As sure it will, for succoure flee
    Under the shadow of his wing;
    And asked who thee forth did bring,
    A Shepheards swaine, saye, did thee sing
    All as his straying flocke he fedde:
    And, when his honour hath thee redde,
    Crave pardon for my hardyhedde.
    But, if that any aske thy name,
    Say, thou wert base-begot with blame;
    For-thy thereof thou takest shame.
    And, when thou art past jeopardee,
    Come tell me what was sayd of mee,
    And I will send more after thee.'

14. *That same framing of his stile to an old rustick language.* E. K. in his Epistle defends the Poet on this point: 'And firste of the wordes to speake, I graunt they be something hard and of most men unused, yet both English, and also used of most excellent authors, and most famous Poetes. In whom, whereas this our Poet hath bene much traveiled and thoroughly redd, how could it be (as that worthy Oratour sayde) but that walking in the sonne, although for other cause he

walked, yet needes he mought be sunburnt; and having the sound of those auncient Poets still ringing in his eares, he mought needes, in singing, hit out some of theyr tunes. But whether he useth them by such casualtye and custome, or of set purpose and choyse, as thinking them fittest for such rusticall rudeness of shepheards, eyther for that theyr rough sounde would make his rymes more ragged and rustical, or else because such olde and obsolete words are most used of country folke, sure I think, and think I think not amisse, that they bring great grace, and, as one would say, auctoritie to the verse.'

Ben Jonson, on the other hand, seems to have disapproved. He says in his *Discoveries*, 'Spenser in affecting the ancients, writ no language: yet I would have him read for his matter; but as Virgil read Ennius.' But though Jonson told Drummond (*Conversations with Ben Jonson*, p. 2) that 'Spenser's stanzaes pleased him not, nor his matter' (i.e. in the *Faerie Queene*); yet Drummond also reports (p. 9), 'He hath by heart some verses of Spenser's Calender about wyne, between Coline and Percye.' I suppose he means (*Shepheard's Calender, October*)

> 'Whoever casts to compasse weightye prise,
> And thinkes to throwe out thondring words of threate,
> Let powre in lavish cups and thriftie bits of meate,
> For Bacchus' fruite is friend to Phoebus wise,
> And, when with wine the braine begins to sweate,
> The nombres flowe as fast as spring doth ryse.'

16. *neyther Theocritus in Greeke.* Theocritus (of Cos or Syracuse circ. B.C. 270), the pastoral poet of Sicily. It is not, I think, fair to quote him in this respect against Spenser. He, too, wrote a language which he did not speak, and which was probably an intentional imitation of the rustic Doric of the Sicilian Greeks.

Virgil's *Eclogues* are more to the point ; for they are written in literary Latin, with few if any condescensions to colloquialism or rusticities.

17. *Sanazar.* See p. 28, l. 23.

18. *Besides these, doe I not remember to have seene but fewe.* Puttenham in his *Arte of English Poesie* (ed. Arber), p. 76—7, mentions some others, Lydgat (abt. 1375—1460), Harding (1378—1465), the author of the Satyr of Piers Ploughman [14th century], Skelton [1460—1529], Sir Thomas Wyat [1503—1542], Lord Vaux [1510—1557], Challener [1515—1565], Sir Walter Rawleigh [1552—1618], Edward Dyar

[1540—1610], Gascon [1536—1577], Phaer [ob. 1560] and Golding [ob. about 1590].

The two last were mainly translators, and it would not come into Sidney's plan to mention chroniclers or satirists, but we might have expected him to name Wyat as well as Surrey.   For another list of the minor poets of the early 16th century, see Webbe's *Discourse* (ed. Arber), p. 33.

23.   *ordering*, 'arranging,' 'planning.'

28.   *excepting Gorboduck.*   The play called *Ferrex and Porrex*, by Thomas Sackville, Lord Buckhurst and T. Norton: printed 1st surreptitiously in 1565, and again with authority in 1571, and several times since.   It was first acted in the Hall of the Inner Temple at Christmas 1561, and in the following January before Queen Elizabeth at Whitehall.   The authorised edition of 1571 will be found reprinted in West's edition of Sackville's works [1859].

It is a play founded on traditional British history.   Gorboduc, king of Briton about B.C. 600, divided his kingdom in his lifetime between his sons Ferrex and Porrex.   The young princes quarrelled : there was a civil war: Porrex slew Ferrex: and their mother Videna revenged her favourite son by entering Porrex's bedchamber and killing him in his sleep.   The people rose in rebellion, and killed both Gorboduc and Videna: and a fresh civil war followed between the nobles and people.

This, perhaps the earliest blank-verse tragedy in English, has been held up by some critics as a model on which later playwrights, including Shakespeare, might with advantage have framed their own dramas; and though Dryden and Oldham spoke of it with contempt, it appears that they had not read it, for they suppose Gorboduc to be a woman. With some faults of construction, to be referred to later on, it has considerable merits,—correctness of diction and metre, with a certain eloquence which helps to carry on the reader: but, like Surrey's blank verse translation of Virgil, the rhythm is too monotonous; the art of varying the pauses, and of continuing the sense through a varying number of lines was not yet hit upon,—that was reserved for Marlowe, whose *Tamburlain the Great* (1587) first shewed of what blank verse was capable.

An unsettled question in regard to *Ferrex and Porrex* is as to the part taken in its composition by Sackville and Norton respectively.   It has been said that the first three acts were by Norton, the last two by Sackville.   But the internal evidence is in favour of a larger share having been taken by Sackville.   For criticisms on the play see

Warton's *History of English Poetry* (ed. Hazlitt), vol. 4, p. 255—266; J. P. Collier, *English Dramatic Poetry*, vol. 2, p. 383; Saintsbury, *Elizabethan Literature*, p. 58.

[T. SACKVILLE (see l. 9), only son of Sir Richard Sackville, was born at Buckhurst in Withyham, Sussex, in 1536; was partly educated by Roger Ascham; studied at St John's College, Cambridge, as well as at New College, Oxford; entered Parliament in 1557 for Westmoreland; and after a period of some extravagance and dissoluteness of living, upon coming into his paternal property (1566), settled down to a sober management of his estate, and to the performance of useful public services. He was created Lord Buckhurst in 1567; served abroad in the diplomatic negociations in France and the Low Countries, as well as in various matters of importance at home; became Chancellor of Oxford in 1591, Lord Treasurer of England in 1599; came into possession of Knole in Kent in 1603 (by a previous grant of Queen Elizabeth), and was created Earl of Dorset by James I. in 1604. He died suddenly at the Council table at Whitehall 19 April, 1608. For a full account of him and his works printed or in MS. see Cooper's *Athenae Cantabrigienses*, Vol. II. p. 484—492.

T. NORTON (1532—1584), a barrister, was a translator of 28 of the Psalms in the version which goes by the name of Sternhold and Hopkins, and the author of other unimportant poems. He was a native of Sharpenhoe in Bedfordshire, and a staunch Calvinist. Some account of him will be found in Wood's *Athenae Oxonienses*.]

PAGE 52.

52   1. *Seneca his stile*, see p. 10, l. 24. Seneca's tragedies, now much neglected and their authenticity doubted, were widely read in the middle ages; and, as we have seen, were the models on which the early tragedy writers formed their plays.

4. *defectious*, 'defective' (Fr. *défectueux*, L. *defectuosus*).

6. *For it is faulty both in place and time.* The 'dramatic unities,' which Shakespeare so often sets at nought, and of which modern play-writers, as well as modern spectators and readers, have learnt to think little, were at this time thought all important by the critics, who accepted Aristotle's rule as final. He says that as Tragedy is a representation (μίμησις) of action, this action must be limited in amount by the time allowed by the play [*Poet.* 7]; and again that 'tragedy tries as far as possible not to extend, or at any rate very little, beyond one revolution of the sun' [ἡ μὲν ὅτι μάλιστα πειρᾶται ὑπὸ μίαν περίοδον

ἡλίου εἶναι ἢ μικρὸν ἐξαλλάττειν c. 5]. From this the rule for unity of time was deduced. Of unity of place Aristotle says nothing ; but he dwells mostly on 'Unity of Fable,' that is practically, Unity of Action. The subject was much discussed in later times, and the strictest rules were formulated by Corneille in his *Essay on the Three Unities* (1659).

What Shakespeare thought of it we may gather from his own words

> 'Vouchsafe to those who have not read the story
> That I may prompt them : and of such as have
> I humbly pray them to admit the excuse
> Of time, of numbers, and the course of things,
> Which cannot in this huge and proper life
> Be here presented. Now we bear the king
> Toward Calais : grant him there; there seen,
> Heave him away upon your winged thoughts
> Athwart the sea.' (*Henry V.* Act v. prol. 1.)

Shakespeare thus fearlessly relies on the imagination of the spectators to justify him: but it is not in this way that Gorboduc sins. Verisimilitude is set at nought in a manner that cannot be amended by any effort of imagination. Thus in Act IV. Sc. 11. the king orders Porrex from his presence, and while continuing his speech, which could have occupied only a few minutes, Marcella comes in and announces that Porrex has been murdered in his sleep by his mother: which involves a change from day to night, Porrex going to bed and falling asleep, and the subsequent murder, all in the space of a quarter of an hour at the most. Sorbière in his *Journey to England* (1662) says of the English plays, 'the poets laugh at the uniformity of place, and the rules of times : their plays contain the actions of five-and-twenty years.' So Jusserand of the novels : 'In these Romances people do not grow old. Pleusidippus has become a man without the least change in his mother's face; she has remained as beautiful as in the first page of the book, and is, according to appearances, still sweet-and-twenty.'

15. *under-kingdoms*, 'inferior kingdoms,' included in the larger name.

that the Player, when he commeth in, must ever begin. See p. 39, l. 15. The arrangement, or rather the want of arrangement, of the stage must be credited with this awkwardness, which was felt also in the time of Plautus. See the prologue to the *Menaechmi* 72 :

> 'Haec urbs Epidamnus est, dum haec agitur fabula :
> quando alia agetur, aliud fiat oppidum ;'

and the *Truculentus* Prol. 10:

> 'Athenae istae sunt, ita hoc est proscenium
> tantisper dum transigimus hanc comoediam.'

Of the plays that Sidney is here attacking few, if any, survive. Probably they were not printed in most cases. The next contributions to the 'legitimate drama' were translations from Euripides, the *Phoenissae*, G. G. Gascoine (1566), and from Seneca, whose ten tragedies were translated by different hands and first collected in 1581. The new school did not begin until after Sidney's death, if we regard Marlowe's *Tamburlaine* (1587) as the first.

24. *with foure swords and bucklers*. Cp. Shakespeare's *Henry V.*, Act 4, Prol. 48:

> 'And so our scene must to the battle fly:
> Where, O for pity! we shall much disgrace—
> With four or five most vile and ragged foils,
> Right ill-disposed in brawl ridiculous,—
> The name of Agincourt. Yet sit and see;
> Minding true things by what their mockeries be.'

For *with* = 'by,' see Index.

29. *traverces*, 'difficulties,' 'crosses.' Cp. 'Love is the theme of his 4th book; and though it is the shortest of the whole Aeneis, yet there he has given its beginning, its progress, its *traverses* and its conclusion.' Dryden. In Shakespeare the verb 'to traverse' is used (1) as a military term 'to march,' (2) in fencing, of a particular mode of parrying; *Merry Wives* 2, 3, 25 'to see thee fight, to see thee firm, to see thee *traverse*.'

Cp. Whetstone, Dedication of *Promos and Cassandra* (1578) 'The Englishman in this quality is most vain, indiscreet, and out of order: he first grounds his work on impossibilities: then in 3 hours runs he through the world, marries, gets children, makes children men, men to conquer kingdoms, murder monsters, and bringeth gods from heaven and fetcheth devils from hell. And (that which is worst) their ground is not so imperfect as their working indiscreet; not weighing, so the people laugh, though they laugh them (for their follies) to scorn: many times (to make mirth) they make a clown companion with a king: in their grave councils they allow the advice of fools: yea they use one order of speech for all persons, a gross indecorum; for a crow will ill counterfeit the nightingale's sweet voice: even so affected speech doth misbecome a clown; for to work a comedy kindly, grave old men should instruct, young men should show the imperfections of youth, strumpets should be lascivious, boys unhappy, and clowns should speak disorderly; intermingling all these actions in such sort as the grave matter may instruct and the pleasant delight: for without this change the attention would be small and the liking less.'

PAGE 53.

4. *containeth matter of two dayes.* The *Eunuchus* of Terence is not alone in this. In the *Heautontimoroumenos* (see p. 59, l. 16) the action also embraces two days.

7. *And though Plautus hath in one place done amisse.* Sidney perhaps means the *Rudens,* in which there is a considerable interval between the 3rd and 4th Acts: or the *Captivi,* in which there is also a long interval between the 3rd and next acts.

19. *Calicut,* the capital of Malabar, was the first port in India known to Europeans: the Portuguese having visited it in 1498.

20. *Pacolets horse.* The magic horse of Pacolet, a dwarf in the old story of Valentine and Orson (or Ursine), an old French Romance, which appears to have been first printed in English by Wynken de Worde. An English interlude founded on it is mentioned as being played 'by hir Majesties players,' written by Raffe Hancock in 1594 [Herbert's *Ames,* p. 1339]; but the modern translations are all modifications of that by Henry Watson [17th cent.]. See p. 131 (ed. 1826) 'Now you shall understand that within this castle where Clerimond was, dwelt a dwarf named *Pacolet,* which she had nourished and brought up of a child, bestowing much cost to have him taught in schools. This Pacolet, being of more age than stature, grew exceeding witty, and at last studied the black art, and therein grew so famous in necromancy, that by enchantment he had composed a little horse made of wood; in the head of which horse he had so artificially conveyed a pin of wood, that every time he mounted on his back to ride abroad, he would turn the pin toward the place he would go unto, and suddenly he would be in the same place without danger; for the horse could run through the air swifter than any bird.' Cp. Chaucer, *Knight's Tale* l. 316, whose 'hors of bras' was also managed by 'trilling a pin.'

22. *Nuncius* (ἄγγελος) 'the messenger' who in Greek tragedies usually announces and describes the catastrophe.

25. *Ab ovo.* Horace, *Ars Poet.* 147 'nec gemino bellum Trojanum orditur ab ovo;' i.e. the egg from which Helen was born.

29. *Polidorus.* In the *Hecuba* of Euripides.

PAGE 54.

54   1. *findeth a slight*, 'finds a trick' or 'contrivance,' a word still in use in our 'sleight of hand.'   (Icelandic, *slaegd*, 'cunning,' *slaegr*, ' sly,' Germ. *schlau*.)

Cf. Skelton, *Against Garnesche*, 2, 150

> 'Dysdaynous, double, ful of deseyte,
>   Liing, spying by suttelte and *slyght*.'

id. the *Bowge of Courte*, v. 302

> 'How he is taken in conceyte,
>   This doctour Dawcocke, Drede, I wene, he hyghte:
> By Goddis bones, but yf we have some *sleyte*,
>   It is lyke he wyll stonde in our lyghte.'

Spenser, *Faerie Queen*, 4, 2, 44

> 'Which when as Blandamon beheld, he sayd:
> "False faitous Scudamour, that hast by *slight*
>   And foule advantage this good knight dismayd."'

Euphues, p. 115 (ed. Arber) 'Lay before thine eyes the *sleightes* and deceits of the lady.'

More, *Eutopia* (ed. Arber), p. 85 'And finally by what *sleight* (artibus) or means the one getteth the victory.'

Chaucer, *Troylus and Cresseid*, 1511

> 'For I mighte have founden a manere
>   *Of sleight* for to cover al the chere.'

So *sleighly* passes on to 'slyly,' ib. 1185

> 'And after noon ful *sleighly* Pandarus
>   Gan drawe hym to the wyndow next the strete.'

Wycliffe's *Bible*, St Matt. 10, 16 'Lo! I sende you as scheepe in the myddil of wolves; therfore be *slig* as serpentis.'

In the next century we find our modern use of the word, cp. Butler's *Hudibras*

> 'As lookers on feel most delight
>   That least perceive the jugglers *sleight*.'

10. *neither right Tragedies, nor right Comedies.* Collier (*Annals of the Stage*, p. 335) quotes Florio's *First Fruits* (1591)

' *G.*   After dinner we will go see a play.

H.   The plays that they play in England are not *right Comedies.*

   T.   Yet they do nothing else but play every day.

   H.   Yea, but they are neither *right comedies nor right tragedies.*

   G.   How would you name them then?

   H.   Representations of histories without any decorum.'

   11. *mingling Kings and Clownes.* See the passage of Whetstone quoted at p. 52, l. 30. Sidney does not seem to be objecting so much to the presence of humbler characters on the stage, when the nature of the plot requires it,—though even that he seems to think questionable, —as to regular jesters or clowns, brought on to make deliberate buffoonery in the midst of tragic action. Cp. Hall's *Satires,* 1, 3, 31

> ' Now lest such frightfull showes of fortune fall,
> And bloudy tyrants rage should chance appall
> The dead-stroke audience, midst the silent rout
> Comes leaping in a self-misformed lout,
> And laughs and grins and frames his mimick face,
> And justles straight into the prince's place.
> Then doth the theatre echo all aloud
> With gladsome noyse of that applauding crowd.
> A goodly hoch-poch, when vile russettings
> Are match with monarchs and with mightie kings;
> A goodly grace to sober tragic muse
> When each base clowne his clumbsie fist doth bruise,
> And show his teeth in double rotten-row,
> For laughter at his selfe-resembled show.'

   The introduction of such professional jesters may have been undignified; but we may be thankful that Shakespeare saw the use of humour even in tragedy. It must be felt for instance that the Porter's speech in *Macbeth,* so far from spoiling the tragic effect, heightens the horror of the scene.

   16. *mungrell,* 'mixed,' connected with 'might,' A. S. *mang,* 'a mixture.' *monger,* 'a dealer' in a mixture of things. The spelling *mun-* appears to have been the ordinary one at this time. Skeat quotes Levins (1570), by whom it is spell *mungril.*

   17. *Apuleius did some-what so.* It is not easy to see what Sidney means by introducing a mention of Appuleius among comedians and tragedians. In his *Apologia* indeed Appuleius says that he had written various poems, Lyrics, Comedies and Tragedies; but of all these we know nothing except such fragments of his verses as he himself quotes in his *Apologia.* The work for which he is chiefly known is the 'Golden

Ass,' a long Romance in xi books, in which Satire, erotic stories, and serious reflexions are mingled. It can only be counted a 'poem' in the wide sense in which Sidney reckons the *Utopia* as such, for it is entirely in prose. His other surviving works are a miscellany called *Florides*, and some philosophical treatises *De deo Socratis, De philosophia Platonis,* and *De Mundo.* Appuleius was born at Madaura in Africa some time in the 2nd century A.D., was educated first at Carthage, and then at Athens, and other places. But we know nothing of his life except what he tells us in his *Apologia,* and it is impossible to feel sure as to how far that is to be trusted. His Latin style is bad, filled with barbarisms, or affected archaisms: but in spite of that the 'Golden Ass' is lively reading, and contains many brilliant descriptions, and one beautiful story, that of Psyche.

20. *The Amphitruo* can only be called Tragi-Comic on the score of the introduction of gods and heroes. In all other respects it is pure comedy. But the presence of these personages was held to remove it from the category of simple comedy. Hence in the Prologue (v. 59) the poet says:

> 'Faciam ut commixta sit haec tragicomoedia :
> Nam me perpetuo facere ut sit comoedia,
> Reges quo veniunt et di, non parabitur.'

22. *very daintily* (dainty, Fr. *dain, digne,* Lat. *dignus*) here seems to mean 'fastidiously,' 'with nice discrimination.' Cp. Shakespeare, *Hamlet,* 5, 1, 78 'The hand of little use hath the *daintier* sense.' *Love's Labour,* 4, 1, 149 'Her feet were much too *dainty* for such tread.'

Horn-pypes, 'merry tunes,' generally for country dances, cp. Shakespeare, *Winter's Tale,* 4, 3, 47 'But one puritan amongst them, and he sings psalms to *horn-pipes.*' Spenser, *Shepheard's Calender,* 5, 22

> 'Before them rode a lusty Tabrere,
> That to the many a *Horne-pype* play'd,
> Whereto they dauncen, eche one with his mayd.
> To see those folkes make such jovysaunce,
> Made my heart after the pype to daunce.'

24. *scurrility,* 'indecency' (Lat. *scurra,* 'a professed jester,' 'a buffoon'). Cp. Shakespeare, *Love's Labour,* 4, 2, 55 'Perge, good master Holofernes, perge: so it shall please you to abrogate *scurrility ;*' ib. 5, 1, 4 'I praise God for you, Sir: your reasons have been sharp and sententious ; pleasant without *scurrility.*'

26. *doltishnes* (*dolt* from 'dull.' A. S. *dol,* 'foolish ').

27. *tract*, 'course' (Lat. *tractus*, 'a drawing out'). Shakesp. *Henry VIII.* 1, 1, 40

> ' As I belong to worship, and affect
>   In honour honesty, the *tract* of everything
>   Would by a good discourser lose some life,
>   Which action's self was tongue to.'

32. *commeth it not of delight.* St Matt. 5, 37 'Whatsoever is more than these *cometh of* evil.' Bacon, *Essays* 51 'The even carriage between two factions *proceedeth* not alwaies *of* moderation, but *of* a trueness to a man's selfe, with end to make use of both.'

PAGE 55.

4. *conveniencie to our selves*, 'suitability,' used in the sense of the Latin *convenientia*, Cicero, *de Amicit.* § 100.

8. *a scornful tickling*, 'a tickling produced by scorn,' Shakespeare, *Hamlet*, 2, 2, 336 'The clown shall make those laugh whose lungs are *tickled* o' the sere.'

10. *We laugh at deformed creatures.* From Aristotle, *Poet.* 5 οἷον εὐθὺς τὸ γελοῖον πρόσωπον αἰσχρόν τι καὶ διεστραμμένον ἄνευ ὀδύνης. Sidney is thinking, I suppose, of such freaks of nature as are made shows.

17. *goe downe the hill agaynst the byas*, i.e. 'take a wrong and un-expected turn:' a metaphor from the game of bowls, the bias properly being 'the slope' [O. F. *biais*]; though it is often used for the weight in the side of the bowl. Cp. Shakespeare, *Shrew*, 4, 5, 25 'Thus the bowl should run, and not unluckily *against the bias;' Richard II.* 3, 4, 5 ' My fortune runs *against the bias.*'

22. *twenty mad Anticks* (L. *antiquus*, 'ancient,' so, 'old-fashioned,' 'odd'). In Shakespeare the word is used, (1) of fantastic representa-tions, *Love's Labour*, 5, 1, 119 'Some delightful ostentation, or show, or pageant, or *antique*, or firework.' (2) Of odd persons, buffoons; *Troilus*, 5, 3, 86 'Like witless *antics.*'

25. *spinning at Omphales commaundement.* For the story of Her-cules, in his infatuation for Omphale, Queen of Lydia, submitting to be dressed as a female slave and to spin wool, see Ovid, *Heroid.* 9, 75

> ' Non fugis, Alcide, victricem mille laborum
>   rasilibus calathis imposuere manum,
>   crassaque robusto deducis pollice fila,
>   aequaque formosae pensa rependis erae?'

28. *scornefulnes*, 'contemptibleness': so *scornefull* in l. 30 is 'productive of scorn,' 'contemptible.' Cp. Shakespeare, *Lucrece*, 520

'So thy surviving husband shall remain
The *scorneful* mark of every open eye.'

PAGE 56.

56   1. *forbidden plainely by Aristotle.* See *Poet.* c. 5. Aristotle defines the ridiculous (τὸ γελοῖον) as 'a mistake or unsightliness which does not give pain and does not cause mischief' (ἁμάρτημά τι καὶ αἶσχος ἀνώδυνον καὶ οὐ φθαρτικόν). Therefore 'sinful things'—which are not ἀνώδυνα (painless) and are φθαρτικὰ (mischievous)—are not the proper subject of laughter: it does not in fact properly apply to 'the vicious' generally (οὐ κατὰ πᾶσαν κακίαν) but only to 'the unsightly' (τὸ αἶσχος).

9. *Nil habet*, etc. Juvenal 3, 152

'Of all the griefs that harass the distrest,
Sure the most bitter is a scornful jest.'   S. Johnson.

11. *busy loving*, 'officious,' 'fussy.'

hartles, 'cowardly.' Thus the heart is used for courage, Shakespeare, *Lear*, 5, 3, 133 'despite thy valour and thy *heart.*' *Henry IV.* 4, 3, 7 'You speak it out of fear and cold *heart*,' i.e. cowardice.

12. *a selfe-wise-seeming schoolemaster.* The pompous and ignorant pedant is a common object of satire. Sidney himself gave a specimen in his *Lady of the May* in which 'Master Rombus' thus speaks:

'Now the thunder-thumping *Jove* transfund his dotes into your excellent formosity, which have, with your resplendent beams, thus segregated the enmity of these rural animals: I am, *potentissima domina,* a school-master; that is to say, a Pedagogue, one not a little versed in the disciplinating of the juvenile fry, wherein (to my laud I say it) I use such geometrical proportion, as neither wanted mansuetude nor correction: for so it is described

Parcere subjectos et debellire superbos.

Yet hath not the pulchritude of my virtues protected me from the contaminating hands of these Plebeians; for coming, *solum modo,* to have parted their sanguinolent fray, they yielded me no more reverence, than if I had been some *pecorius asinus.* I, even I, that am, who am I? *Dixi; verbus sapiento satum est.* But what said *Trojan Aeneas,* when he sojourned in the surging sulks of the sandiferous seas?

Haec olim memorasse jubebit.'

Shakespeare's Sir Hugh Evans and Holofernes will furnish other speci-
mens.

a awry-transformed Traveller, 'a man corrupted by travel;' a travel-
ler who has adopted foreign manners, dress, etc., and done it wrongly
(More's *Utopia*, ed. Arber, p. 60 'wordes of the lawe or a *wrythen* and
wrested understanding of the same.' Hall's *Satires*, 6, 1, 194 'And
hang'd my head for fear they deeme *awry*').

The writers of the age are full of satire on the travelled Englishman
who aped foreign manners.   Cp. Hall's *Satires*, 3, 1, 63 (1590)

> 'But thou canst maske in garish gauderie
> To suit a fooles far fetched liverie.
> A French head join'd to neck Italian,
> Thy thighs from Germanie, and brest from Spain:
> An Englishman in none, a foole in all,
> Many in one, and one in severall.'

Roger Ascham, *Scholemaster* (ed. Mayor), p. 68, 79 'But I know as
many mo, and sometime very deare frends, for whose sake I hate
going into that countrey the more, who partying out of England fervent
in the love of Christes doctrine and well-furnished with the feare of
God, returned out of Italie wors *transformed* than ever was any in
Circe's Court'...'If you think we judge amisse and write to sore against
you, heare what the Italian sayth of the Englishman, what the master
reporteth of the Scholer: who uttereth playnlie what is taught by him,
and what is learned by you, saying, *Englese Italianato e un diabolo in-
cornato.*' *Euphues* (ed. Arber), p. 314 'How if an English-man be infected
with any mys-demeanour, they say with one mouth hee is Italianated'.
Shakespeare, *Henry VIII.* 1, 3, 18 ...'our travelled gallants That fill
the court with quarrels, talk, and tailors.' *As You Like It*, 4, 1, 33
'Farewell, Monsieur Traveller; look you, lisp, and wear strange suits,
disable all the benefits of your own country, be out of love with your
nativity, and almost chide God for making you that countenance you
are, or I will scarce think you have swam in a gondola.' Chapman,
Monsieur d'Olive, 2, 1

> 'These same travellers
> That can live anywhere, make jests of anything:
> And cast so farre from home, for nothing else
> But to learn how they may cast off their friends.'

13.   *these if we sawe walke in stage names, which wee play naturally,*

'if we saw these characters, which we support in real life, represented on the stage.'

15.   *teaching delightfulnes,* 'pleasure which is also instructive.'

as in the other, i.e. the serious or tragic part of poetry.

the Tragedies of Buchanan, see p. 48, l. 17.

19.   *none so much used in England.* The evidence for the early and extensive use of plays in all parts of England is abundant, beginning with Miracle and Passion plays or Mysteries, going on to Moralities and Interludes, at least as early as the 12th century. These were gradually superseded by the representation of historical and legendary subjects. They were played by wandering players, or by troupes collected and trained in the villages, in churchyards or even churches, village greens, or barns. See the passage quoted on p. 54, l. 10. Cp. Froude, *History of England,* vol. i. p. 71.

'No great general ever arose out of a nation of cowards; no great statesman or philosopher out of a nation of fools; no great artist out of a nation of materialists; no great dramatist except when the drama was the passion of the people. Acting was the especial amusement of the English, from the palace to the village green...The mystery plays came first; next the popular legends; and then the great figures of English History came out upon the stage, or stories from Greek or Roman writers; or sometimes it was an extemporised allegory. Shakespeare himself has left us many pictures of the village drama. Doubtless he had seen many a Bottom in the old Warwickshire hamlets; many a Nathaniel playing "Alissander," and finding himself a little "o'er parted." He had been with Snug the joiner, Quince the carpenter, and Flute the bellows-mender, when a boy, we will not question, and acted with them and written their parts for them.'

See also J. P. Collier, *English Dramatic Poetry and Annals of the Stage,* vol. i. p. 1—64, for the notices of acting in England before the reign of Henry VIII. : and Warton's *History of English Poetry,* vol. 3, p. 292 sq. (ed. Hazlitt). Stubbes, *Anatomy of Abuses* (1583), p. 140—6 sq. (ed. Furnivall) 'Away then with so infamous an art! for goe they never so brave, yet are they counted and taken for beggers. And is it not true? live they not upon begging of everyone that comes? Are they not taken by the lawes of the Realm for rogues and vacabounds? I speake of such as travaile the cuntries with playes and interludes, making an occupation of it, and ought so to be punished, if they had their deserts.'

23.   *Other sorts of Poetry almost have we none.* Sidney seems to

mean of actually living writers, yet he has already mentioned the *Mir-rour for Magistrates* and Spenser's *Shepheardè's Calender*.

24. *Lyricall kind of Songs and Sonnets.*   Mostly in the anthologies, the first of which was *Tottel's Miscellany* (1557): *the Paradise of Dainty Devises* (1576): *A Gorgious Gallery of Gallant Inventions* (1578): *A Handful of Pleasant Delights* (1584).   See Introduction to *England's Helicon*, ed. A. H. Buller.

PAGE 57.

1—7.   Sidney's criticism of the love poetry of the day may be com- **57** pared with that of Hall, *Satires*, 1, 7

> 'The love-sicke poet, whose importune prayer
> Repulsed is with resolute despaire,
> Hopeth to conquer his disdainfull dame
> With publicke plaints of his conceived flame.
> Then powres he forth in patched sonnettings
> His love, his lust, and loathsome flatterings;
> As though the staring world hang'd on his sleeve,
> When once he smiles to laugh; and when he sighs to grieve.
> Careth the world, thou love, thou live, or die?
> Careth the world how faire thy faire one be?'

Sidney refers to the same idea in *Astrophel and Stella*, LIV.

> 'But you, fair maids, at length this true shall find,
>   That love's right badge is but worn in the heart:
> Dumb swans, not charping Pies, do lovers prove.'

But in spite of the truth of these criticisms, the touches of nature, and the perfection of form in many of these lyrics, so far overcome the tedium which the monotony of theme and attitude naturally produces, that we still read many of them with pleasure.

1. *new budding occasions*, 'subject-matter ever fresh.' Shakespeare, *Love's Labour's*, 2, 69 'His eye begets *occasion* for his wit.'

6. *hang together.*   Cp. *Euphues*, p. 248 (ed. Arber) 'In faith, Euphues, thou hast told a long tale; the beginning I have forgotten, the middle I understand not, and the end *hangeth not together.*'

8. *then that in truth they feele those passions.*   Sidney has himself hit the secret of true passion in poetry.   See *Astrophel and Stella*, Sonnet I.

> 'I sought fit words to paint the blackest woe,
>   Studying invention fine her wits to entertain:

S.   II

Oft turning others leaves, to see if thence would flow
   Some fresh and fruitful showers upon my sun-burnt brain.
But words came halting forth, wanting inventions stay,
   Invention, nature's child, fled step-dame study's blows,
And others feet still seem'd but strangers in my way.
   Thus great with child to speak, and helpless in my throws,
Biting my truant pen, beating myself for spite,
   Fool! said my muse to me, *look in thy heart, and write.*'

16. *honny-flowing*, 'mellifluous'. Cp.'melliflui canit oris Homerus,' Boethius, *Consolatio*, v. 2. *Arcadia*, Book I. p. 3 'And yet is nothing, compared to the *honey-flowing* speech that breath doth carry.'

18. *farre fette*, see p. 27, l. 10.

20. *with coursing of a Letter*, i.e. as in acrostics, the initial letter of the several lines spelling some word. For instance in ch. I. of Tusser's *Five-hundred Points of Good Husbandry* (1573), the initial letters of the first 16 verses spell 'Thomas Tusser made me'. So in Tottel's *Miscellany* (ed. Arber), p. 105, the initial letters spell 'Damascene Awdley.'

'D eserts of Nymphs, that áuncient Poets showe,
A r not so kouth as hers: whose present face,
M ore than my Muse, may cause the world to knowe
A nature nobly given: of woorthy race:
S o trayned up, as honour did bestowe.
C yllene in sugerd speech gave her a grace.
E xcell in song Apollo made his dere,
N o fingerfeat Miuerve hid from her sight.
E xprest in look, she hath so soverain chere,

A s Cyprian once breathed on the Spartan bright.
W it, wisdom, will, woord, work and all, I ween,
D are nomans pen presume to paint outright,
L o luyster and light: which if old time had seen,
E ntroned shyne she should, with goddesse Fame.
Y eeld, Envie, these due prayses to this dame.'

But this was not the only way of 'coursing a letter,' cp. Puttenham, *Arte of English Poesie* (ed. Arber), p. 30 'The posteritie taking pleasure in this manner of Simphonie had leasure as it seemes to devise many other knackes in their versifying that the auncient and civill poets had not used before, whereof one was to make every word of a verse to begin with the same letter, as did Hugobald the Monke, who made a large poem to the honour of *Carolus Calvus*, every word beginning with C. which was the first letter of the king's name, thus:

Carmina clarisonae Calvis cantate camenae.

And this was thought no small peece of cuning.' In *Notes and Queries*
III. 7, 43 a poem is quoted in which only one vowel occurs. So G.
Harvey, vol. I. p. 18, in a letter to Spenser talks of 'hunting the letter'
when writing a string of alliterative adjectives.

22. *with figures and flowers*, with the lines so arranged as to
form some figure, such as a flower, an altar, or wings. In the Greek
Anthology, Book xv. we have thus a Pandean pipe or syrinx (21), a
pyramid (27), an axe (22), wings (24), and an altar (25 and 26). In a
collection of Poems published at Dôle in 1592 (*Sylvae quas vario carmi-
num genere primarii Scholastici Collegii Dolani S. J., in publica totius
civitatis gratulatione laetitiaque extempore obtulerunt*), there are Greek
and Latin poems in the shape of wings, altars, spectacles, circles,
angles and triangles. *Notes and Queries*, VI. 3, 146, 297. Thus, too,
number 13 of George Herbert's Poems is arranged as two Easter Wings.
G. Puttenham gives a regular scheme of rules for this sort of composi-
tion. *Arte of English Poesie* (ed. Arber), p. 104

'Your last proportion is that of figure, so called because it yelds an
ocular representation, your meeters by good symmetrie reduced into
certain Geometricall figures, whereby the maker is restrained to keep
him within bounds and sheweth not onely more art, but serveth also
much better for briefnesse and subtiltie of devise.' He then goes on to
give the forms thus used: 'the Lozange called Rhombus, the Fuzie or
spindle called Rhemboides, the Triangle called Tricquet, the Square or
quadrangle, the Pillaster or Cillinder, the Spire or taper called piramis,
the Rondel or sphere, the Egge or figure Ovall, the tricquet reversed,
the tricquet displayed, the Taper reversed, the rondel displayed, the
Lozange reversed, the Egg displayed, the Lozange rabbated.' He gives
diagrams of all these and some specimens. Of them all he prefers the
'Piller, Pillaster or Cillinder;' of which his specimen is here given:

'The Piller is a figure among all the rest of the Geometricall most
beawtifull, in respect that he is tall and vpright and of one bignesse
from the bottom to the toppe. In Architecture he is considered with
two accessarie parts, a pedestall or base, and a chapter or head, the
body is the shaft. By this figure is signified stay, support, rest, state
and magnificence, your dittie then being reduced into the forme of the
Piller, his base will require to beare the breath of a meetre of six or
seuen or eight sillables: the shaft of foure: the chapter egall with the

base, of this proportion I will giue you one or two examples which may suffise :

Her Maiestie resembled to the crown-
ed piller.   Ye must read vpward.

    Is blisse with immortalitie.
    Her trymest top of all ye see,
      Garnish the crowne
      Her iust renowne
      Chapter and head,
      Part that maintain
      And   womanhead
      Her mayden raigne
      In te gri tie :
      In ho nour and
      With ve ri tie :
      Her roundnes stand
      Strengthen the state.
      By their increase
      With out de bate
      Concord and peace
      Of her sup port,
      They be the base
      With   stedfastnesse
      Vertue and grace
      Stay and comfort
      Of Albi ons rest,
      The sounde Pillar
      And seene a farre
      Is plainely exprest
    Tall stately and strayt
    By this no ble pour trayt

Philo to the Lady Calia, sendeth this
Odolet of her prayse in forme of a Pil-
ler, which ye must read downeward.

    Thy princely port and Maiestie
    Is my   terrene dei tie,
      Thy wit and sence
      The streame & source
      Of e lo quence
      And deepe discours,
      The faire eyes are
      My bright loadstarre,
      Thy speache a darte
      Percing my harte,
      Thy face a las,
      My loo king glasse,
      Thy loue ly lookes
      My prayer bookes,
      Thy pleasant cheare
      My sunshine cleare,
      Thy ru full sight
      My darke midnight,
      Thy will the stent
      Of my con tent,
      Thy glo rye flour
      Of myne ho nour,
      Thy loue doth giue
      The lyfe I lyue,
      Thy lyfe it is
      Mine earthly blisse :
    But grace & fauour in thine eies
    My bodies soule & souls paradise.'

30. *Nizolian Paperbookes,* i.e. note-books with collections of phrases, such as the *Thesaurus Ciceronianus* of Marius Nizolius, first published under the title of *Observationes in M. Tullium Ciceronem* in 1535. Of the keeping of such books see Roger Ascham, *Scholemaster* (ed. Mayor), p. 153. Erasmus is said to have compiled from Cicero an Alphabetical Dictionary of each occurrence of every word, with its context, another of every phrase, and an index of the metrical feet used at the beginning, middle, or end of periods or clauses, with the variations of rhythms according to the sense.

Marius Nizolius was born at Brescello in the Duchy of Modena, in 1498; gave lectures in Rhetoric at Parma, and was afterwards Principal of the University of Sabionetta. Besides his Ciceronian thesaurus he wrote on Cicero's philosophy, *de veris principiis et vera ratione philoso-phandi,* re-edited by Leibnitz in 1670.

31. *figures.* In the grammatical or rhetorical sense, such as zeugma, hypallage, aposiopesis, etc. a list of which is given by Putten-ham at the end of his book. Cp. Elyot's *Governour* (ed. Croft), vol. 1, p. 55 'And what doubt is there but so may he as some speak good latin as he may do pure frenche, which nowe is broughte into as many rules and *fiugres*, and as long a grammar as is latine or greke.'

PAGE 58.

1. *like those Indians.* See Hakluyt's *Voyages* (ed. 1600), p. 369 'At the ende of these four dayes I entred into a valley very well inhabited by people. At the first village there met me many men and women with victuals, and all of them had Turqueses hanging at their nostrils and eares.'

2. *at the fit and naturall place.* But, after all, rings in the ears are no more 'fit and natural' than in the nose. In both cases the propriety is the result of convention.

6. *Vivit,* &c. Cicero, *in Catil.* 1, § 2 'O tempora, O mores! Senatus haec intelligit, consul videt: hic tamen vivit. Vivit? immo vero in senatum venit,' etc.

13. *similiter cadences.* Applied first to rhyme in poetry. Puttenham, p. 93 'This *cadence* is the fal of a verse in every last word with a certain tunable sound which being matched with another of like sound do make a concord.' For its use in oratory he says, p. 27 'Yea their Oratours' proses nor the Doctours' Sermon's were acceptable to Princes nor yet to the common people unlesse it went in manner of tunable rime or metricall sentences, as appears by many of the auncient writers, about that time and since.'

15. *dainteness,* cp. p. 54, l. 22.

16. *Sophister.* A University term for students of a certain standing to dispute in the schools. Cp. Pope, *Dunciad,*

> 'Three College *Sophs,* and three pert Templars came,
> The same their talents, and their tastes the same.'

17. *would prove two eggs three.* The story has been often repeated in various forms as a satire on logical quibbling. I find it quoted recently in the following form, with glasses of wine instead of eggs:

A conceited young scholar from Oxford, drinking with two gentlemen, must needs be forming syllogisms. He bade them fill two glasses, which they did. 'Now,' said he, 'I will prove those two glasses to be three. Thus: is not one here?' 'Yes,' says one. 'And here another; that's two,' says he. 'Yes,' says the other gentleman. 'Why then,' says the scholar, 'one and two are three; so 'tis done.' 'Very well,' says one, 'I'll have one glass, and my friend here shall have the other, and you shall have the third for your pains in finding it out.' Perhaps this story (with eggs) accounts for a phrase in R. Robinson's translation of More's *Utopia* (ed. Arber), p. 56 'Another comes in with his five eggs,' i.e. with subtle and specious proposals.

21. *fineness*, 'ingenuity,' 'subtlety.' Shakespeare, *All's Well*, 5, 3, 270 'Thou art too *fine* in thy evidence.' *Troilus*, 1, 3, 209 'Those that with the *fineness* of their souls by reason guide his execution.'

24. *all Herbarists, all stories of Beasts, Foules, and Fishes.* Sidney seems here to be referring distinctly first to Gosson's *Schoole of Abuse*, and secondly to Lyly's *Euphues*. In both these works the trick of piling up a series of illustrations from a curious and wonderful natural history is conspicuous. For instance, in the first page of the *Schoole of Abuse* we have: 'The Scarabe flies over many a swete flower and lights in a cowshard: It is the custome of the flye to leave the sound places of a horse and suck at the botch: the nature of *Colloqueritida*, to draw the worst humours to itselfe: the manner of swine to forsake the fayre fieldes, and wallow in the myre'—and all this to express the iniquity of the Poets in 'dispersing theyr poison through the world.' So *Euphues* (ed. Arber), p. 110:

'Thinke this with thyself that the sweete songs of Calipso were subtile swans to entice Ulisses; that the crab then catcheth the oyster when the sun shineth; that Hiena, when she speaketh like a man, deviseth most mischiefe; that women when they be most pleasant pretend most treacherie.' 'In the Euphues,' says Jusserand, 'the similes are for the most part borrowed from an imaginary natural history, a sort of mythology of plants and stones, to which the most extraordinary virtues are attributed.' *The English Novel in the time of Shakespeare*, p. 107.

PAGE 59.

59   2. *Antonius and Crassus. Marcus Antonius* (grandfather of the Triumvir) was born B.C. 145, celebrated a triumph over the Cilician pirates in B.C. 102, was Consul in B.C. 99, Censor B.C. 97. He belonged to the Aristocratic party, and was more than once accused of bribery and other crimes, and was finally put to death by Marius in B.C. 87. Cicero speaks of him as one of the greatest Roman orators, and makes him one of the interlocutors in the dialogue *de Oratore*.

P. Licinius Crassus Dives Mucianus, son of P. Mucius Scaevola, but adopted by P. Licinius Crassus, was born in B.C. 175, Consul B.C. 175, and Pontifex Maximus. He was celebrated as an orator and jurist. Of him Gellius says that he possessed five of the greatest advantages of life, 'he was very rich, very high born, very eloquent, a very excellent jurist, and Pontifex Maximus.'   He was killed near Smyrna B.C. 131 in a war against Aristonicus, who opposed the Roman occupation of Pergamus.

4. *as Cicero testifieth of them.* See *de Orat.* lib. ii. § 1 'Opinio fuit L. Crassum non plus attigisse doctrinae, quam quantum prima illa puerili institutione potuisset; M. autem Antonium omnino omnis eruditionis expertem atque ignarum fuisse.'

5. *not to set by it*, 'not to value it,' cp. 1 Sam. xviii. 30 'David behaved himself more wisely than the servants of Saul, so that his name was much *set by*.' More's *Utopia* (ed. Arber), p. 58 'That their lawes were had in contempt and nothing *set by* or regarded.'
Skelton, *Dyties Solacions*

> 'Wyth bound and rebound, bounsyngly take up
>   Hys jentyll curtoyl, and *set nought by* small naggys.'

id. Magnyfycence, v. 295

> 'In fayth, I *set not by* the world two Douncaste cuttys.'

Ps. xv. 4 (P. B.) 'He that *setteth not by* himself.'

9. *knacks*, 'trick,' 'ornaments,' properly of dress, and so of oratory.
Bullen's *Lyrics*, p. 129

> 'Some do long for pretty *knacks*
>   And some for strange devices
> God send me what my lady lacks
>   I care not what the price is.'

Stubbes' *Anatomy of Abuses* (ed. Furnivall), p. 53

'And these sheets (sometimes it happeneth) are wrought throughout with necle work of silk, and suche like, and curiouslie stitched with open seame, and many other *knackes* besydes, mo than I can describe.'

Gosson, *Straunge newes out Affrick* (ed. Arber), p. 63 'There is ever a new *knack* in a knaves hood, or some kind of monster to be seen in Affrik.'
G. Chapman, *Caesar and Pompey*, Act 2, Sc. 1

> 'As if good clothes were *knacks* to know a knave.'

Puttenham, p. 30 'they had leasure, as it seemes to devise many other *knackes* in their versifying.' (Cp. our *knick-knack*. Skeat connects it with Gael. *cnac*, Irish, *cnag*, 'a crack,' Welsh, *cnec*, 'a snap,' and says it meant (1) a snap, (2) a snap with the finger, (3) a jester's trick, (4) a joke, trifle, or toy.)

14. *smally*, 'little.' R. Ascham, *Scholemaster*, p. 6 (ed. Mayor) 'But now commonlie, in the best Scholes of England, for wordes right choice is *smallie* regarded.'

Stubbes' *Anatomy of Abuses* (ed. Furnivall), p. 24 'But how little this esteemed of, and how *smally* regarded, to consider, it greeveth me to the very harte, and there is almost no life in mee.'

20. *to hide Art.* 'Ars est celare artem,' a proverb which does not appear to occur in any classical author. The nearest is Ovid, *A. A.* 2, 313 'si latet ars prodest.' Cp. Puttenham, *Arte of English Poesie* (ed. Arber), p. 308 'We doe allow our Courtly Poet to be a dissembler only in the subtilties of his arte; that is, when he is most artificial, so to disguise and cloak it, as it may not appeare, nor seeme to proceede from him by any studie or trade of rules, but to be his natural.'

22. *deserve to be pounded.* The 'pound' (A. S. *pund*, 'an enclosure') maintained formerly in each village for strayed cattle.

24. *wordish consideration*, see p. 57, l. 15.

31. *awry*, 'out of the straight,' 'wrong,' see note on p. 56, l. 12.

PAGE 60.

60   4. *it wanteth Grammer.* It is not of course true that English is without grammar, or these differences of cases, &c., as Sidney says: though the tendency of an analytical language is to get rid of them to a great extent. The earliest treatise on English grammar seems not to have been published till some time after Sidney's death, when appeared in Cambridge, printed by J. Legatt (1594), a Latin treatise, *Grammatica Anglicana praecipue quatenus a Latina differt ad unicam P. Rami methodum concinnata, in qua perspicue docetur quicquid ad hujus linguae cognitionem requiritur.* There was also an appendix of *vocabula Chauceriana quaedam selectiva.*

9. *a peece of the tower of Babilons curse.* The tower of Babel is thus called from a notion that it was part of Babylon, Gen. xi. 4. For *peece*, see p. 2, l. 3.

13. *that hath it equally with any other tongue in the world.* The capability of English for the purposes of poetry it had been the fashion to depreciate in comparison with Latin. Elyot's *Governour* (ed. Croft), vol. I. p. 129 'I could recite a great nombre of semblable good sentences out of these and other wanton poets (Ovid, Martial, &c.), who in the latine do expresse them incomparably with more grace and delectation to the reder than our Englishe tonge may yet comprehende.' And

Puttenham, *Arte of English Poesie* (ed. Arber), p. 21, finds it necessary to start by asserting 'our language being no less pithie and significative than theirs'...'our language admitting no fewer rules and nice diversities than theirs' (i.e than the Greeks and Romans)...'Poesie therefore may be an Art in our vulgar, and that verie methodicall and commendable.'

Webbe, Preface to *A discourse on English Poetry* (ed. Arber), p. 19 'But is our speeche so course, or our phrase so harshe, that poetry cannot therein finde a vayne whereby it may appear like it selfe? Why should we think so basely of this?'

Such was the depreciation of English as compared with the classical languages. But it was also decried in comparison with the modern European languages.

'According to some, travelling increased in a certain number of Englishmen, the tendency to feel contempt towards their mother tongue. "There are persons," wrote George Pettie in 1581, "who will set light by my labours, because I write in English: and there are some nice travellers who returne home with such quaesie stomachs that nothing will downe with them but French, Italian or Spanish...they count our tongue barren: they count it barbarous, they count it unworthy to be accounted of."' Jusserand, *English novel in the time of Shakespeare*, p. 72.

13. *in compositions of two or three words together.* Sidney's own practice in this respect will not perhaps always commend itself to a modern reader. For a list of the *compound words* used by him in this essay, see Index. The critics of the next generation looked upon the use of these compounds as a fashion introduced by Sidney in his *Arcadia.* See Hall, *Satires*, VI, 255

> 'He knows the grace of that new eloquence
> Which sweet *Philistides* fetch'd of late from France,
> That well beseem'd his high-styled Arcady;
> Though others marr'd it with much liberty,
> In epithets to joyne two words in one,
> Forsooth, for adjectives cannot stand alone:
> As a great poet could of Bacchus say
> That he was Semele-femori-genita.'

It has generally been supposed that this habit was ridden to death by Lyly in his *Euphues* (1579). But the English of that book to me at least appears singularly pure and melodious. The marked peculiarity of it, which tends to weary the reader, is not its language, but the habit of piling up illustrations from a fanciful natural history, which has been spoken of before. Still the imitators of Sidney and Lyly no doubt made themselves ridiculous, and helped to bring ridicule on their supposed models. Hence we have de Armado's letter in *Love's Labour's Lost,* and the far grosser exaggeration of Scott's Sir Percy Shafton.

21. *with some regarde of the accent.* It was the insufficient regard to accent that makes much of the early English poetry rough and unpleasing. George Puttenham's ch. viii. bk. ii. in the *Art of English Poesie* is headed, 'How the good maker will not wrench his word to help his time, either by *falsifying his accent* or by untrue orthographie.' W. Webbe, preface to *A discourse on English Poetrie,* p. 19 'If English poetry were truely reformed, and some perfect platforme or Prosodia of versifying were by them ratifyd or sette downe: eyther in immitation of Greekes or Latines, or, where it would scant abyde the touch of theyr Rules, the like observations selected and established by the natural affectation of the speech.'

23. *Ryme* or *rime.* A. S. *rim,* 'number,' it is misspelt *rhyme* from confusion with 'rhythm' ($\dot{\rho}\nu\theta\mu\dot{o}s$ 'flow'). This mistake puzzled William Webbe, *A discourse of English Poetrie* (ed. Arber), p. 56 'The falling out of verses together in one like sounde, is commonly called in English, Ryme, taken from the Greeke word $Pv\theta\mu os$, which surely in my judgment is very abusively applyed to such a sence: and by thys, the unworthinesse of the thing may well appeare, in that wanting a proper name, wherby to be called, it borroweth a word farre exceeding the dignitye of it, and not appropriate to so rude or base a thing.' Puttenham, ch. vi. more correctly defines rithme as 'numerosity,' and connects it with $\dot{a}\rho\iota\theta\mu\dot{o}s$, but does not appear to distinguish the derivation of ryme and rhythm. 'The error contained in the spelling *rhyme* does not occur before 1550.' Skeat.

26. *lively,* as adv., cp. Shakespeare, *Gentlemen of Verona,* 4, 4, 174 'which I so *lively* acted.'

PAGE 61.

61   3. *sweet slyding,* Puttenham, *Arte of English Poesie* (ed. Arber), p. 91 'This point grew by the smooth and delicate running of their feete, which we have not in our vulgare, though we use as much as may be the most flowing words and slippery sillables.'

4. *The French, in his whole language,* &c. See Brachet's *Dictionary,* Introduction, p. LII., speaking of the fundamental laws for the transformation of Latin into French: 'In words accented on the ante-

penult, as *orácula, tábula, artículus, durábilis,* the penultimate vowel is necessarily short in Latin; this vowel was scarcely sounded at all: the refined Roman may have given it a slight sound, but the grosser popular voice neglected altogether such delicate shades of pronunciation.   In all the remains of popular Latin that have come down to us (the graffiti of Pompeii, inscriptions, epitaphs, &c.), the short penultimate is already gone: we find *oraclum, tabla, postus, moblis, vincre, suspendre;* and when this common Latin passed into French the words thus contracted became *oracle, table, poste, meuble, vaincre, suspendre.*   Indeed by the *law which forbids the French language to throw the accent farther back than the penultimate syllable,* it was compelled, if it would retain the Latin accent in its proper place in words formed from *oráculum, tábula,* &c., to suppress the short *u* of the penultimate, and to say *oracle, table,* &c.'

9.   *ryme* here = ' rhythm.'

10.   *the accent,* see p. 60, l. 21.

12.   *caesura.*   The pause at some point in a verse secured by dividing a foot between the last syllable of one word and the first of the next: as

> And all the wind | y clamour of the daws.

16.   *the Italian cannot put in the last silable.*   The Italian rhyme is on the *two* last syllables.   For example:

> 'Ecco la notte e' l cielo tutto s' imb*runa*
>
> E gli alti monti le contrade adomb*rano,*
>
> Le stelle n' accompagno e la *luna*
>
> E le mie pecorello il bosco sgomb*rano*
>
> Insieme ragunate, che ben *sanno*
>
> Il tempo, e l' ora che la mandra ingomb*rano*.'
>
> (Sanazarro).

The French use alternately the masculine and female rhyme, but the *e* mute is taken to constitute the female; as

> 'Sans habits, sans argent, ne sachant plus que *faire,*
>
> Vient de s'enfuir, chargé de sa seule mis*ére.*
>
> Et, bien loin des sergents, des clercs, et du pal*ais,*
>
> Va chercher un repos qu'il ne trouva jam*ais.*'
>
> (Boileau.)

19.   *Sdrucciola,* 'slippery,' 'sliding' syllable, a term applied to tri-syllable rhyme.   The *Sdrucciola sillaba* or *sdruecciolo verso* is defined by Alberti thus: Versi sdruccioli, quellé che dopo l' ultimo accento hanno piu sillabi brevi, 'short syllables after the last accent,' as

'Dico gli antichi: quasi l' onor debbia
D' esse il loro oscurár, come il sol nebbia.'

(Arioso.)

Cp. G. Chapman, *All Fooles*, Act II. sc. 1

'I could have written as good Prose and verse,
As the most beggarlie Poet of em all,
Either accrostique, *Exordion,*
Epithalamions, Satyres, Epigrams,
Sonnets in Doozens, or your *Quatorzaines*
In any Rime Masculine, Feminine,
Or Sdruciolla or cooplets, Blancke Verse.'

PAGE 62.

62   2. *toy*, 'trifle'. Shakespeare, *Two Gentlemen*, 1, 2, 82 'Set as little by such *toys* as possible.' Cp. p. 32, l. 18.

7. *beleeve with Aristotle, that they were the auncient Treasurers of the Græcians Divinity.* No passage in Aristotle is exactly reproduced by this sentence. In the *Metaphysics*, A. 3. 983^b, Aristotle says of poets that they were πρῶτοι θεολογήσαντες, 'first who formulated accounts of the gods.' Sidney, I fancy, was quoting second-hand from Landin (whom he mentions immediately afterwards). See in *P. Virgilii Maronis allegorias*, p. 1 'Qua quidem re Aristotelem, virum excellenti ingenio et doctrina post Platonem omnino singulari, motum crediderim, ut eosdem priscis temporibus Theologos poetasque fuisse affirmet.' 'And this caused Aristotle, I believe, to affirm that in primitive times Theologians and Poets were the same.'

8. *Bembus*, see p. 48, l. 16.

9. *civilitie*, 'civilisation,' 'culture,' as opposed to barbarism; see Puttenham, p. 206, quoted at p. 3, l. 18.

10. *with Scaliger*, in his *Poetics*, see p. 36, l. 3.

12. *Clauserus, the Translator of Cornutus. Lucius Annaeus Cornutus* was b. at Leptis in Africa, and coming to Rome as a slave was manumitted by some member of the family of the Annaei. He flourished in the reign of Nero, by whom he was banished in A.D. 68. He was the instructor of the poets Persius and Lucan. His chief works seem to have been commentaries on Aristotle; but he also wrote a grammatical commentary on Virgil. The only works of his which are even partially extant are two treatises, Ἑλληνικὴ θεολογία, and περὶ τῆς τοῦ θεοῦ φύσεως. This last was published at Basle with a Latin translation by *Clau-*

serus (Conrad Clauser, of Zurich) apparently in 1543: *Cornuti sive Phurnuti de Natura deorum gentilium commentarius e graeco in latinam conversus per Conradum Clauserum Tigurinum.* It is from the Preface to this work that Sidney is quoting (p. 2):

'Nec hi (philosophi) sane primi hanc docendi viam invenerunt, etiam docti omnes qui temporibus priscis floruerunt eandem observaverunt, istis que in censu quasi per manus successione mutua lampada tradiderunt. Et qui illi? Hesiodus, Homerus, a quibus initium omnis humana philosophia sumpsit, et per quos SUPREMO NOMINI eam divulgari placuit, philosophiae praecepta nobis sub fabularum velamento representant. Quaeris dialecticam, imo logicam, id est totum disserendi rationem? eam reperies in poetarum fabulis. Quaeris physicam seu naturalem philosophiam? Ea prodit quam pulcherrime, veluti e thalamo pulchrè exornato, e poetarum fabulis. Quaeris Ethicam, id est moralem philosophiam cum suis partibus? Eam largissimam in poetarum fabulis reperies.'

18. *Landin.* Cristofero Landino (1424—1504) was born in Florence, and was protected and favoured by Cosmo and Pietro de Medici, and appointed by the latter tutor to his famous son Lorenzo. His works were, I. *Disputationes Camuldulenses* (1475—1480), a series of dialogues supposed to be held between Landino, his brother, Lorenzo and Giuliano de Medici, and Leo Battista Alberti in a monastery in the wood of Camaldoli. It is in four Books: (1) *De vita activa et contemplativa.* (2) *De summo bono.* (3) and (4) *In Publii Virgilii Maronis allegorias* (2nd edit., Strasburg, 1508). II. Latin Poems, notes on Virgil, Horace and Dante. For this last he was rewarded by the public donation of a villa on the hill of Casentino near Florence. See Roscoe's *Life of Lorenzo de Medici*, pp. 91, 98, 241, 247 (ed. 1875). The passage in Landin to which Sidney refers seems to be from the part of his *disputationes* devoted to Virgil (p. 3003 in Hortensius' Virgil, 1577), 'quam quidem rem divinam potius quam humanam esse cui potius quam Platoni crediderim? Ille enim in Ione dicit poesim non arte humana tradi, sed *divino furore* nostras mentes irrepere.' 'For Plato says in the Ion that poesy is not taught by human art, but finds its way into our minds by a *divine fury.*'

28. *Libertino patre natus.* Horace, *Sat.* 1, 6, 45 'nunc ad me redeo libertino patre natum.'

Herculea proles, 'descendant of Hercules,' i.e. royal, as were the royal families of Sparta.

30. *si quid*, &c. Virgil, *Aen.* 9, 446.

31. *with Dantes Beatrix*, i.e. in Paradise. *With Virgils Anchises*, i.e. in the Elysian fields.

PAGE 63.

63   1. *the dull making Cataract.* In Cicero's *Somnium Scipionis*, c. v. he speaks of the music of the spheres. 'Hoc sonitu oppletae aures hominum obsurduerunt.   Nec est ullus hebetior sensus in vobis, sicut, ubi Nilus ad illa, quae Catadupa nominantur, praecipitatur ex altissimis montibus, ea gens, quae illum locum adcolit, *propter magnitudinem sonitus sensu audiendi caret.*' Seneca, *Naturales Quaest.* 4, 2, § 5, says that a tribe settled near the Cataracts of the Nile were so deafened by the noise that they had to be removed to a quieter place.

2. *Plannet-like Musick.* The 'Musick of the Spheres' produced by the rotation of the Planets, each planet giving a note higher than that next it, and the seven spanning the whole octave, was a doctrine of Pythagoras. See Plato, *Republ.* x. 617. It is explained by Cicero, *Somnium Scipionis*, c. v.; and, though early discredited, was more or less discussed and maintained in the 16th century.

Shakespeare, *M. of Venice*, 5, 1, 58
> 'Look how the floor of heaven
> Is thick inlaid with patines of pure gold:
> There's not the smallest orb which thou beholdst
> But in his motion like an angel sings,
> Still quiring to the young-eyed cherubin.'

Antony and Cleopatra, 5, 2, 84
> 'His voice was propertied
> As all the tuned spheres.'

Job xxxviii. 7 'The morning stars sang together.'

Sir Thomas Browne, *Religio Medici*, pt. ii. p. 111 (ed. Greenhill), says: 'For there is a musick where ever there is a harmony, order, or proportion; and thus far we may maintain the music of the Sphears; for those well-ordered motions, and regular paces, though they give no sound into the ear, yet to the understanding they strike a note most full of harmony.'

Pope, *Essay on Man*, i. 202
> 'If nature thunder'd in his op'ning ears
> And stunn'd him with the music of the spheres,

> How would he wish that heaven had left him still
> The whisp'ring zephyr, and the purling rill?'

In his note to this last passage Mr Mark Pattison has collected many illustrative passages.

5. *such a* Mome, *as to be a Momus of Poetry.* The two words are identical, but are used differently. A *mome* is a 'stupid person.'

Spenser, *F. Q.* VII. 6, **49**

> 'Yet he poore soule! with patience all did beare;
> For nought against their evils might countervaile:
> Ne ought he said, whaever he did heare
> But hanging down his head did as a *Mome* appear.'

Shakespeare, *Comedy of Errors*, III. 1, 35 '*Mome*, malt-horse, capon, coxcomb, idiot, patch!'

Also a sulky disagreeable person. Bullen's *Lyrics* (Nic. Breton), p. 89

> 'Now Xmas draweth near, and most men make good cheer,
>   With heigh-ho care away!
> I like a sickly *mome*, in drowsy dumps at home
>   Will naught but fast and pray.'

But *Momus* (Greek μῶμος, 'blame,' 'ridicule') is personified in Hesiod's Theogeny (214) as the son of Night. Hence he is used for the impersonification of the *critical* spirit.

Cp. Rainolde, *Overthrow of Stage Plays* (1593), p. 2 'Although I confess myself to have written those things, which those who speak are stained with *Momus'* name by you.' Id. p. 39 'For what is the discipline of *Momus* but the school of carping, nipping, depraving and reprehending of every good thing?'

6. *the Asses eares of Midas.* Midas was a king of Phrygia, whose enormous wealth was the subject of numerous legends (Ovid, *Metam.* XI. 90). The story was that, being chosen as one of the judges to decide between the musical abilities of Apollo and Marsyas, he differed from the other judges in awarding the prize to Marsyas. Apollo to punish him changed his ears into those of an ass. He hid them under his Phrygian cap from everyone but his barber; who was so oppressed by the secret, that he dug a hole and whispered it to the earth. But by and by reeds grew up from the hole, which as they waved in the wind pronounced the words 'Midas has asses' ears.' Ovid, *Metam.* XI. 146.

8. *Bubonax.* Sidney is referring to the tale of Hipponax (an

Iambic poet of Ephesus about B.C. 500), of whom one story was that he satirized the statuary *Bupalus* so bitterly that he hanged himself. By some confusion of mind or printer he has combined the two names *Hipponax* and *Bupalus* into 'Bubonax.' A similar story is told of Archilochus and the daughter of Lycambes.

8. *rimed to death, as is sayd to be doone in Ireland.* He seems to refer to the supposed power of the bards, of whom the Irish peasants had a superstitious fear. See Hardiman's *Irish Minstrelsy*, p. 358 'To the present day the rural Irish dread nothing so much as the satirical severity of their bards.' Ib. Introd. p. xxxv. 'Among the ancient Irish, the principal species of musical composition was termed *Avantri-reach*. It consisted of three parts: *Geautraighe*, which excited to love; *Goltraighe*, which stimulated to valour and feats of arms; and *Suan-traighe*, which disposed to rest and sleep.' For the Irish Bards, see on p. 5, l. 2. This power of rhyme in Ireland is alluded to in Shakespeare *As You Like It*, 3, 2, 185 'I was never so be-rhymed since Pythagoras' time, that I was an Irish rat.'

GLOSSARIAL INDEX.

[The references are by pages and lines of the text. Two dates after a name are those of birth and death, unless otherwise notified.]

Abiders 'men able to hold out' (A.-S. *ábídan* 'to wait'), **1**, 17

ab ovo, quotation from Horace, 'from the egg,' i.e. from the earliest point in a story, **53**, 25

Abraham, the Patriarch, **19**, 24; **41**, 5

absolute (Lat. *absolutus*) 'perfect,' **12**, 14; **41**, 5

abuse (Lat. *abusus*) 'corruption,' **30**, 6; **37**, 19; **40**, 10; **41**, 9, 31; **45**, 23

abuse, to, 'to misuse,' 'to corrupt,' **40**, 7, 30; **41**, 11; **45**, 19; **47**, 24; **56**, 20; **59**, 21

Academie of Plato, **15**, 16

accent in modern verse, **60**, 21

accomplish, to (Lat. *ad complere*), 'to attain to fully,' **19**, 17

accomplished 'finished,' 'perfect' **23**, 12

accord, to (L. L. *accordare*, O. F. *acorder*, Lat. *cor* 'a heart'), 'to reconcile,' **15**, 5

actors and players of nature, **7**, 26

Adam, **9**, 27

admiration (Lat. *admiratio*), 'astonishment,' **1**, 13

Adrian, Roman emperor (A.D. 76—138), **48**, 12

advocate, long gown of, **12**, 21

Aeneas, **9**, 4; **20**, 31—2; **21**, 6; **25**, 30; **32**, 28; **33**, 11; **40**, 5

affectation (Lat. *affectare*), **57**, 18

affects 'feelings' (Lat. *afficio*), **31**, 4

Affrick 'Africa,' **44**, 4; **52**, 14

after-livers 'posterity,' **29**, 12

Agamemnon, **18**, 17, 24

Agincourt, battle of (1415), **15**, 18

Agrippa, Menenius (Roman Consul B.C. 501), **27**, 4

Agrippa, Henry Cornelius, German writer (1486—1535), **35**, 17, 21

Ajax, **18**, 15

Albinus, Clodius, Roman officer (about A.D. 160—197), **6**, 6

Albion, ancient name of Britain, **42**, 9

Alcibiades, Athenian statesman (ob. B.C. 404), **20**, 20

Alexander the Great (B.C. 356—323), **21**, 10; **29**, 10; **43**, 9, 12; **46**, 32; **55**, 21

Alexander, tyrant of Pherae (ob. B.C. 359), **31**, 11

aloes, as a medicine, **25**, 25

Alphonsus, Alphonzo king of Aragon (1385—1458), **15**, 28

Amadis de Gaule, **26**, 9

Amphion, **3**, 16; **10**, 21

Amphitrio, 'Amphitruo' father of Hercules. Title of a play of Plautus, **54**, 20

anatomie (Gk. ἀνὰ- τέμνειν 'to cut up) 'analysis,' 'close examination,' **13**, 2

Anchises, **18**, 11; **26**, 13

anger, a short madness, **18**, 14

anticks (Fr. *antique.* Lat. *antiquus*) 'tricks,' **55**, 23

Juvenal quoted, **49**, 23; **56**, 9

Katholou, Kathekaston (καθ' ὅλου, καθ' ἕκαστον), 'universal,' 'particular,' **20**, 15—17
kennell (O. F. *chenil*, F. *chien.*, Lat. *canis*), **23**, 29
kinde, those, **35**, 7
knacks, 'tricks,' 'fanciful ornaments,' **59**, 9 (Welsh *Cnec*, 'a snap')

Lacedaemonians, inhabitants of Sparta and Laconia, **32**, 8
Landin, 'Cristofero Landino,' an Italian writer (1424—1504), **62**, 18
language, capability of the English, **59**, 32
larded, 'trimmed,' 'ornamented,' **40**, 12
larges, 'largess,' 'liberal distribution,' **14**, 19 (Lat. *largitio*)
Latine, 'Latin,' **43**, 29
laudes, 'praises' (Lat. *laus*), **31**, 28
layde upon, 'quoted against,' 'opposed to,' **44**, 9
Lazarus, **19**, 20, 23
learning, definition of, **13**, 4—7; its obligation to poetry, **2**, 25 sqq.; a chaine shot against, **42**, 11
Lelius, 'Caius Laelius,' Roman jurist and statesman (b. B.C. 186), **47**, 1
libertino patre natus, 'son of a freed-man,' **62**, 28
Linus, **3**, 8
literas nescivit, 'he knew not literature,' **23**, 22
lively, adv. 'in a lively manner,' **60**, 26
Livie, T. Livius, Roman historian (B.C. 59—A.D. 17), **60**, 26
Livius Andronicus, Roman dramatist (about B.C. 240), **3**, 19
loden, 'laden,' **1**, 11; **15**, 1
Lucan, M. Annaeus Lucanus, Roman poet (A.D. 39—65), **11**, 1
Lucrecia, wife of Collatinus, **11**, 15
Lucretius, T. Lucretius Carus,

Roman poet (B.C. 95—55), **10**, 30
lute, a stringed musical instrument like a guitar. The word is said to be of Arabian origin, cp. Portuguese *alaude*, (Skeat), **15**, 24
lyricke, the, 'the Lyric poet' (lyra, 'a lyre'), **31**, 23

Macedon, **32**, 19
maister, 'master' (Fr. *maître*, Lat. *magister*), **1**, 16; **2**, 16
make, to, 'to compose poetry,' **11**, 26
maker, a 'poet,' **7**, 19; **9**, 17, 21; **48**, 6
Manilius, Roman astronomical poet (1st cent. A.D.), **10**, 32
many formed, 'manifold,' 'various,' **13**, 12
Marathon, battle of (B.C. 490), **15**, 18
margent, 'margin,' (Lat. *margo*), **25**, 14
Marius, Caius, Roman general (B.C. 157—86), **23**, 15
Mars, god of war, **49**, 6
Mary, 'marry,' 'by Mary', **42**, 9; **50**, 3
masculine ryme, **61**, 17
masking rayment 'disguise' or 'clothing assumed' as in a masque, **26**, 24
mathematickes, the, **13**, 19
matter, 'subject' (Lat. *materies*, 'timber'), **8**, 11; **12**, 17
Medaea, wife of Jason, **18**, 27
meere, 'pure,' 'nothing but,' (Lat. *merus*): meerely, 'purely,' 'entirely,' **6**, 29; **11**, 26
meete with, to, 'to agree with,' **7**, 19
Melancthon, 'Philip Schwartzerd,' German scholar and reformer (1496—1560), **48**, 17
Meliboeus, a character in Virgil's Eclogues, **29**, 2
men mostly childish, **25**, 27
Menelaus, king of Sparta, **18**, 17

Menenius Agrippa, Roman consul B.C. 501, **27**, 4

metaphysick, the, 'the metaphysical philosopher' (Gr. μετὰ, 'beyond,' φύσις, 'nature'), **8**, 14

Midas, a king of Phrygia renowned for wealth, **63**, 7

middest, 'midst' (a strengthened form of *middes*), **18**, 11

Milciades, 'Miltiades,' the victor at Marathon (ob. B.C. 489), **23**, 10

mimesis, μίμησις, 'imitation,' **10**, 7

Mirrour of Magistrates (or mirrour *for* Magistrates), the title of a collection of poems first published in 1559, **51**, 9

miserere, the, Psalm li. (from the first word in the Latin version), **28**, 1

mislike, to, 'to dislike,' **11**. 1; **23**, 6; **28**, 31; **31**, 20; **43**, 20, 22, 32

misomousoi, μισόμουσοι, 'haters of the muses,' **35**, 1

mistie, 'obscure,' **16**, 31; **32**, 32

moderator, 'one who decides between two disputants in the Schools,' **16**, 1

mome, 'a sulky,' or 'ill-natured person,' **63**, 5

Momus, 'disparagement,' impersonified in Hesiod as the god Momus (Μῶμος), **63**, 5

moral philosophers, **14**, 12

Moore, Sir Thomas (properly *More*), Chancellor to Henry VIII., and author of Utopia, etc. (1480—1535), **19**, 4

Moses, Jewish lawgiver, **10**, 16

mountibanks of Venice, sellers of quack medicines or the like (*monier*, 'to mount,' *banco*, 'a bench'), **49**, 2

mungrell, 'mixed' (cp. mingle, A.-S. *mang*, 'a mixture'), **54**, 16

Muretus, a French scholar and writer (1526—1583), **48**, 19

Musaeus, Greek poet, **3**, 5

musicke, **13**, 18; **25**, 18

names wrongly given by Sidney, **22**, 10 (*Abradates*); **63**, 8 (*Bubonax*); **32**, 20 (*Olympus*)

Nathan, the prophet, **27**, 24; **39**, 10

nature, to follow, **8**, 4

naughtie, 'wicked,' **30**, 4; naughtiness, 'wickedness,' **16**, 20; **29**, 25 (*naught*, 'nothing;' *naughty*, 'nothing-like,' 'worthless')

Nilus, the river Nile, **63**, 1

Nisus, a hero in Virgil's Aeneid, **18**, 21

Nizolian paper-books, 'note-books of phrases,' like those of Nizolius or Nizzoli (1498—1566) to Cicero, **57**, 30

Normans, the, **5**, 18

note, a, 'distinguishing mark,' **12**, 25

nothing, to say, 'to advance a false argument,' 'to make a groundless assertion,' **41**, 30

numbrous, 'metrical,' **12**, 8

nuntius, 'a messenger,' **53**, 22

occidendos esse, 'that they must be killed,' **23**, 25

Oedipus, king of Thebes, **18**, 23

of, Sidney uses this preposition in various meanings, where in later English 'from' or 'by,' 'on,' or 'concerning' would be used:

(1) stole or usurped *of* poets, **4**, 24

derived *of* carmina, **6**, 12

scoffing commeth not *of* wisdom, **35**, 26

yet commeth it not *of* delight, **54**, 33

followed *of* imitation, **45**, 33

(2) makers *of* themselves, not takers *of* others, **48**, 6

an example *of* myself, **2**, 10

(3) depended most *of* poetry, **4**, 9

of purpose, **62**, 17

(4) Plato meant it not *of* poets, **46**, 10

VERBAL QUOTATIONS.

CAMBRIDGE UNIVERSITY PRESS.

THE PITT PRESS SERIES.

*** *Many of the books in this list can be had in two volumes, Text and Notes separately.*

I. GREEK.

Aristophanes. Aves—Plutus—Ranæ. By W. C. GREEN, M.A., late Assistant Master at Rugby School. 3*s.* 6*d.* each.

Aristotle. Outlines of the Philosophy of. By EDWIN WALLACE, M.A., LL.D. Third Edition, Enlarged. 4*s.* 6*d.*

Euripides. Heracleidae. By E. A. BECK, M.A. 3*s.* 6*d.*

——— **Hercules Furens.** By A. GRAY, M.A., and J. T. HUTCHINSON, M.A. New Edit. 2*s.*

——— **Hippolytus.** By W. S. HADLEY, M.A. 2*s.*

——— **Iphigeneia in Aulis.** By C. E. S. HEADLAM, B.A. 2*s.* 6*d.*

Herodotus, Book V. By E. S. SHUCKBURGH, M.A. 3*s.*

——— **Book VI.** By the same Editor. 4*s.*

——— **Books VIII., IX.** By the same Editor. 4*s.* each.

——— **Book VIII. Ch. 1—90. Book IX. Ch. 1—89.** By the same Editor. 3*s.* 6*d.* each.

Homer. Odyssey, Books IX., X. By G. M. EDWARDS, M.A. 2*s.* 6*d.* each. BOOK XXI. By the same Editor. 2*s.*

——— **Iliad. Book XXII.** By the same Editor. 2*s.*

——— ——— **Book XXIII.** By the same Editor. [*Nearly ready.*

Lucian. Somnium Charon Piscator et De Luctu. By W. E. HEITLAND, M.A., Fellow of St John's College, Cambridge. 3*s.* 6*d.*

——— **Menippus and Timon.** By E. C. MACKIE, M.A. [*Nearly ready.*

Platonis Apologia Socratis. By J. ADAM, M.A. 3*s.* 6*d.*

——— **Crito.** By the same Editor. 2*s.* 6*d.*

——— **Euthyphro.** By the same Editor. 2*s.* 6*d.*

Plutarch. Lives of the Gracchi. By Rev. H. A. HOLDEN, M.A., LL.D. 6*s.*

——— **Life of Nicias.** By the same Editor. 5*s.*

——— **Life of Sulla.** By the same Editor. 6*s.*

——— **Life of Timoleon.** By the same Editor. 6*s.*

Sophocles. Oedipus Tyrannus. School Edition. By R. C. JEBB, Litt.D., LL.D. 4*s.* 6*d.*

Thucydides. Book VII. By Rev. H. A. HOLDEN, M.A., LL.D. [*Nearly ready.*

Xenophon. Agesilaus. By H. HAILSTONE, M.A. 2*s.* 6*d.*

——— **Anabasis.** By A. PRETOR, M.A. Two vols. 7*s.* 6*d.*

——— **Books I. III. IV. and V.** By the same. 2*s.* each.

——— **Books II. VI. and VII.** By the same. 2*s.* 6*d.* each.

Xenophon. Cyropaedeia. Books I. II. By Rev. H. A. HOLDEN, M.A., LL.D. 2 vols. 6*s.*

——— ——— **Books III. IV. and V.** By the same Editor. 5*s.*

——— ——— **Books VI. VII. VIII.** By the same Editor. 5*s.*

London: Cambridge Warehouse, Ave Maria Lane.

50/12/90

II. LATIN.

Beda's Ecclesiastical History, Books III., IV. By J. E. B.
MAYOR, M.A., and J. R. LUMBY, D.D.   Revised Edition.   7s. 6d.

—————— **Books I. II.**   By the same Editors.   [*In the Press.*

Caesar. De Bello Gallico, Comment. I. By A. G. PESKETT,
M.A., Fellow of Magdalene College, Cambridge.   1s. 6d.   COMMENT. II.
III.   2s.   COMMENT. I. II. III.   3s.   COMMENT. IV. and V.   1s. 6d.   COMMENT.
VII.   2s.   COMMENT. VI. and COMMENT. VIII.   1s. 6d. each.

—————— **De Bello Civili, Comment. I.**   By the same Editor.   3s.

Cicero. De Amicitia.—De Senectute.   By J. S. REID, Litt.D.,
Fellow of Gonville and Caius College.   3s. 6d. each.

—————— **In Gaium Verrem Actio Prima.**   By H. COWIE,
M.A.   1s. 6d.

—————— **In Q. Caecilium Divinatio et in C. Verrem Actio.**
By W. E. HEITLAND, M.A., and H. COWIE, M.A.   3s.

—————— **Philippica Secunda.**   By A. G. PESKETT, M.A.   3s. 6d.

—————— **Oratio pro Archia Poeta.**   By J. S. REID, Litt.D.   2s.

—————— **Pro L. Cornelio Balbo Oratio.**   By the same.   1s. 6d.

—————— **Oratio pro Tito Annio Milone.**   By JOHN SMYTH
PURTON, B.D.   2s. 6d.

—————— **Oratio pro L. Murena.**   By W. E. HEITLAND, M.A.   3s.

—————— **Pro Cn. Plancio Oratio,** by H. A. HOLDEN, LL.D.   4s. 6d.

—————— **Pro P. Cornelio Sulla.**   By J. S. REID, Litt.D.   3s. 6d.

—————— **Somnium Scipionis.**   By W. D. PEARMAN, M.A.   2s.

Horace. Epistles, Book I.   By E. S. SHUCKBURGH, M.A.,
late Fellow of Emmanuel College.   2s. 6d.

Livy. Book IV.   By H. M. STEPHENSON, M.A.   2s. 6d.

—————— **Book V.**   By L. WHIBLEY, M.A.   2s. 6d.

—————— **Books XXI., XXII.**   By M. S. DIMSDALE, M.A., Fel-
low of King's College.   2s. 6d. each.

—————— **Book XXVII.** By Rev. H. M. STEPHENSON, M.A.   2s. 6d.

Lucan. Pharsaliae Liber Primus.   By W. E. HEITLAND,
M.A., and C. E. HASKINS, M.A.   1s. 6d.

Lucretius, Book V.   By J. D. DUFF, M.A.   2s.

Ovidii Nasonis Fastorum Liber VI.   By A. SIDGWICK, M.A.,
Tutor of Corpus Christi College, Oxford.   1s. 6d.

Quintus Curtius.   A Portion of the History (Alexander in India).
By W. E. HEITLAND, M.A., and T. E. RAVEN, B.A.   With Two Maps.   3s. 6d.

Vergili Maronis Aeneidos Libri I.—XII.   By A. SIDGWICK,
M.A.   1s. 6d. each.

—————— **Bucolica.**   By the same Editor.   1s. 6d.

—————— **Georgicon Libri I. II.**   By the same Editor.   2s.

—————— —————— **Libri III. IV.**   By the same Editor.   2s.

—————— **The Complete Works.**   By the same Editor.   Two vols.
Vol. I. containing the Introduction and Text.   3s. 6d.   Vol. II. The Notes.   4s. 6d.

—————

London : Cambridge Warehouse, Ave Maria Lane.

III. FRENCH.

Corneille. La Suite du Menteur. A Comedy in Five Acts. By the late G. MASSON, B.A. 2s.

De Bonnechose. Lazare Hoche. By C. COLBECK, M.A. Revised Edition. Four Maps. 2s.

D'Harleville. Le Vieux Célibataire. By G. MASSON, B.A. 2s.

De Lamartine. Jeanne D'Arc. By Rev. A. C. CLAPIN, M.A. New edition revised, by A. R. ROPES, M.A. 1s. 6d.

De Vigny. La Canne de Jonc. By Rev. H. A. BULL, M.A., late Master at Wellington College. 2s.

Erckmann-Chatrian. La Guerre. By Rev. A. C. CLAPIN, M.A. 3s.

La Baronne de Staël-Holstein. Le Directoire. (Considérations sur la Révolution Française. Troisième et quatrième parties.) Revised and enlarged. By G. MASSON, B.A., and G. W. PROTHERO, M.A. 2s.

—————— —————— **Dix Années d'Exil. Livre II. Chapitres 1—8.** By the same Editors. New Edition, enlarged. 2s.

Lemercier. Fredegonde et Brunehaut. A Tragedy in Five Acts. By GUSTAVE MASSON, B.A. 2s.

Molière. Le Bourgeois Gentilhomme, Comédie-Ballet en Cinq Actes. (1670.) By Rev. A. C. CLAPIN, M.A. Revised Edition. 1s. 6d.

—————— **L'École des Femmes.** By G. SAINTSBURY, M.A. 2s. 6d.

—————— **Les Précieuses Ridicules.** By E. G. W. BRAUNHOLTZ, M.A., Ph.D. 2s.

—————— —————— **Abridged Edition.** 1s.

Piron. La Métromanie. A Comedy. By G. MASSON, B.A. 2s.

Racine. Les Plaideurs. By E. G. W. BRAUNHOLTZ, M.A. 2s.

—————— —————— **Abridged Edition.** 1s.

Sainte-Beuve. M. Daru (Causeries du Lundi, Vol. IX.). By G. MASSON, B.A. 2s.

Saintine. Picciola. By Rev. A. C. CLAPIN, M.A. 2s.

Scribe and Legouvé. Bataille de Dames. By Rev. H. A. BULL, M.A. 2s.

Scribe. Le Verre d'Eau. By C. COLBECK, M.A. 2s.

Sédaine. Le Philosophe sans le savoir. By Rev. H. A. BULL, M.A. 2s.

Thierry. Lettres sur l'histoire de France (XIII.—XXIV.). By G. MASSON, B.A., and G. W. PROTHERO, M.A. 2s. 6d.

—————— **Récits des Temps Mérovingiens I.—III.** By GUSTAVE MASSON, B.A. Univ. Gallic., and A. R. ROPES, M.A. With Map. 3s.

Villemain. Lascaris ou Les Grecs du XVe Siècle, Nouvelle Historique. By G. MASSON, B.A. 2s.

Voltaire. Histoire du Siècle de Louis XIV. Chaps. I.— XIII. By G. MASSON, B.A., and G. W. PROTHERO, M.A. 2s. 6d. PART II. CHAPS. XIV.—XXIV. 2s. 6d. PART III. CHAPS. XXV. to end. 2s. 6d.

Xavier de Maistre. La Jeune Sibérienne. Le Lépreux de la Cité D'Aoste. By G. MASSON, B.A. 1s. 6d.

IV. GERMAN.

Ballads on German History. By W. WAGNER, Ph.D.   2*s.*

Benedix. Doctor Wespe. Lustspiel in fünf Aufzügen. By KARL HERMANN BREUL, M.A., Ph.D.   3*s.*

Freytag. Der Staat Friedrichs des Grossen. By WILHELM WAGNER, Ph.D.   2*s.*

German Dactylic Poetry. By WILHELM WAGNER, Ph.D.   3*s.*

Goethe's Knabenjahre. (1749—1759.) By W. WAGNER, Ph.D. New edition revised and enlarged, by J. W. CARTMELL, M.A.   2*s.*

———— **Hermann und Dorothea.** By WILHELM WAGNER, Ph.D.   New edition revised, by J. W. CARTMELL, M.A.   3*s.* 6*d.*

Gutzkow. Zopf und Schwert. Lustspiel in fünf Aufzügen. By H. J. WOLSTENHOLME, B.A. (Lond.).   3*s.* 6*d.*

Hauff. Das Bild des Kaisers. By KARL HERMANN BREUL, M.A., Ph.D., University Lecturer in German.   3*s.*

———— **Das Wirthshaus im Spessart.** By A. SCHLOTTMANN, Ph.D.   3*s.* 6*d.*

———— **Die Karavane.** By A. SCHLOTTMANN, Ph.D.   3*s.* 6*d.*

Immermann. Der Oberhof. A Tale of Westphalian Life, by WILHELM WAGNER, Ph.D.   3*s.*

Kohlrausch. Das Jahr 1813. By WILHELM WAGNER, Ph.D.   2*s.*

Lessing and **Gellert. Selected Fables.** By KARL HERMANN BREUL, M.A., Ph.D.   3*s.*

Mendelssohn's Letters. Selections from. By J. SIME, M.A.   3*s.*

Raumer. Der erste Kreuzzug (1095—1099). By WILHELM WAGNER, Ph.D.   2*s.*

Riehl. Culturgeschichtliche Novellen. By H. J. WOLSTENHOLME, B.A. (Lond.).   3*s.* 6*d.*

Schiller. Wilhelm Tell. By KARL HERMANN BREUL, M.A., Ph.D.   2*s.* 6*d.*

———— ———— Abridged Edition.   1*s.* 6*d.*

Uhland. Ernst, Herzog von Schwaben. By H. J. WOLSTENHOLME, B.A.   3*s.* 6*d.*

V. ENGLISH.

Ancient Philosophy from Thales to Cicero, A Sketch of. By JOSEPH B. MAYOR, M.A.   3*s.* 6*d.*

An Apologie for Poetrie by Sir PHILIP SIDNEY. By E. S. SHUCKBURGH, M.A. The Text is a revision of that of the first edition of 1595.   3*s.*

Bacon's History of the Reign of King Henry VII. By the Rev. Professor LUMBY, D.D.   3*s.*

Cowley's Essays. By the Rev. Professor LUMBY, D.D.   4*s.*

London: Cambridge Warehouse, Ave Maria Lane.

Milton's Comus and Arcades.   By A. W. VERITY, M.A., sometime Scholar of Trinity College. *3s.*

More's History of King Richard III.   By J. RAWSON LUMBY, D.D. *3s. 6d.*

More's Utopia.   By Rev. Prof. LUMBY, D.D. *3s. 6d.*

The Two Noble Kinsmen.   By the Rev. Professor SKEAT, Litt.D. *3s. 6d.*

VI. EDUCATIONAL SCIENCE.

Comenius, John Amos, Bishop of the Moravians.   His Life and Educational Works, by S. S. LAURIE, A.M., F.R.S.E. *3s. 6d.*

Education, Three Lectures on the Practice of.   I. On Marking, by H. W. EVE, M.A.   II. On Stimulus, by A. SIDGWICK, M.A.   III. On the Teaching of Latin Verse Composition, by E. A. ABBOTT, D.D. *2s.*

Stimulus.   A Lecture delivered for the Teachers' Training Syndicate, May, 1882, by A. SIDGWICK, M.A. *1s.*

Locke on Education.   By the Rev. R. H. QUICK, M.A. *3s. 6d.*

Milton's Tractate on Education.   A facsimile reprint from the Edition of 1673.   By O. BROWNING, M.A. *2s.*

Modern Languages, Lectures on the Teaching of.   By C. COLBECK, M.A. *2s.*

Teacher, General Aims of the, and Form Management.   Two Lectures delivered in the University of Cambridge in the Lent Term, 1883, by F. W. FARRAR, D.D., and R. B. POOLE, B.D. *1s. 6d.*

Teaching, Theory and Practice of.   By the Rev. E. THRING, M.A., late Head Master of Uppingham School.   New Edition. *4s. 6d.*

British India, a Short History of.   By E. S. CARLOS, M.A., late Head Master of Exeter Grammar School. *1s.*

Geography, Elementary Commercial.   A Sketch of the Commodities and the Countries of the World.   By H. R. MILL, D.Sc., F.R.S.E. *1s.*

Geography, an Atlas of Commercial.   (A Companion to the above.)   By J. G. BARTHOLOMEW, F.R.G.S.   With an Introduction by HUGH ROBERT MILL, D.Sc. *3s.*

VII. MATHEMATICS.

Euclid's Elements of Geometry. Books I. and II.   By H. M. TAYLOR, M.A., Fellow and late Tutor of Trinity College, Cambridge. *1s. 6d.*

———— ———— **Books III. and IV.**   By the same Editor. *1s. 6d.*

———— ———— **Books I.—IV.,** in one Volume. *3s.*

Elementary Algebra (with Answers to the Examples).   By W. W. ROUSE BALL, M.A. *4s. 6d.*

Elements of Statics.   By S. L. LONEY, M.A. *5s.*

Elements of Dynamics.   By the same Editor.   *[Nearly ready.*

Other Volumes are in preparation.

London: Cambridge Warehouse, Ave Maria Lane.

The Cambridge Bible for Schools and Colleges.

GENERAL EDITOR: J. J. S. PEROWNE, D.D.,
BISHOP OF WORCESTER.

"*It is difficult to commend too highly this excellent series.*—Guardian.

"*The modesty of the general title of this series has, we believe, led many to misunderstand its character and underrate its value. The books are well suited for study in the upper forms of our best schools, but not the less are they adapted to the wants of all Bible students who are not specialists. We doubt, indeed, whether any of the numerous popular commentaries recently issued in this country will be found more serviceable for general use.*"—Academy.

Now Ready. Cloth, Extra Fcap. 8vo. With Maps.

Book of Joshua. By Rev. G. F. MACLEAR, D.D. 2*s.* 6*d.*

Book of Judges. By Rev. J. J. LIAS, M.A. 3*s.* 6*d.*

First Book of Samuel. By Rev. Prof. KIRKPATRICK, B.D. 3*s.*6*d.*

Second Book of Samuel. By the same Editor. 3*s.* 6*d.*

First Book of Kings. By Rev. Prof. LUMBY, D.D. 3*s.* 6*d.*

Second Book of Kings. By Rev. Prof. LUMBY, D.D. 3*s.* 6*d.*

Book of Job. By Rev. A. B. DAVIDSON, D.D. 5*s.*

Book of Ecclesiastes. By Very Rev. E. H. PLUMPTRE, D.D. 5*s.*

Book of Jeremiah. By Rev. A. W. STREANE, M.A. 4*s.* 6*d.*

Book of Hosea. By Rev. T. K. CHEYNE, M.A., D.D. 3*s.*

Books of Obadiah & Jonah. By Archdeacon PEROWNE. 2*s.* 6*d.*

Book of Micah. By Rev. T. K. CHEYNE, M.A., D.D. 1*s.* 6*d.*

Haggai, Zechariah & Malachi. By Arch. PEROWNE. 3*s.* 6*d.*

Book of Malachi. By Archdeacon PEROWNE. 1*s.*

Gospel according to St Matthew. By Rev. A. CARR, M.A. 2*s.*6*d.*

Gospel according to St Mark. By Rev. G. F. MACLEAR, D.D. 2*s.* 6*d.*

Gospel according to St Luke. By Arch. FARRAR, D.D. 4*s.* 6*d.*

Gospel according to St John. By Rev. A. PLUMMER, D.D. 4*s.*6*d.*

Acts of the Apostles. By Rev. Prof. LUMBY, D.D. 4*s.* 6*d.*

Epistle to the Romans. By Rev. H. C. G. MOULE, M.A. 3*s.* 6*d.*

First Corinthians. By Rev. J. J. LIAS, M.A. With Map. 2*s.*

Second Corinthians. By Rev. J. J. LIAS, M.A. With Map. 2*s.*

Epistle to the Galatians. By Rev. E. H. PEROWNE, D.D. 1*s.* 6*d.*

Epistle to the Ephesians. By Rev. H. C. G. MOULE, M.A. 2s. 6d.

Epistle to the Philippians. By the same Editor. 2s. 6d.

Epistles to the Thessalonians. By Rev. G. G. FINDLAY, M.A. 2s.

Epistle to the Hebrews. By Arch. FARRAR, D.D. 3s. 6d.

General Epistle of St James. By Very Rev. E. H. PLUMPTRE, D.D. 1s. 6d.

Epistles of St Peter and St Jude. By Very Rev. E. H. PLUMPTRE, D.D. 2s. 6d.

Epistles of St John. By Rev. A. PLUMMER, M.A., D.D. 3s. 6d.

Book of Revelation. By Rev. W. H. SIMCOX, M.A. 3s.

Preparing.

Book of Genesis. By the BISHOP OF WORCESTER.

Books of Exodus, Numbers and Deuteronomy. By Rev. C. D. GINSBURG, LL.D.

Books of Ezra and Nehemiah. By Rev. Prof. RYLE, M.A.

Book of Psalms. Part I. By Rev. Prof. KIRKPATRICK, B.D.

Book of Isaiah. By Prof. W. ROBERTSON SMITH, M.A.

Book of Ezekiel. By Rev. A. B. DAVIDSON, D.D.

Epistles to the Colossians and Philemon. By Rev. H. C. G. MOULE, M.A.

Epistles to Timothy & Titus. By Rev. A. E. HUMPHREYS, M.A.

The Smaller Cambridge Bible for Schools.

The Smaller Cambridge Bible for Schools *will form an entirely new series of commentaries on some selected books of the Bible. It is expected that they will be prepared for the most part by the Editors of the larger series (The Cambridge Bible for Schools and Colleges). The volumes will be issued at a low price, and will be suitable to the requirements of preparatory and elementary schools.*

Now ready.

First and Second Books of Samuel. By Rev. Prof. KIRKPATRICK, B.D. 1s. each.

First Book of Kings. By Rev. Prof. LUMBY, D.D. 1s.

Gospel according to St Matthew. By Rev. A. CARR, M.A. 1s.

Gospel according to St Mark. By Rev. G. F. MACLEAR, D.D. 1s.

Gospel according to St Luke. By Archdeacon FARRAR. 1s.

Acts of the Apostles. By Rev. Prof. LUMBY, D.D. 1s.

Nearly ready.

Second Book of Kings. By Rev. Prof. LUMBY, D.D.

Gospel according to St John. By Rev. A. PLUMMER, D.D.

London : Cambridge Warehouse, Ave Maria Lane.

The Cambridge Greek Testament for Schools and Colleges,

with a Revised Text, based on the most recent critical authorities, and English Notes, prepared under the direction of the

GENERAL EDITOR, J. J. S. PEROWNE, D.D.,
BISHOP OF WORCESTER.

Gospel according to St Matthew. By Rev. A. CARR, M.A.
With 4 Maps. 4*s. 6d.*

Gospel according to St Mark. By Rev. G. F. MACLEAR, D.D.
With 3 Maps. 4*s. 6d.*

Gospel according to St Luke. By Archdeacon FARRAR.
With 4 Maps. 6*s.*

Gospel according to St John. By Rev. A. PLUMMER, D.D.
With 4 Maps. 6*s.*

Acts of the Apostles. By Rev. Professor LUMBY, D.D.
With 4 Maps. 6*s.*

First Epistle to the Corinthians. By Rev. J. J. LIAS, M.A. 3*s.*

Second Epistle to the Corinthians. By Rev. J. J. LIAS, M.A.
[In the Press.

Epistle to the Hebrews. By Archdeacon FARRAR, D.D. 3*s. 6d.*

Epistle of St James. By Very Rev. E. H. PLUMPTRE, D.D.
[Preparing.

Epistles of St John. By Rev. A. PLUMMER, M.A., D.D. 4*s.*

London: C. J. CLAY AND SONS,
CAMBRIDGE WAREHOUSE, AVE MARIA LANE.
Glasgow: 263, ARGYLE STREET.
Cambridge: DEIGHTON, BELL AND CO.
Leipzig: F. A. BROCKHAUS.
New York: MACMILLAN AND CO.

CAMBRIDGE: PRINTED BY C. J. CLAY, M.A. AND SONS, AT THE UNIVERSITY PRESS.

9 780521 166218